THE OLDEST EUROPEANS

by J. F. del Giorgio

Acknowledgements

First, I would like to thank José Luis (Koldo) Leizaola. He regaled me with an impromptu speech on the meaning of certain names in the Mesopotamia. It happened nearly three decades ago. I did not know it at the time, but it was the seed that started this book.
Marek Wesolowski, Armando Azpúrua and the late Moisés Szponka helped me with spontaneous material.
I had readers generous with both their time and their advice: Judith Pérez de Albrizzio, Martha Luchsinger, Electra Sklyris, Mercedes (Kikina) Titeau, Carlos Albrizzio, Luc Bramaud de Boucheron, Robert Hutchinson and Antonio Segovia.
Norman Oder made a kind note and supplied information.
Sweet Victoria Walker and Jerzy Gintel gave me technical advice.
Soledad Mendoza and Otoniel Escobar contributed unselfishly with their valuable experience.
Julio Dominguez improved an illustration and gave advice with his usual professional skill.
Nicolás Risso did a wonderful job with the cover and was very patient.
A nice panel helped with their vote for the art part, among them: Aniuska Dominguez, Carolina Risso, Marcela Quintieri, Marianela Romero-Servigna, M.E. Marcelina del Giorgio, Boris Dominguez and Victor Maldonado.
My daughter Paola del Giorgio contributed in all the phases and was a good critic.
My wife Anita contributed in absolutely every step and detail. She made this book possible.

THE OLDEST EUROPEANS

J. F. del Giorgio

A. J. Place

THE OLDEST EUROPEANS
by J. F. del Giorgio

FIRST EDITION

Copyrighth© 2005 by J. F. del Giorgio
All Rights Reserved

On the cover, and Fig 11, Venus of Willendorf, © Naturhistorisches Museum Wien, courtesy
On the back cover, and Fig. 37, The Cerne Abbas Giant, from Celtic Mysteries by John Sharkey, Published by Thames and Hudson, London and New York
On the flap, female charioteers from a fresco from Tiryns, 13th century B.C.

Cover design
Nicolás Risso, nicorisso@fibertel.com.ar

Illustrations, except when otherwise indicated, J. P. Hannah

ISBN: 980-6898-00-1
Depósito Legal No. lf252200542860
Printed in Caracas, Venezuela, using acid free paper, by Gaudeamus 2003 C.A., December 2005

A.J. Place
Ed. Mengal Ap. 8 -C Av. La Salle
Los Caobos. Caracas 1052 - Venezuela

Thousands of years ago	Event
37	First Homo sapiens sapiens in Europe
28	Oldest written record; the Blanchard Bone calendar
26	Dolni Vestonice
14	Lescaux
10	Early agriculture in North Egypt
8	Indo-European tribes start to invade Europe Ninkasi's recipe for beer
5	Skara Brae is built by the sea
4	Indo-European tribes start to enter Greece (Ionians-Eolians)
3.5	Achean invasion-Santorini eruption-Troyan War Moises Exodus-Tutankhamen
3.1	Dorians invade Greece-Iliad and Oddissey Ionian Rebirth
2.753	Romulus and Remus found Rome
2.4	Pericles and Peloponesian War-Mausolus' Tomb Alexander-Hannibal
2.115	Etruscan cities get Roman citizenship
2.09	Sula strips Etruscan liberties
2.05	Julius Caesar and Cleopatra
2	Birth of Jesus

Cyclades

Minoan

Year	Event
0	Birth of Jesus
563	Saint Columba erects a church in Iona
584	Visigoth King Leovigild conquers "all" the Iberian Peninsula
711	Arabs invade Spain
778	Battle of Roncesvalles
c850	Burial of two women in the Oseberg ship beside the Oslo fjord
857	Major outbreak of ergotism in the Rhine Valley
921	The Caliph of Bagdad sends Ibn Fadlan to Bulgaria
1040	Macbeth kills his cousin, King Duncan I
1057	King Macbeth dies
1152	Eleanor of Aquitania marries Henry II of England
1282	The almogavars expel Charles of Anjou from Sicily
1494	Charles VIII of France invades Italy
1534	Jean Cartier explores North America
1581	Catherine de Medici and her ladies dance the Ballet Comique de la Reine
1611	Birth of d'Artagnan
1619	Birth of Cyrano de Bergerac
1657	Posthumous publication of Cyrano's "A voyage to the moon"
1673	Death of d'Artagnan at the siege of Maastricht
1722	Ergot poisoning saves the Ottoman Empire from Peter the Great's army
1901	Sabino de Arana Goiri proposes the extended meaning of Euzko
1937	German Nazi planes bomb Guernica
1940	Discovery of the Rh blood factor
1952	Grabaulle man es found in Denmark

Table of Contents

Acknowledgements 2
Chronological Tables 5
Introduction
The old people ♦ The men who beat the Romans ♦ The warriors from *The Song of Roland*, the *Iliad*, the *Odyssey* and the *Eneid* ♦ The birth of civilization ♦ The incredible travelers ♦ Discovering America ♦ Circumnavigating the world ♦ Famous ancient women ♦ The roots of Europe. 15
1-The Oldest Europeans
The city of the wolves ♦ D'Artagnan goes to Paris ♦ Touché! The magic of Cyrano ♦ The *Song of Roland* ♦ The terrible almogavars. 22
2-The Men from the Stone
Words straight from the Stone Age ♦ Ice Age survivors ♦ Sheep raisers and wine makers ♦ The "discoveries" of Jean Cartier ♦ The men who circumnavigated the world ♦ Dances from the Paleolithic ♦ The ancestral Euzkos. 32
3-The Blood Trail
The Early-European blood group ♦ What the geneticists are telling ♦ Boyd and the Early European Race ♦ Basques, Scots and Scandinavians ♦ Irish and Welsh ♦ Etruscans and Pelasgians ♦ Meet a warrior from

antiquity: the name is Bond, James Bond ♦ The cryptic language of the ancient stone masons ♦ The Pompeii from the Neolithic. 40

4-The Italian Euzkos

The Roman kings ♦ The stone builders ♦ Creating and training the Roman Legions ♦ The expansion of Rome ♦ The Etruscan legacy ♦ Bishops, tribes and fasci ♦ The double ax ♦ The music people: histrios and subuli ♦ The masterpieces which inspired the Renaissance ♦ The Sino-Caucasian group of languages and its link with a living tongue. 49

5-The Greek Euzkos

An unparalleled window to the past ♦ The building Cyclops ♦ The Indo-Europeans are coming!! ♦ The Minoan civilization ♦ Bulls, rituals and the good life ♦ The double ax again ♦ Eolians and Ionians or some Aryans really like to go native ♦ Acheans and the end of a civilization ♦ Dorians and harsh rule 63

6-Rebirth

The rebirth of a civilization: the Ionian world ♦ The racial war ♦ The siege of Troy ♦ Philosophers, poetry and music ♦ Nice harbor at Samos ♦ Water supply at Pergamon ♦ Go plan a city Hippodamus! ♦ Athens and Sparta ♦ The Peloponnessian conflict ♦ The Pelasgian language of Lemnos. 75

7-Cherchez la Femme...

What makes the Europeans different? ♦ The shocking European woman ♦ The Latin-Greek macho tradition ♦ The peculiar Etruscan and Pelasgian females ♦ The Indo-European family: burning widows in India ♦ The Euzkan inheritance ♦ Women's rights and Rh distribution ♦ Of Roman kings (and queens' daughters) ♦ The prehistoric Basque family ♦ Women's rights among the ancient Basques. 85

8-The Old Religion

The ubiquitous Venus figurines ♦ The incoming gods ♦ The names of the Goddess ♦ Sacred numbers and chimeras ♦ Nymphs and beer producers ♦ The priest of Diana at Nemi ♦ Snake processions today? ♦ The Great Mother and the Hero ♦ The king must die ♦ Hey, how many Hercules can there be? ♦ Herodotus and his doubts ♦ A mistletoe for Christmas ♦ Sacred islands and Charon ♦ Blowing the tuba at royal funerals ♦ Mara succeeds Laima ♦ A sacrifice in Minoan Crete ♦ Sacrificial kings in Lascaux and Trois Freres? ♦ Bull games in Crete ♦ The Olympic games have started ♦ The right way to choose a king. 97

9-The Founding Fathers
Herodotus and his troubles ◆ The vanishing leaders ◆ Why those Acheans? ◆ Some help from Washington and Lincoln ◆ Oracles and sun-moon cycles ◆ The new kings: why to die if you can live longer? 123

10-The Beginning of the End
How to become a Hero by killing a monster ◆ Logos and chimeras ◆ Bellerophon, Theseus and Hercules ◆ Getting a date with Hippolyte ◆ The reluctant Hero ◆ How to maroon a Hercules ◆ The Garden of the Hesperides ◆ Medea and her crush for Jason ◆ An advice from the Centaurs maybe can help a troubled marriage ◆ Deianeira and her solution ◆ The one and only but not the last Hercules or how to confuse people. 129

11-The Fall
War at Troy ◆ All for just a woman ◆ Homer, the master storyteller ◆ The counsels of Jove must be fulfilled ◆ The pious killers ◆ Where were you during the sacred war? ◆ The art of literary tricks 139

12-Orea Eleni
The best way to kidnap a princess ◆ Helen, the dream girl ◆ Portrait of a Queen-Priestess at Lacedemonia ◆ Herbs, rituals and business managing ◆ Hallucinogens anyone? ◆ Chignons, indiscreet moles and tiaras ◆ What a dress!! ◆ The dazzling beauty parades at the procession ◆ To be the social and political center ◆ Some marriages can be difficult ◆ Helen makes a political move ◆ Menelaus looks for help ◆ Priam's ambitions ◆ Pelasgian backing? ◆ The fall ◆ Julius Caesar's revenge ◆ Agamemnon gets the double ax ◆ Menelaus and his worries ◆ Helen's viewpoint ◆ The last days of Helen ◆ The last feminine political bastion ◆ Sudden night for women ◆ Basques had said it all. 145

13-The Wanderer
Odysseus goes to the west ◆ Telemachus needs some help ◆ The Metonic cycle or replacement time has arrived ◆ Let's kill a priestess ◆ "Go implore Arete!" says Nausicaa ◆ Why was Homer told to choose Odysseus? ◆ Penelope takes her time ◆ The wisdom of a priestess. 164

14-The Witch Hunt Starts
Never heard of a wizard hunt? ◆ The old craft of the witches ◆ Victims and victories ◆ Purifying sacred islands or how to be one of the Seven Sages of Greece ◆ Iona: Macbeth and Duncan, together at last ◆ Dionysiac fraternities and Mysteries ◆ Cybeles ◆ The coming of Christianism ◆ Mari of the Caves ◆ The Prolific Mother ◆ Carnival and Halloween ◆ Renaming the solstice ◆ Lycanthropy at full moon ◆

Euripides, hallucinogens and Apollo priestesses ◆ The remarkable fungus ◆ Licking toads and other pastimes ◆ Befriending cobras in India ◆ Apollo slays Pytho ◆ An Arab travels through Viking lands ◆ Public coition among the Euzkans ◆ Ergotism, epidemics and witch hunting ◆ Bog mummies ◆ Witch trials in Basque land. 173

15-*Our Own Stone Roots*
The ancient roots of language ◆ To skin a sheep ◆ Azkonas and skeans ◆ Love and hate prehistory ◆ Words from the Cro-Magnon and Neandertals? ◆ Tsk, tsk ◆ Getting hide and shelter ◆ The words of our forefathers. 194

16-*An Astonishing Map*
Hey, Vosgos can't be Basque! ◆ The problem with that boar... ◆ Rivers, valleys and fossil names ◆ München is in a mound! ◆ Names, names, names everywhere 204

17-*The Oldest Language*
Oldest surviving language in the world ◆ From woman to woman and from man to man...◆ How to climb a philogenetic tree ◆ The age of Eve ◆ Paleolithic roots ◆ Looking in Saudi Arabia ◆ Watch out! Opportunists are entering Europe! ◆ Cromagnons really like ivory! ◆ How to touch a Cromagnon today ◆ Disaster at Last Glacial Maximum ◆ A handful of survivors ◆ Let's talk an Aryan language now ◆ Crossing the Atlantic before Columbus ◆ The way Asterix's ancestors traveled 209

18-*What Homer did not Tell*
The Euzko heritage ◆ Venus statuettes from the Gravettian ◆ Isis-Adonis and the coming of Aton-Rah ◆ Sleeping naked on earth ◆ The Chartres tradition ◆ The Polish Virgin ◆ The Road of St. James ◆ Basques, Scots, Irish and Welsh ◆ Basques and Neandertals ◆ A tomb in Arkhanes ◆ Getting buried in a ship ◆ The beauty from Lulan ◆ The lady from the kurgan and her weapons ◆ Amazing Amazons ◆ Penthesileia and her friends ◆ Why you didn't tell it all, Homer? .221

19-*Return*
Courtly love ◆ Eleanor d'Aquitaine ◆ Catherine de'Medici ◆ The unusual man-woman relationship in Europe and some of its former colonies ◆ The Giant from Cerne Abbas ◆ We are all one, at least! 240

20-*Further Readings*
A quick glance ◆ A pictorial travel ◆ Magazines ◆ References 247

21-*Index* 259

LIST OF ILLUSTRATIONS

Fig. 1. Antler fragment from the Magdalenian period with incisions resembling a *sorginguaiza* (witch's scissors) 37
Fig. 2. GENE MAP shows the *Rh*-negative factor to be most common among the Basques and less common further west 42
Fig. 3. Etruscan warrior 52
Fig. 4. Etruscan lands 55
Fig. 5. Etruscan sarcophagus from Cerveteri (600 B.C.) 58
Fig. 6. GENEALOGICAL CHART relates entire families of languages to proposed superfamilies ...61
Fig. 7a. Long-horn fighting bull 70
Fig. 7b. A typical beef-producer bull 71
Fig. 8. Map of the Pelasgian World 73
Fig. 9. Map of Indo-European Greece 76
Fig. 10. La Parisienne, found at Knossos 92
Fig. 11. Venus of Willendorf, (about 24000 BP) 97
Fig. 12. Cretan priestess or goddess with snakes (c. 1500 B.C.) 99
Fig. 13. Woman holding wheat stalks. Mycenae (c. 1300 B.C.) 100
Fig. 14. Fresco from the palace at Knossos (c. 1400 B.C.) 100
Fig. 15. Fresco from Thera (Santorini) (c.1500 B.C.) 101
Fig. 16. Gold ring with feminine figures 101
Fig. 17. Two goddesses. Mycenae. (c. 1400 B.C.) ...102
Fig. 18a. Stag man of Trois Frères 117
Fig. 18b. The only human figure in the Lascaux cave 118
Fig. 19. Sketch from a fresco found in Thera (Santorini) (c.1500 B.C). 145
Fig. 20. Sketch from a fresco found in Thera (c. 1500 B.C.) 146
Fig. 21. Sketch from a fresco found in Thera (c. 1500 B.C.) 146
Fig. 22. Sketch from a gold ring from Isopata with a representation of a dance of worship 148
Fig. 23. Sketch from a fresco found in Thera (c. 1500 B.C.) 149

Fig. 24. Sketch of a scene from a gold ring. (Tyrins, c. 1500 B.C.) 150
Fig. 25. Sketch from a fresco from Thera (c. 1500 B.C.) 150
Fig. 26. Sketch of a fresco from the Queen Apartments in the Palace at Knossos (c. 1500 B.C.) 151
Fig. 27. Sketch of a gold brooch from a tomb at Mycenae (c. 1500 B.C.) 152
Fig. 28. Sketch of a snake goddess. (c. 1600 B.C.) ...152
Fig. 29. Sketch of a fresco from Tyrins (c. 1300 B.C.) 153
Fig. 30. Sketch of a faience figurine from the central shrine at Knossos c. 1500 B.C. 153
Fig. 31. Sketch of a fresco from the acropolis at Mycenae. Their queens, including famous Clytemnestra, must not have looked much different. (c. 1300 B.C.) 160
Fig. 32. Lions' Gate at Mycenae. A Minoan ring print ... .176
Fig. 33. Godess from Mari 180
Fig. 34a. Pingri woman offering her arm 187
Fig. 34b, c. After the bite the woman rests. Her assistant watchs carefully... 187
Fig. 35. Map of currents with Basque linguistic elements in their names 206
Fig. 36. Map of survivors' migration from the Pyrenees after the Last Glacial Maximum 217
Fig. 37. The Cerne Abbas Giant, hill figure, Cerne Abbas, Dorset, England, perhaps c. 1st century B.C. .244

SKETCHES, END OF CHAPTERS
Table of Contents:
Venus in mammoth ivory, Gravettien period 14
Introduction:
Horse, Altamira Cave, about 16000 B.P. 21
1-The Oldest Europeans:
Two mammoths, Rouffignac Cave, about 18000 B.P. .31
2-The Men from the Stone:
Bison, Altamira Cave, about 16000 B.P. 39

3-*The Blood Trail*:
Stone utensils .... .48
4-*The Italian Euzkos*:
Dancers from Tomb of the Lionesses c. 420 B.C., Piper from Tomb of the Triclinium c.520 B.C. All from Tarquinia .... .62
5-*The Greek Euzkos*:
Dolphins from the Palace of Knossos, c. 1500 B.C. ...74
6-*Rebirth*:
Piper, Ionian artist, c. 450 B.C. .... .84
7-:*Cherchez la Femme...*:
Athene from the Parthenon, c. 450 B.C. .... .96
8-*The Old Religion*:
Athene from Chalcidian amphora, c. 540 B.C. .... .122
9-*The Founding Fathers*:
Olympic Zeus (Phidias) c. 440 B.C. .... .128
10-*The Beginning of the End*:
Herakles killing Nessus, from Attic amphora, c. 620 B.C. .... .138
11-*The Fall*:
Murder of Polixena, sarcophagus from Çanakkale, 6th century B.C. .... .144
12-*Orea Eleni*:
Athene from Attic amphora, c. 525 B.C. .... .163
13-*The Wanderer*:
Odysseus and Circe, from a vase, c. 500 B.C. ...... .172
14-*The Witch Hunt Starts*:
Romulus and Remus (medieval Italian sculpture) ...193
15-*Our Own Stone Roots*:
Steps on the moon .... .203
16-*An Astonishing Map*:
Rhinoceros from Rouffignac cave, about 12-15000 B.P. .... .208
17-*The Oldest Language*:
Bison in mammoth ivory from Rouffignac, about 13000 B.P. .... .220

18-What Homer did not Tell:
Amazons from the sarcophagus of Ramtha Huzcnai, Tarquinia, 5th century B.C. 239
19-Return:
Cerne Abbas Giant, hill figure, Cerne Abbas, Dorset, England, perhaps c. 1st century B.C. 246
20-Further Readings:
Female charioteers from a fresco from Tiryns, 13th century B.C. 258
21-Index:
Ship from a fresco from Akrotiri, 16th century B.C. . . .276

TRACKS CHAPTER 15-OUR OWN STONE ROOTS:

Lizard 194
Norway rat 195
Opossum 196
Gibbon 197
Orangutan 198
Gorilla 199
Chimpanzee 200
Bonobo 201
Human 202
Human 203

Introduction

The Old People

In the sixties a comic strip appeared in France: *The adventures of Asterix the Gaul*. Asterix, the cunning hero of those adventures, was a small warrior; all perilous missions were immediately trusted to him and to his inseparable friend Obelix, a menhir-delivery man. The time was 50 B.C., when Gaul was entirely occupied by the Romans. Well, actually not entirely. There was this small village of indomitable Gauls, Asterix and his friends, still holding out the invaders. And life was not exactly easy for the legionaries unlucky enough to be garrisoning the Roman camps in the Gauls' neighborhood.

The comic strip was an immediate success in France. It has been translated into many languages and became a bestseller in many countries. It is still a bestseller. With an inspired text by the late Goscinny and superb drawings by Uderzo, it has touched a special cord everywhere.

What made it so successful?

One of the many reasons may be the timing of its story. These are times when nations are almost disappearing, absorbed by giant superstructures or minimized by superpowers.

Common citizens in all lands are feeling themselves powerless in front of immense, almost inhuman corporations and institutions. A time when people everywhere feel mega forces far beyond their control menace their life-styles. So, the message of these wild, warring Gauls, resisting successfully the most technologically advanced superpower of their times, and managing to maintain their obsolete and crazy customs, found a response in the heart of readers all around the world.

In the celebrated strip the Romans, unable to defeat the rebellious Gauls, content themselves with surrounding their village with camps, whose legionaries are always scared at the prospect of a courtesy visit by Asterix and his band.

Actually, these wild Gauls are almost all the time savagely quarreling among themselves, a continuous fight that is interrupted only by any happy chance of beating up the poor Roman invaders.

In the strip they are not always fighting the Romans. Sometimes they are their allies; sometimes they join them as mercenaries. Living by the sea, they are fond of traveling, often going as far as America.

The best gag in the strip is the ambition of Roman generals to be able to tell Julius Caesar "All of Gaul has been vanquished." Whenever this happens, the skeptic Caesar invariably asks: "All?" Then the proud general, or his messenger, will vainly state "All." The "All" always meaning that at least these troublemaking villagers have been taught to behave. Of course, soon Asterix and his gang also invariably prove them wrong.

Where is this indomitable village located? Apart from the fact that it is by the sea, nothing else is said about the place. The reader is left to choose, according to his imagination, the most suitable region.

There is an amazing, unbelievable fact about this successful strip. As it always happens, reality beats fiction. The incredible fact is: there were people like that living in the French territory during Roman times.

Yes, even if it is very difficult to accept, there did exist a bunch of wild, ever–quarreling people that continually resisted the Roman troops. After many battles, the Romans finally contented themselves with surrounding the irreducible rebels with garrisons, to protect their commercial routes, and then resignedly left them to carry on with their own life. As in the comic strip, sometimes they were allies. At other times they served as mercenaries in the Roman legions. Latin authors have described well their ferocity and uses, their appearance and garments.

They were also excellent sailors, among the best of all times. They traveled everywhere. Some scientists think they had been visiting America for some millennia.

According to history, they were among the first to circumnavigate the world.

They were deeply connected to the Gauls and shared most of their cultural traits. They were the survivors of a much, much older European population. They had been in that land thousands of years before the Latins came to Europe. Long before any Aryan, Indo-European tribe came into the continent.

So, unlike the strip, those few survivors in France also defeated the Romans in defense of their land, as they would defeat the Vandals after the Romans, and then the Visigoths, the Franks, the Moors, the Goths and, more recently, even resist the attacks of the Nazi aviation as some of the first victims of World War II. That is precisely the most amazing part of the whole story: *they are still among us*, keeping many of their age-old customs.

Some of them still speak their ancient tongue. It is a language with words so old that many of their terms have been considered to come directly from the Stone Age.

The influence of their religious beliefs is felt and evident in all the present major religions.

Their ancient myths are still the most celebrated in the arts.

The regions where they managed to keep some of their population, by intermarriage or political arrangements with the new cultures, have been traditionally the birthplace of the arts, sciences and philosophy.

All the major cultural and artistic revivals have taken place among them, even recently. Some of the most celebrated literary pieces of all times have them as their main characters or describe a confrontation with them. That is not a casual event. They were counted among the most famed warriors. Consider these: the *Iliad*, the *Odyssey* and the *Aeneid* either describe their adventures or narrate battles against them. Their bravery was the birth of the French *Song of Roland*.

Everything concerning them leaves us in wonder.

If those literary references can be considered astonishing, what can be said about an even more astounding aspect: they *still* keep generating literary characters so strong that are known for producing best sellers. They have now won over the radio, cinema and TV.

An exaggeration? Maybe, but whenever a warring, fighting character is needed it is a notable coincidence that writers and script-writers from all times do insist in picking up people from that very ancient stock. Are a few modern examples needed? What about D'Artagnan and Cyrano de Bergerac? Maybe some of their adventures have been exhibited recently. Not enough? Well, let's mention a more recent character. The name is Bond, James Bond—Commander Bond, at Her Majesty's Secret Service.

Good Heavens! What has Commander Bond to do with D'Artagnan and all those people in the *Iliad*? What has made authors from Homer and Alexander Dumas to Ian Fleming continuously choose that people as characters? They appear whenever the authors need a good fight, and, above all, a good fighter.

Who were that people? Unfortunately, most of their languages are extinct.

From the few, very few cases where their languages survived, or at least just enough words of them to allow present specialists to classify them, we know that their languages differed among themselves. Just as French, Spanish, English or Swedish do, in spite of common ancestors some thousand years ago.

Let's start with the remnants of their population. At one of the apparently few spots in Europe where they still keep many of their traditions alive and, most important of all, some of those ancient tongues are still being spoken.

This small group of survivors had fame since ancient times not only as fierce warriors, but also as wonderful shepherds and the best of navigators.

Some scholars attribute to a few sailors of that race the fact that Christopher Columbus, who carried them in his crew, was able to cross the Ocean and discover America. In fact, Jean Cartier, the explorer who "discovered" the coast of North America, as far as Canada, found in his exploring trip, and much to his disgusted surprise and understandable consternation, a ship belonging to these ancient people in the northern American waters. To the "discoverer's" relief they were there not to compete in the discovery business or to claim some American territory for any European crown. They were just fishing.

Many readers would consider that a wonder. It was not. It was just tradition. There are irrefutable scientific reasons to believe that crossing the Atlantic Ocean was a habit of this people thousands of years before Columbus.

These astounding people are the remnant of a once much larger Paleolithic population. Anthropologists once thought they were the primitive Europeans before they were slowly displaced by the successive waves of Indo-European tribes or else merged with them.

They spoke a group of tongues with scarce links to those presently spoken in Europe.

The cultural legacy of all those tribes and nations that inhabited Europe some millennia ago is immense. Many of the oldest stories, which children still enjoy, come from them. Those tales have been with us for many thousand years, and can still be easily identified.

Many, if not most, of the customs and institutions that the West is proud to carry on were their own. That includes a very important one that seems to be deceivingly modern: *the freedom and equality of women.*

If the men they produced were remarkable, their women were no less impressive. In many aspects they surpassed the men of their times.

Many of those females have left names, which are famous today, easily recognizable even by people with scant knowledge of history. Their lives also have been the subject of plays, essays, and now uncountable movies and TV plays.

The psychic, cultural legacy left by those formidable women still influences most aspects of our life. The diminishing political influence of their ancient states meant the fall of women's rights in most lands. Women all around are still struggling to recover this ancient legacy.

Male or female, these oldest Europeans have left their powerful imprint on almost everything. In spite of some of them having been at war with the Romans, not a few of the Roman customs and institutions are theirs in origin. Roman legions were founded and trained by them. The Romans were indebted to them for their marmoreal palaces and buildings, for their splendid aqueducts and irrigation works. Present traditional foods and beverages, including those delicious French wines carry their indubitable mark.

The architecture of some of the buildings they have left in the islands of the Mediterranean Sea, still surprises the experts. Their concept of light and air, embedded in their palaces, was so modern that only in the twentieth century were some of them rediscovered and fully appreciated. City planning started with them.

They have left their mark in everything: art and religion, philosophy and science, architecture and jewelry, folklore and customs, traditions and legends, institutions and family.

There is scarcely any trait of modern European culture that has not been influenced. In fact, the way of life and attitudes that distinguishes present Europeans from other peoples are, mostly, a heritage from these almost unknown ancestors.

Nothing about Europe can be understood without referring to them, the oldest Europeans.

1

The Oldest Europeans

In southern France, in the region of Armagnac, whose wines and cognacs enjoy justly deserved world fame, there is a small village: Loupiac. Its name means city of the wolves. A name, as it will be seen in the last pages of this book, that carries some extraordinary old connotations. Some four miles from Loupiac, down a narrow country road, there is a small, attractive *chateau*, with two modest towers: the chateau of Castelmore, where some signs warn the tourists not to trespass. The chateau belongs to the Batz family. There, in 1611, was born Charles Batz de Castelmore. He was probably baptized in the chapel of St. Jacques in Loupiac. A discrete plaque reveals that Bertrand de Batz built both the chapel and an *albergue* in 1605. Bertrand was surely one of Charles' forebears, maybe his father. The albergue was destined to the many pilgrims who followed the then famous *Chemin de St. Jacques*—the Way of Saint James.

Charles Batz de Castelmore grew up and went to Paris, where he became a *mousquetaire* at his Majesty's service. Madame Marie de Rabutin-Chantal, Marquise de Sevigné—a lady in the court of Louis XIV—wrote letters to her daughter that are considered a French literary treasure. In one of them she describes the imprisonment of *monsieur* Fouquet, the king's treasurer, brought down by the charges of corruption and emptying the royal coffer.

Le Roi Soleil, the Sun King, trusted this delicate mission to one close to him, and paradoxically, also one of Fouquet's friends: our Charles Batz de Castelmore. Madame de Sevigné did not use that name in her letter. She preferred the name that Charles himself used. It was a *nom de guerre* well known at that time and still famous nearly four hundred years later: *monsieur le chevalier* d'Artagnan. After many years of distinguished service the King named him Count of Artagnan. He became for a while the temporary military-governor of Lille. He had a soldier's death—at the siege of Maastricht, on June 25, 1673. The mention of his name immediately brings to mind the clash of swords, linked to temerity and adventure.

He was not the only one from his region to be distinguished both by his courage and loyalty. Take, for example, Hercule Savinien Cyrano de Bergerac, better known as Cyrano de Bergerac. Contemporary of d'Artagnan, he also served valiantly, distinguishing himself at the battles of Mouzon and Arras. Twice wounded, he had to retire from the army. He then turned to philosophy, becoming a reputed writer. Cyrano had a very long nose, but very few, if any, dared to point out that fact, at least while he was present—his sword was much longer than his nose. He was well known for his quick temper and his ability at fencing. His love of philosophy and poetry did not make him any softer. Like d'Artagnan, he was prone to duels.

Both d'Artagnan and Cyrano keep fighting nowadays. We can appreciate their mastery at swordsmanship in many movies and TV series. Their lives inspired Alexandre Dumas and Edmond Rostand to write books and plays about them. There was something in their lives that made all the legend about them credible. Both d'Artagnan and Cyrano came from families from a well-known region. Readers in France already knew that soldiers or adventurers coming from the same region were all easily aroused and ready to fight at any excuse, and frequently without much of an excuse. The region had been traditionally famous, and not only in France, for the kind of soldiers it produced.

When Charles VIII, sovereign of France, invaded Italy in 1494, a century before d'Artagnan and Cyrano were born, his troops created havoc whenever they encountered the enemy. No wonder they did. French troops had this disturbing habit of killing the enemy. That was considered very impolite behavior by the Italian *condottieri* of that time, which preferred the much more civilized method of taking prisoners and then asking for a nice ransom. It is understandable, then, the panic that these unpolished French soldiers caused, when they exterminated any rider who had had the bad fortune of being dismounted. Among the French, there were certain soldiers that were much more feared than the rest. A Florentine, describing the parade of Charles VIII's troops, aptly mentioned them: "...and then came the ferocious Gascons."

Ferocious Gascons! Their fame had been established much, much earlier than that. Curiously, that same expression, ferocious, kept popping up throughout the centuries. Anyone who had the bad fortune to confront them, and the good fortune to live long enough at least to tell the story, usually used the same word, ferocious. What they inspired in battle was just that—fear. That was the stock where d'Artagnan and Cyrano came from— the fiery Gascons. Both of them contributed to keep alive the already old fame of their countrymen. The Gascons were famous already, for the same motive, in Roman times. Who were these Gascons?

These quarrelsome people were established in the south of France and the north of Spain, at both sides of the western Pyrenees Mountains. Some scholars believe that for the pronunciation of their name they used a consonant whose sound was intermediate between *b* and *g*. So, in the *Chronicles of Fredegar* (8th century A.D.) they were called Wascones, and their country Wasconia. In France they became the Gascons and their region the Gascoigne. They also occupied the Aquitaine, farther to the north. In Spain, they became the Vascones.

The Romans recorded the presence of the tribe of the Vascones in the North of Spain, in lands of the province of Navarre. They took note that the Vascones and the Aquitanians spoke languages close to each other or dialects of the same language. They also left record of their fieriness. The Romans contented themselves with installing a number of camps surrounding them and mainly with retaining the control of the passes between Spain and France. Painfully aware of their warring qualities, they used them as mercenaries whenever possible. They always kept having trouble with them.

With the decline of the Roman Empire, the Visigoths, who had come to Spain in 418 A.D. as auxiliaries to the Roman Legions, had their turn at trying to tame this impossible people.

The Visigoth mercenaries attempted, as Rome weakened, to take everything over. The Visigothic monarch Leogivild succeeded in uniting the whole Iberian Peninsula in 584 A.D.

The entire peninsula? Well... any comic resemblance to the Asterix strip is attributable only to the Visigothic writers. From the Visigoth kings' chronicles, we may assume they succeeded. Almost from their first king on it is possible to find in the royal curricula, written by compliant court biographers, this remarkable sentence: *"...perdomuit feroces vascones"* (he subdued the ferocious Vascones).

We might have to excuse historians if they heartily express their doubts about it. As that Latin expression is used in the Visigoth chronicles to describe the victories of king after king, historians have long concluded that maybe the Vascones were indeed ferocious, but not at all subdued. People can be conquered only once. All that subduing really meant the Vascones kept fighting and were relatively free.

In fact, when the Arabs were invading the Iberian peninsula in 711, the Visigoth king Roderick was still trying to conquer the city of Pamplona, which had been one of the main Roman camps and which controlled one of the most important routes: the Roncesvalles pass. The pass was soon to become famous as the scene of one of the most significant battles in European history.

The Visigoths had occupied Pamplona in 448. But Pamplona was again at that time in the hands of those not very much subdued and still ferocious people who had inhabited the region long before any written history: the Vascones, or as they are called today, the Basques.

It only took three years for the Arabs to arrive to the Basque lands, after annihilating the Visigothic kingdom in Spain, as a consequence of their victory in the battle of Guadalete in 711. The attempt of Roderick to make true that "perdomuit feroces vascones" had cost him his throne, for not paying adequate attention to the Arabs invading from the south. When Roderick decided it was time to temporarily forget the combative Basques, he went hurriedly to confront the invaders and was killed in Guadalete by Tarik's Berbers. The victor was the same Tarik to whom Gibraltar owes its name (Gebel-al-Tarik, Tarik's mountain).

From 714 on it was the Arabs' turn to try to tame the unruly Basques. Their cultured chroniclers became aware of that wild people "whose men live naked, just like the beasts with whom they cohabitate." The wild tribes met by the Arabs do not seem to have impressed them much. The Arabs never considered them their main adversaries. It was a quite reasonable vision. The Basques were always quarreling among themselves and it was not possible for them to unite enough to menace their new powerful Muslim neighbors. They never raised great armies.

As the Romans had discovered before, the Basques were not a major threat for the control of most of the peninsula. No doubt that some Basque leaders might have had some visions or ambitions, but no one appeared able to unite them into a great power.

But these people, whose strange and peculiar tongue, not similar to any their different adversaries had found before, kept baffling all non-Basques who tried to speak it, and who were no match in a struggle for overall dominance in Spain or France, exhibited a terrible energy when others tried to occupy their lands. Romans, Vandals and Visigoths had had a taste of it. Now it was the turn of both the Arabs and the main power in Europe at that time: the Western Holy Roman Empire. The strongest European leader, Charlemagne, accepted the invitation of some Arab rebels to intervene in Spain. There he went with his formidable army in 778.

The emperor Charlemagne, king of the Franks, had crushed the revolts in Aquitaine. Farther to the southwest, the Basques, who controlled one of the routes into Muslim Spain, were as usual at their favorite pastime—making trouble in the Gascoigne and beyond the Pyrenees. The Arabs outside Saragossa halted Charlemagne's army, and he was obliged to retreat. They retired into France way of the Roncesvalles pass. There he suffered a most unexpected and humiliating experience. The rear of his army was totally annihilated by the Basques. Many of the emperor's leading warriors were killed.

It was a total surprise. Later the court singers started praising the courage and other qualities of the vanquished Frank knights who had met their doom in the pass. The *Chanson de Roland*, the most celebrated of all French *chansons de geste*, which marked the birth of French literature, sings of the bravery of all those who perished that day. Roland, Charlemagne's nephew, was the legendary hero, succumbing to the treacherous attack... of none less than the Arabs! Now, what had *any* Muslim army to do with that massacre? The answer is nothing at all.

It is difficult to find a more embarrassing moment in the history of war than the Roncesvalles defeat. Which poet or court singer would have dared to state the truth? How could they have explained to their countrymen that the state-of-the-art army of the greatest power in Europe had been irremissibly dusted not by the superb Arab troops but by just a bunch of peasants?

The object of the expedition was to force the Arabs out of Spain. The Basques were considered a minor obstacle. For the expedition leaders they were bothersome and wild people whose lands had to be crossed but not representing any real danger. Everyone knew they had no standing army. Reality proved itself so shameful that for centuries the court bards attributed the defeat to the Arabs.

Even more embarrassing, the Basques were not disputing any kind of political supremacy, or trying to tilt any balance of power. They were just angry for the same reason that they were also successfully fighting the Arabs: trying to keep foreigners off their lands. They had rolled boulders over the cliffs and then fallen over the already disrupted forces of Charlemagne.

Surprise could explain some things, but how could they beat the most seasoned troops of Europe? The well-trained soldiers of Charlemagne had successfully dealt with the best that Saxons, Lombards, Bavarians and Avars could put in the field. No wonder that the legend attributed their defeat to the powerful Muslim army. The political outcome, however, was the same. The massacre was key to the permanence of the Arabs in Spain.

The disaster probably dissuaded Charlemagne from attempting the domination of the Iberian Peninsula. Scholars have debated about how long could the Arabs have held it without that unexpected setback suffered by the Franks.

In spite of the Charlemagne's troops disregard for the Basques, that slaughter was not a novel experience for the Franks in their dealing with the bellicose Basques.

Some scholars think that many of the elements of the *Chanson of Roland* come from other disasters preceding and following Charlemagne's military debacle. They believe, for instance, that the fiction of the twelve peers, fighting to their deaths in the song, was inspired by the massacre of an earlier unlucky expedition, that of the duke Harembert.

Twelve Frank chiefs led that expedition, sent by king Dagobert against the Basques in 636-637. They were annihilated in the valley of Subola, identified with Mauléon, near Roncesvalles.

Also in the same neighborhood similar encounters, under almost identical circumstances, took place in 813 and again in 824—all with the same frightening consequence, an unmerciful carnage.

The epic beating suffered by Charlemagne's men in 778 was far from being an isolated incident. But there was no glory in being defeated by rustics wearing no protection, and whose weapons were truly primitive. So, the true heroes of the battle were excluded from the song.

One of the most curious things about the Basques is that there is some peculiar cloud of silence about them. Historians, anthropologists and philologists seem to have established, just as the bards who sang the *Chanson of Roland*, a tacit pact not to mention them.

A demonstration of the terrible fighting power of the fearless mountaineers from the Pyrenees was given to Charles *the Lame* in 1282. He would become Charles II, King of Naples and Sicily in 1289. But in 1282 Charles *the Lame* had some reasons to be worried. His father, Charles de Anjou, King of Naples and Sicily, had been utterly defeated by a troop of *almogavars* in Sicily. Peter III of Aragon had sent the *almogavars* there. In spite of being grossly outnumbered, more than 15 to 1, and not having cavalry, the *almogavars* had crushed the well-armed soldiers of Charles de Anjou in a few months and freed Sicily from them.

Charles *the Lame* was in charge of Calabria at that time and he knew that a small detachment of the triumphant *almogavars* had been now sent against him. One morning he was told that his men had captured an *almogavar*. He ordered to bring the prisoner and his weapons immediately to him. When they did, young Charles *the Lame* felt completely disappointed. The almogavar was dressed with just rags—no shield, no helmet and no armor. His weapons were a few azkonas, small throwing darts or small knives, and a coltell, a long knife. He was, from his appearance and manners, obviously not a knight.

Charles, we are told, contemplated the shabby rustic in front of him with scorn. "Are these the soldiers with which the King of Aragon intend to make war to us?" he said with disdain, according to the chronicler.

The *almogavar* did not understand his words but Charles's gestures were clear enough. The ragged captive demanded to know the meaning of the prince's words. When his captors succeeded in explaining their lord's comments the prisoner was visibly incensed. He demanded his weapons and to be allowed to fight one fully armed knight.

The chronicler did not mention it but we may imagine the hubbub among Charles' knights at the challenge. The chronicle only states that all the knights felt offended and asked their commander permission to chastise the offender. The prisoner and the aroused knights were all granted their wish.

The almogavar was given his azkonas and his coltell.

One cavalier was fully armed and then the unequal encounter took place in front of the prince and the rest of the knights.

As the heavy war-horse was running implacably, carrying the fully armored rider with his lance, ready to pierce the seemingly defenseless prisoner, there must have been a sadistic, anticipated rejoicing among Charles' troops.

Everybody knew that no unarmored man on foot could stand such a charge. Without any shield or helmet he was considered practically dead almost before the combat started.

The well-protected and experienced rider did not even need to recur to his spear, neither to use his sword, axe nor mace. Just the formidable impact of the big charger, trained to kill with its hooves, would suffice to swiftly turn the arrogant, ragged captive into a bloody pulp.

Some Roman centurion, who had had the unpleasant experience of encountering peasants like the prisoner near the Pyrenees, would have warned the cheering knights. A Visigoth knight would have heatedly expressed his doubts and told these far away cousins not to be so confident. Any of Charlemagne's riders could have told them that horses seemed not to make such a difference to these weird fighters. Disappointed Arabs could have added that these crazy people seemed to need no armor whenever they fought. All of them would have agreed that his rustic, unwarlike appearance was not to be trusted.

Anyway, the combat was short.

When the horse approached him, the *almogavar* threw an *azkona* not to the rider but straight to the chest of the horse, bringing down the animal. He then walked to the fallen knight and was ready to cut his throat when the combat was stopped.

Charles *the Lame* released the prisoner and presented him with a dress.

No doubt that both Cyrano and d'Artagnan would have approvingly cheered their countryman's performance. *Touché!*

Most probably, after the surprising outcome of so uneven confrontation, the prince and his riders must have reconsidered their former optimism about the coming conflict against the *almogavar* force. If so, they were right. Soon after they were thrown out of Calabria.

The *almogavars* were guerrilla warriors or shock troops under the crown of Aragon. They were of mixed origin—recruited mostly among people from Navarre and Catalonia in the Pyrenees. There were even Arabs among them, as their name proclaims (from *al-muggabi*, Arab for scout or guerrilla soldier). The name of their weapons also points to their different nationalities: *azkona* (Basque, throwing dart or knife), *coltell* (Catalan, knife).

Latin writers had attributed the same equipment, clothes and habits in war to the always-unrestful Vascones. Their tactics in front of heavy cavalry were simple. They killed the horses. Then they turned against the riders, who were pinned down by the weight of their armor. The dismounted horsemen were then at their complete mercy. Unfortunately for fallen knights, the fierce mountaineers never had a great fame for their mercifulness.

The Romans writers knew of the portentous agility of the Basques and their deadly skill in the use of their scarce and limited weaponry. Their temerity was legendary and also their fierceness in the defense of their land. In spite of being devoted Christians, until a few centuries ago, even bishops were in danger if they attempted to pass through their land without adequate permission.

The Basque tongue is extremely difficult for any foreigner. Their words and structure do not resemble any of the Indo-European tongues or dialects. It puzzled the Romans and still disconcerts linguists today. Among its many peculiar features there is one that calls the attention of many philologists: many of the words seem to imply that the Basque language has been spoken from very ancient times. It carries sounds that seem to have come directly from the Stone Age.

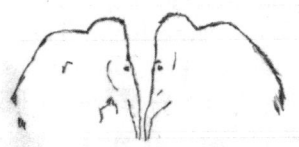

2

The Men from the Stone

Inchauspe, a French-Basque priest from Bayonne, was the first to point out a peculiarity—common in many Basque words for instruments used in cutting and digging. Both the roots *aitz* and *arri*, which mean stone, were present in them. Today it is widely accepted that the reason for those roots to subsist is that metal instruments were not available at the time the words originated. To put it in other way, those words come straight from the Stone Age.

A few examples: *aizkora* (axe), *aisto* (stone+small =small knife), *aitzur* (stone+sharp=hoe), *azpil* (round stone =dish, platter), *aizturrak* (scissors), *aitzurrotz* (stone+keen edge=trident), *nabar* (revolving+stone=plow-share), *zula-kaitz* (chisel), *zaparri* (percussion+stone=mortar).

From these revealing words it is not difficult to see where their tableware and tools came from. They tell us more clearly than a history book the kind of life the Basques' ancestors led over some thousand years ago—how they lived, worked and ate.

In an extraordinary time travel, those words transport us back to Stone-Age usage and also to the colder climate of the Ice

Age. *Orma* means wall in the Viscayan dialect. In the Guipuscoan and Labourde ones it means ice, also thin ice crust. *Ormasoi* is a refuge close to the wall—*Ormagin*, mason. *Lei*, which means ice, enters into *leiza* (cave), *leihor* (refuge). Yes, it really is a language from cave people from the Ice Age.

For quite different reasons, some scholars also attribute the Basques an extraordinary antiquity. They believe the Basques are the descendant of the Cro-Magnon cave dwellers. That they come from the same stock that left those wonderful Paleolithic paintings in Altamira, Lascaux, and other places throughout France and Spain. That means Basques are thought to have been in their lands for more than 20,000 years—quite a time. Others think Basques have been in the region for a much, much longer time, no less than... 40,000 years!! They quote the archaeological evidence of continuous occupation of the Pyrenees by people with the same anthropological characteristics.

It is not easy to dispute such assertions. Anthropometry tells us that present Basque skulls, for instance, have a striking similarity to skulls found in very old strata. The skeleton of the face is distinctively narrow and orthognathism, or absence of forward protrusion of the jaws, is also very marked—long faces and long, narrow noses.

Such a prolonged period of continuous occupancy is so unusual that it defies imagination. It would nearly make the Basques survivors of two Ice Ages.

Anyway, in spite of the understandable discussion among anthropologists and archaeologists, almost everybody agrees that Basques have been in the region for at least 5,000 years. Even by this extremely conservative estimation the Basques come out as the oldest surviving ethnic group in Europe.

New scientific methods have now extended that already long period. Recent DNA studies indicate that they had been there for some 35.000 thousand years. They are the oldest Europeans.

Where do they come from? There are hints, in their DNA, pointing to a much earlier Asiatic migration. For many reasons, some scientists think they are the remnant of the people who were in Europe before the Indo-Europeans or Aryans came to slowly displace them. They are the people that modern anthropologists are beginning to call the Old Europeans. The Basques call themselves Euskaldunak, their country Euskalherria and their language Euskera.

Some Basque thinkers have used the word *Euzko* to name their people, and they extended that name to other peoples in Europe who they thought were ethnically related to them or had the same origin. That will be the meaning of Euzko in this book.

We will see that Euzkos have left an impressive inheritance in the world. Practically everything points to them—art, culture, customs, technology, science, philosophy and religion. All bear their mark. Almost everything started with them.

The Basques show the traits that seem common to most Euzkos. They are splendid shepherds. The sheep is one of the first domestic animals, if not the first. Even sheep keeping in both North and South America, is associated to the sons of immigrating Basques.

They have loved wine and enjoyed a reputation as good drinkers since ancient times. The region of Bordeaux, for instance, has been considered the greatest wine-exporter of the world. Bisturi grapes were already famous in Roman times. Cabernet Sauvignon comes from them. That is the country of the famous Château wines: Laffite, Latour, Margaux, Mouton-Rothschild and Haut-Brion. The Gascon region has a lot more names to its glory. Poets have been singing its wines for nearly two thousand years. Not that they were not celebrated before that. It just means that there are no older written records.

Another common Euzko trait: they are wonderful navigators. Basque fame is well established in that field. Jean Cartier had an annoying experience in 1534. Sent to explore the northern coast of America, he found a French Basque ship in a Labrador bay he was supposed to be "discovering". Fortunately for his ambitions, the Basque sailors where not interested in claiming any discovery right or fame. They rather preferred to keep doing their business as quietly as possible—no need to reveal their fishing waters to strangers. They had nearly extinguished whales off their coast and in the central Atlantic. So, they had crossed nearly 2,000 miles of Atlantic waters to continue fishing their very remunerative prey.

Were the Basques in America before Columbus?

There is archaeological evidence of at least ten Basque whaling ports and establishments along the Labrador coast. They were there from the beginning of the 16th century A.D., maybe a little before. There is no definite proof however that they had arrived there before Columbus.

Some scholars speculate whether or not, according to some old traditions, the genial Genovese was following some Basque whaler route. Others point to some arguable epigraphic evidence of much earlier Basque travels to America.

Pre-Columbian traveling to America seems to have been a tradition among Euzkos. We will see that while commenting on other Euzkos.

Basques were irrefutably among the first to circumnavigate the world. When Ferdinand Magellan died in the Philippines, captainship of his expedition fell upon the master of the ship *Concepción*—44 year old Juan Sebastián Elcano. He brought home the survivors the following year. Elcano was from Guetaria, a Basque city and port, where each year there is a celebration enacting the return of the *Victoria*, the first ship to circle the globe—the only one from the original five to come back from the adventure.

Spaniard kings favored Basque ships and sailors, due to their magnificent sea qualities. Basques took part in all Spanish expeditions of discovery and conquest.

They sailed with Columbus. Some scholars believe that the *Santa María* owner and master, Juan de la Cosa, may have been a Basque. They sailed and fought with Pizarro and Cortés. They frequently commanded expeditions, as Juan de Garay, who founded Buenos Aires, or Juan de Oñate, who explored New México.

Basque ships and sailors were the main force of the ill-fated *Armada Invencible*, sent by Phillip II to conquer England. Most of its ships were sunk by storms before reaching their objective. They had sailed mostly from Basque ports.

The Basque language, apparently a Stone Age tongue surviving alive and well into the Space Age, is still spoken by some 700.000 people, most of them in Spain (provinces of Álava, Vizcaya, Guipúzcoa and Navarra), the rest in France (Labourd, Basse-Navarre and Soule). There are still 3.000.000 people of Basque descent in the coast of the gulf of Biscay and in the western foothills of the Pyrenees.

The Basque tongue comprises a large number of varieties of speech, all showing the same essential features of language structure. They are grouped in eight dialects. Viscayan differs considerably from all the others.

There is a revival of the Basque language, now freely spoken on TV and radio programs. Some TV and radio channels are only in the Basque tongue. Sounds straight from the Stone Age presently flow from some ultramodern electronic sets.

Since ancient times, writers have coincided that the Basques are simple and honest people. A promise given is never broken. They are proud; their sense of dignity is easily aroused. Their tenaciousness is proverbial, as their taste for wine. Loyal, discreet, industrious and with an eye for detail, they were considered optimal for secretarial and clerkly duties. Their seafaring and warrior prowess were legendary.

Basques love song and dance. Their dances have a rigorous, mathematical structure. If their language brings sounds from Stone-Age man, the *sorginguaiza* (witch's scissors) used to decorate costumes of some of their dances and celebrations are the exact replica of an engraving found on a deer horn from Isturitz (Fig. 1) considered to be from the last upper Paleolithic culture, the Magdalenian. The *sorginguaiza* most probably points to a Stone-Age-religion origin of some dances.

As the warriors who defeated Charlemagne's troops, dancers show and cultivate an extraordinary agility.

In the Dance of the Goblet, the Zamalzain (horseman) leaps and pirouettes, unable to see his feet beneath the hobby-horse worn at his waist, yet at the climax he hops upon a wine goblet, balances a few seconds on it with one foot, making the sign of the cross with the other, and then bounds clear without ever spilling its content (even a drop lost would mean great shame).

Children show outstanding agility in their games. They play a traditional kind of hopscotch where one of the squares, the one they must avoid, is marked with a swastika, the ancient pre-Christian religious symbol. Nevertheless the Nazi aviators bombed them, during the Spanish civil war that preceded World War II. *Guernica*, the world-famous painting by Pablo Picasso, presents the tragedy of the civil war as a nightmare, denouncing the bombing of the homonymous city. The Basques joined the Republican side, in spite of their traditional religiosity, trying to regain their regional rights, lost during the Carlist Wars. Franco stripped them of their remaining rights as a punishment. Basque language and culture were proscribed in Spain for nearly four decades. The present Spanish Constitution has reestablished their rights and allows Basque to be an official tongue. There is a rebirth of Basque culture.

Fig. 1. Antler fragment from the Magdalenian period with incisions resembling a *sorginguaiza* (witch's scissors)

Basque social and family life has a remarkable quality. Each member of a family is referred not by the family name but by his connection to his dwelling—the House. It includes all the buildings and the land. Persons are known as master, mistress, son or daughter of a House or dwelling.

A peculiarity of Basque names is that practically all of them, with very few exceptions, are *toponyms*—they describe the place where the dweller lives. That custom is unique. Among other people a name can point to a dwelling or town, but more frequently it means (or was intended to mean) an attribute of the person. A few names in the Anglo-Saxon culture come from places. Milton, for instance, means mill town. But most names point to a quality, like Charles, from Teutonic origin, meaning strong. Fletcher was the dart maker. Karen comes from the Greek, meaning pure. Among the Basques such names are extremely rare. Almost all of them are connected with a place. The name describes the place or one of its characteristics: *Chevarria* (the new house), *Bolívar* (flat lowland with a mill), *Garaycoechea* (the house in the heights).

Let's stop considering the Basques, those Euzko survivors from the Stone Age, at least for a while. What about the other Euzkos?

Philologist Wilhelm von Humboldt proposed that Basques were *Euzkos*. Those two words were the same in his opinion. Basque intellectuals Miguel de Unamuno and Sabino de Arana Goiri agreed with Humboldt and others in 1886.

Arana Goiri extended the meaning of that name in 1901, proposing that *there were other peoples of probable Euzko origin*. He pointed to a linguistic singularity—the *sk* sound. He included its phonetic variants—*sg* for instance. All people who had that sound in their national, traditional names, if not of Indo-European origin, might come from that stock, such as the Etru**sc**ans, the Pela**sg**ians. A singularity among singularities, Euzko, the word chosen to designate the Basques and their kin was not a toponym. It meant a people, not a place.

Euzkos seem to recognize Euzkos, in spite of certain differences. Arana Goiri claimed in 1901 that not only non-Indo-European peoples whose name carried that root *sk* were Euzkos but also some apparently Indo-European peoples who had that sound in their names were related to them. He pointed, for instance, to the **Sc**ots and the **Sc**andinavians.

It was not much of a proof. That weak linguistic linkage did not seem more than an adventurous, ill-based proposition. It was never taken seriously outside some Basque intellectual circles. Nevertheless, it kept proving surprisingly true. Arana's propositions survived successive tests posed by the ever-developing scientific methods during all the following century.

The Scots related to the Basques? Good grief!!! What on earth could the Scots possibly have to do with the Basques, those ever-warring mountain shepherds, well known for their frugality, their belief in witches, and who repeatedly thrashed the Romans? Is that not also a precise description of the Scots? Oops! Sorry! It was probably a coincidence. As it will be seen later, those are not the only cultural coincidences. All through history, most Euzkos seem to have shared other most important cultural traits. The intuition of Arana Goiri was proved right a few years later by a totally unexpected and new scientific path, which had nothing to do with philology. It was hardly a surprise. After all, anything tied to those bellicose Euzkos, the Basques, the Scots, and others, must have left a trail somewhere. Coming from such a warring people it must be a really bloody trail.

And so it is.

3

The Blood Trail

Arana Goiri made those extravagant claims that Basques, Scots and Scandinavians were related peoples in 1901. He was probably unaware that a transcendental discovery had been made the year before. Karl Landsteiner had found the classical four blood–type groups: *A, B, AB* and *O*.

Due to their importance in transfusions, a great number of analyses were performed promptly around the globe. As an enormous amount of data kept flowing and conferences took place, a pattern soon became clear: blood groups were not evenly distributed among the world's population.

There are regional variations in the distribution of blood groups. In a general way, it can be said that a high frequency of type *O* is found in northwestern Europe, southwest Africa, parts of Australia, and in the Indians of South and Central America. The frequency of *B* rises in the eastward direction across Europe into Asia, and the maximum is reached in central Asia and northern India.

Type *B* blood is practically nonexistent among the Basques. They have one of the highest incidences of type *O* blood in

Europe. What really sets them apart is another blood characteristic.

Landsteiner and A.S. Wiener in 1940, almost half a century after Arana Goiri's speculations, experimenting with guinea pigs, rabbits and Rhesus monkeys, made a new discovery: the Rhesus-blood-group system—more simply put, the *Rh*.

The new factor proved to be of great importance to pregnant women. *Rh*- females, when married to a *Rh*+ male, after their first or second pregnancy may develop antibodies to the next fetus blood, originating a hemolytic disease in the newborn. When that was understood, a great number of *Rh* tests were performed throughout the world. The results brought a surprise: *Rh*- serum was the first extremely geographically localized blood-trait.

Rh- falls to nearly zero in non-European populations. Only along the Mediterranean coast of Africa (the Berebers have the highest rates), and in a few locations of that continent there is a small spread of *Rh*-. The *Rh*- turned to be an almost exclusive European characteristic.

If the location of the *Rh*- was surprising, its distribution among the European population was also baffling: it is highest among the Basques (30% of the population carry it). It is also high in other fringe areas of Western Europe, such as parts of Ireland (notably in the north), northern Wales and Scotland, Iceland, Norway and part of Germany (Fig. 2, see next page). In all those parts about a 15% of the population is *Rh*-.

In the rest of Europe the percentage falls to 1-2%, decreasing gradually from the western coast to fade away almost totally past the Ural Mountains.

The unique distribution of *Rh*- led scientists to an interpretation: the Basques were the remnant of a once widespread population, an earlier European stock.

The much higher *Rh*- frequency in the western coast of Europe indicated that migrants coming from the East had displaced them.

It was totally coherent with the non-Indo-European tongue spoken by the Basques and their different traditions.

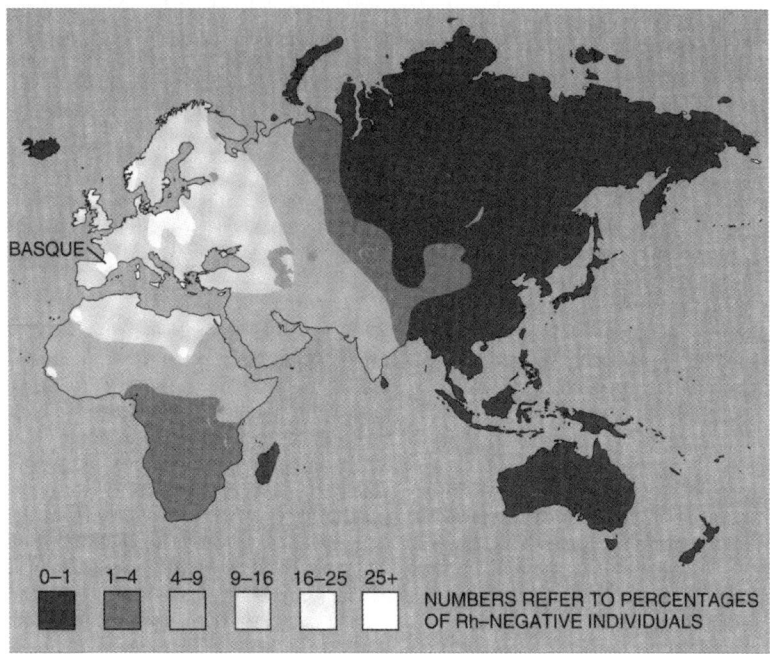

Fig. 2. "GENE MAP shows the *Rh*-negative factor to be most common among the Basques and less common further west. Such data suggest that the Basques preserve vestiges of an early European population that later mixed with newcomers from Asia." (from Genes, Peoples and Languages by Luigi Luca Cavalli-Sforza, Illustration by Laurie Grace, *Scientific American*, November 1991)

It became a classical example, in present Genetic texts, of human-gene-marker variation and displacement. Soon, some concepts were derived from it. In the fifties, the Basques or Euzkos came to be considered a race apart from all others.

Based on that remarkable gene-frequency distribution, W.C. Boyd, an influential American scientist, postulated six races: Caucasoid, Negroid, Mongoloid, Amerindian, Australoid and, of course, the Early European or Basques.

Had Arana Goiri been alive he would have gone into ecstasies. For centuries the Basques had insisted that they were different from all other Europeans—that their roots were different. They had been fighting heartily to remain that way. Suddenly they found they were considered not only different Europeans but also a different race. It was quite a change.

Boyd's postulations lasted only until the sixties. Today the number of human-gene-markers is in the hundreds. Their distribution is extraordinarily complex and nobody is talking about races anymore. Apart from any politically correct intention, the increasing number of markers, whose physiological or genetic importance is mostly unknown, makes it very difficult to use the old idea of race in Biology as a scientific-model tool for the interpretation of results.

Nevertheless, the assertion about the Basques being the remainder of an earlier European stock is still widely accepted, and continues to be used.

So, more than fifty years after Arana Goiri, based on philological considerations, pointed to the probable relationship among Basques, Scots and Scandinavians, an unexpected and solid confirmation came from obvious biological ties. Both Scotland and Scandinavia show a remarkably high frequency of Rh-.

Other more modern studies irrefutably show that Scots and Basques are kin. All the Celts (Irish, Welsh, Scots and Gauls, for instance) seem to be genetically related to the Basques. Scientists who analyzed the linkage between Celts and Basques concluded that *their DNAs were practically the same*. (A more detailed description of the DNA studies and their implications for the European prehistory will be found in chapter 17)

So, in a certain way Asterix was Celt and Basque at the same time. Both peoples are strongly connected.

These Celtic tribes differed in some cultural traits but all had an extraordinary coincidence among them and with the Basques in some remarkable qualities that deeply separated them from the Indo-Europeans. These important cultural disparities will be discussed in further chapters.

Some of the similarities between Basques and Scots have been mentioned. One of them was the failure of the Romans to subdue the tribes of what is now known as Scotland. The Romans found two groups of tribes there (Caledonians and Maeatae). Romans mostly named them Picts by 310.

Roman writers described some new tribes the following century—the Scots. They were Irish who came across to Britain first as allies of Picts and raiders of the Roman province of Britannia, then as settlers. They began to dispute the power to the Pict tribes. Their stormy relationship lasted some centuries, with alternating fortunes. Kenneth mac Alpin finally overcame the Picts in 843.

Burials, weapons, adornments and many descriptions indicate that Picts and Scots had similar cultures. The Pict tongue is lost to us. From inscriptions, names and place-names, it seems that the Picts spoke essentially a British Celtic language, distantly related to Welsh rather than to the Scots Gaelic. It retained many elements derived of an older, non-Celtic speech.

The Scots' fighting customs made them suitable material for every writer looking for daring characters. From Walter Scott to Ian Fleming, the Scot warrior became a familiar figure in literature. Take Bond, Mr. James Bond, for instance.

As any typical Euzko this literary character is a navigator: Commander Bond, Royal Navy, serving at Her Majesty's Secret Service. He is intensely loyal to a queen, a highly significant Euzko trait, for reasons that will be shown later.

Scottish actor Sean Connery, the most successful Bond, shows some particular features. His face is rather longer than wide. His forehead is also a typical Euzkan one, high and vertical, replacing the old human model with a flattened one. The back of his skull is pronounced, to balance the inconvenience of that new human acquisition, the steep forehead's weight. His nose is long and thin, apt for people who needed to warm the cold air during the glacial period. Curiously, his hair color is neither the straw-white of the Vikings nor the copper-blonde of the Celts but the black of the Picts, which were still controlling Scotland until the eighth century.

Tending sheep with a proper beret, Mr. Connery would pass perfectly as a Basque shepherd in the Pyrenees.

The secret agent exhibits in fiction the loyalty and agility that characterized Euzko warriors at all times—once incited they fought to the death. D'Artagnan would have been delighted with such a companion. Not surprisingly, Ian Fleming's creation has found a comfortable place in the collective subconscious.

The Pict tribes quarreled and raided each other and formed a loose confederacy, just like the Basques. The Picts were unable to coalesce enough to form a menacing nation, but were incredibly fierce when it came to defend their land and their old customs.

There are many other markers, apart from the genetic ones, that indicate a relationship between those Picts and Basques. One of them was the perennial tendency to use stones as building material and for monuments. Wherever Euzkos were on the scene, stones were skillfully used for many purposes. Stones and Euzkos are linked all through history and geography.

J. Caro Baroja has pointed that Basque stone workers were famous in Spain. If the job required workers skilled in wood or plaster, people turned to the Moors, who were very good at it. Since the 15th century at least, those who needed stonecutters looked for some Basque *arguiña*. They formed wandering bands that executed different kinds of stone works even in faraway places. People from the region or some other places usually joined them. Sometimes they settled in one of their working places. For instance, the father of one famous painter, Zurbarán, did so and remained in Badajoz, in the Extremadura region. Other stone workers returned to the Basque country.

Apart from their skill, those stonecutter bands stood out from their contemporaries for an interesting feature: there was some kind of secrecy in their association.

They used signs and marks, left many times engraved in their works. Their contemporaries thought it was a secret language. Perhaps what was called a "secret" language was merely the original tongue of the Basque masters. They did not need any special language to disguise their talk in the presence of foreigners. Euskera is famous for the difficulties it presents to outsiders.

The stoneworker bands working in the Galician zone of the Iberian Peninsula used a peculiar jargon, for instance. Galicians wittily called it *latin dos canteiros* (Latin of the stonecutters). Baroja has pointed that they are practically Basque words. A few examples: *arria* (stone, Basque *arri*), *ascorea* (ax, B. *aizkora*), *ureta*, *ura* (water, B. *ur*), *andio* (big, B. *and*), *bai* (yes, B. *bai*), *ez* (no, B. *ez*). Most words of the jargon are just Basque words. Sometimes they change a little, phonetic or semantically, but the original Basque word can be easily spotted.

These special or professional jargons were used to identify the user as belonging to the trade—status marks. Some authors believe that the legend of the secret language, attributed to masons and temple builders in ancient times, may have started this way. As there is such a tradition among Freemasons, this coincidence may be significant.

Among the Picts, stone constructions and monuments were common. But Picts were living in Roman times. There are other constructions from a far older past with a strangely familiar name.

Where are the best preserved stone buildings in Europe? They where found in the windswept Orkney Islands of northern Scotland.

Several dwellings of unmortared flagstone, linked by covered passages, were buried there by some sudden catastrophe. It became a Neolithic version of Pompeii. A huge storm tore away the cliff in 1850 and revealed houses from five thousand years ago. Its inhabitants were fishermen, who also raised cattle and sheep.

Without using metal tools, they left hearths and impressive stone furniture, including a two-shelved bureau. Astounding indoor toilets with a functional sewage system might fascinate tourists.

The name of the place? *Skara Brae*. Arana Goiri would have immediately recognized it. Skara is more than familiar. It is a family name.

The Celt tongue has Indo-European roots. The almost completely non-Indo-European genes of the Celts immediately tell us some story.

Some of the earliest Indo-European migrants must have *intermarried* with the locals. They surely took advantage of the peculiar Euzkan leadership structure.

So the migrants became the Celtic aristocracy and imposed their language over a far more numerous people. The remarkable Euzkan family and tribal structures allowed such incorporations, as it will be seen in later chapters.

The newcomers adopted most of the old customs.

The Celts have always confused historians. Celtic traditions and legends show many traits of a mixed heritage. As it will be seen, such intermarriages happened many times in ancient Europe.

Linguists and archaeologists believe that Celtic tongues, spoken by Scots, Welsh, Irish and Gauls among others, were some of the earliest Indo-European languages spoken in the continent.

The Celts kept many Euzkan uses and beliefs. The French still say *quatre-vingt* (four-twenty) for counting eighty. They also say *quatre-vingt-dix* (four-twenty-ten) to count ninety. It is an Euzkan inheritance. Basques still use a 20-based numeration instead of the 10-based one of Indo-Europeans. Thirty is twenty-ten, forty is two-twenty, sixty is three-twenty. The Gauls counted like that. The Scandinavian Danes also retained that old system.

Once the Euzkans and Indo-Europeans mixed, the resulting tribes showed a marked resistance to adopt more orthodox Indo-European uses.

As we will see later, Celts closely resembled in that behavior the history of the Ionian and Eolian tribes in Greece, which confronted the last waves of Indo-Europeans—the Dorians.

The Celts in Ireland, Wales, Scotia resisted firmly the Romans. The Roman Empire hired Celt troops as mercenaries.

Celts were good navigators, with some scholars postulating that they also had anticipated Columbus in his discovery.

A lot of North American navigable river names, between

then the Merrimack and the Potomac, sound suspiciously Celt. They have no equivalent in Amerindian names. Epigraphists have said that Celtic runes had been found in stone inscriptions in America. They have pointed also to some mounds and some peculiar stone temples. Julius Caesar judged the Celtic ships as able to sail into the ocean.

Were they?

We know now that crossing the Atlantic in remote times was possible. *We actually know it happened.*

The confirmation did not come from any archaeological find. It was through the study of some old language characteristics that we positively know that some of Asterix ancestors had crossed the ocean.

Before telling that story, let's see some of the other Euzkan peoples.

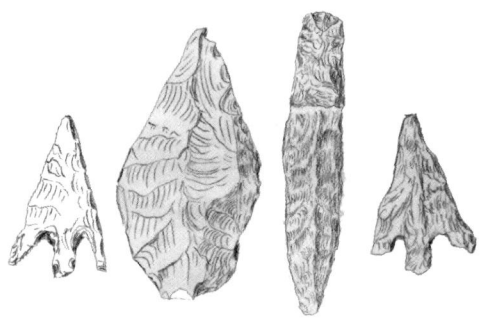

4

The Italian Euzkos

Arana Goiri had indicated that ancient people who had lived in Italy, the Etruscans, also were Euzkos. They carried in their name that revealing sound— the *sk*.

The Etruscans were an enigma to the Greeks, who were completely puzzled by their language, their customs and their origin. Herodotus claimed they were Lydians, who had immigrated to Italy from Asia Minor.

Some modern scholars disagree. The Etruscan language was clearly non-Indo-European. Lydian was an Indo-European one. Was Herodotus wrong? It is not an easy question. Maybe he was right, and Lydians had arrived, and then *intermarried* with other tribes just like, as it will be shown later, it happened in Greece.

The Romans were not so baffled by the Etruscans. After all, *the Romans were partly Etruscans.* They called the Etruscan *tusci* and Tuscany the region in northwestern Italy where they lived, which still keeps its ancient name.

Rome came into existence as a hybrid city. According to its historians, Latins and then Sabines inhabited the city. Maybe this was an Indo-European politically correct version—these two peoples were both from Indo-European stock. From their language differences and similarities, we know today that their origin was common, and that they had been separated for a relatively short historical period. Etruscan joined these two peoples, Roman historians tell us. According to them, merchants and others from Etruria came to reside in the new city, which had been founded again in 753 B.C. Maybe what really happened was exactly the opposite—the Etruscans as first inhabitants.

Excavations have shown that there had already been a continuous occupation of the place for some millennia before that. Discussions about the nature, culture and origin of those first villagers are still in vogue. Were they from the Etruscan tree or Latins? Archaeology shows no clear answer to this. Nevertheless, in spite of a previous occupation, a new foundation could have taken place. A city is not merely a place where some people live together. To subsist, particularly in rough times, there must be a minimum of communal participation and some regulations. Almost from its beginnings, Rome showed certain peculiarities. There were difficulties among the people, who seemed to be quite a quarreling lot. They showed also a remarkable common sense to solve those social difficulties.

Dionysus of Halikarnassos believed that a migrating band of young men from the city of Alba Longa had founded or taken the city. That is quite coincident with the story of the composition of their Senate. Tulius Hostilius, the third king, incorporated the defeated nobility of Alba Longa as senators. It tells a lot about the Roman way of expanding their influence: sharing more than forcing. It also shows a formidable veneration for their ancestors.

The Alba Longa origin could explain the initial deficit in women and the warring nature of their inhabitants. It also points to some Euzkan origin.

Romans were, in a sense, revolutionary in their social conceptions. When the plebeian class arose, Rome gave them land and political power. This allowed the city to raise a numerous army of citizens, whose interest and loyalty were indissolubly tied to it. Then came a most revolutionary innovation, which would give Rome preeminence all over the Mediterranean world: they extended their citizenship to the people they conquered. The inability of the competing cities to do this was one of the main reasons why they failed to stop the Roman advance.

Etruscan cities, instead, formed a loose confederacy. Roman writers mentioned an Etruscan League formed by twelve cities (*duodecim populi Etruriae*). They were princely fiefdoms that could seldom unite on matters beyond religion.

Before Rome achieved preeminence, the Etruscans dominated by sheer weight of their combined opulence, by their powerful navies and their active commerce.

Paradoxically, the Etruscans gave the Romans what would be one of their greatest assets in their future development. Roman historians quoted a period when the city was ruled by Etruscan kings, the Tarchinians. This was thought to be a legend, just like the war of Troy, until the discovery of tombs and inscriptions lent it credibility.

Three Etruscan kings ruled from 616 B.C. to 509 B.C. Now, what could happen to that newly founded (or founded again) city under Euzko dominance? What could be the legacy of that stone-loving, fighting race? Rome became a stone city: it was mainly under those Euzko kings that their marble buildings came to be. From a village of mud and huts it suddenly became a real city, in less than a century, with impressive public buildings and stone-paved roads.

According to tradition, those new masters carried out the first public works, such as the walls of the Capitoline Hill, in order to also build there Rome's first monumental temple, dedicated to Jupiter. Rome also owes to those kings the Cloaca Maxima, which drained the marsh where the Forum was built.

Many of the Etruscan traditions are known just because Romans adopted or kept them and transmitted them to us.

A momentous contribution from those warring Euzkos was the Roman Legion. They formed, trained and first put into operation that powerful tool.

The *fasci* emblem of power, carried by the disciplined legions and resurrected two and a half millennia later by Mussolini's fascists, was also an Etruscan religious symbol, discovered in some tombs in Tuscany.

Fig. 3. Etruscan warrior with a *bipennis* (from a sarcophagus in a Vetulonian tomb)

The *fasci* were iron bars tied around a double ax (*bipennis*—identical to the ancient *labrys* of the Greeks). Other Roman power emblems are also of Etruscan origin: the golden crown, the *toga palmata*, the cetrum and the throne (*sella curulis*), the triumphal rites and the processions.

Even when the kings were finally expelled and the Republic arrived, the Euzko influence was far from ended. Many, if not most, of the leading families that ousted the kings were of Etruscan origin. Monarchy and the royal house were forced to part, not the Euzkos (or Etruscans).

An Euzkan nobility remained, and Euzkan names could still be found many centuries later among the influential senators and other powerful administrators (for instance: the Larsii, the Licinii, the Minuccii, the Volumnii, the Sempronii, the Herminii, etc). A family that left a deep historical mark—the Julia—was also of Euzkan origin.

From the three components of the Roman people came many of the terms we still use in our languages.

They evidence their formidable cultural influence and the unique agreement that Etruscans, Latins and Sabines reached in that wonderful social experiment which became Rome.

From the three-people system came *tribe, tribune, tribunal,* terms where the *tri* prefix reminds us of an ancient, difficult truce and of an astoundingly conscious decision to share rights and responsibilities equally.

The Roman legions also showed the legacy of that old accord.

Romulus had divided the people into three tribes and thirty

curiae, each of which in turn was composed of families.

At the beginning, each ethnic group contributed with a levy of citizens—a thousand marching men (ten centuries) and one hundred horsemen—for a total of 3,300 soldiers. Soon the whole Mediterranean region would shudder when the frightening creation of those Euzko rulers started to extend the Roman influence all over those lands.

Etruscans also exerted an extraordinary religious influence upon the Romans, and consequently upon the rest of Europe. Anyone using the word *temple* is recognizing it. The area of the sky that augurs set apart for an individual omen of lightning or bird flight was called a *templum* and became the Roman word for temple.

Every Christian bishop participating in a procession and carrying his staff, both inherited from the Romans, is also reminding us of the Etruscan rituals and ceremonies.

Those Euzkos used to study the liver of sacrificial victims to divine. Livy declared that there was no nation more religious than the Etruscans. It seems to be true. Religiosity is a typical Euzkan trait.

In their religion the funeral rituals and a cult of the dead were preeminent. That was a widespread practice in ancient Europe. Most of what is known about the Etruscans has reached us through their numerous tombs. Their inscriptions (some 11,000, mostly proper names), their paintings, pottery and even architecture, as many of their tombs were modeled after houses or contained small house models for the supposed delight of the dead.

Religion controlled every aspect of their life. According to Seneca, "the difference between Romans and the Etruscans is this: we believe that lightning are produced when the clouds collide, they think that clouds collide in order to produce lightning—as they refer everything to the divinity—they think that things have no meaning by their existence, but that they exist in order to have a meaning."

Their religious conceptions influenced even their continuity. They believed that their civilization would last only eight "centuries" (not exact periods of about a hundred years) and that in each century the same patterns recurred. It is currently thought that their belief in cycles, pointing to an unavoidable collapse or "death" of their culture, must have accelerated their end. It probably weakened their resolution to confront some aggressive neighbors they had helped to surge—the Romans.

"The Etruscans had almost all Italy under their power," wrote Cato, referring to pre-Roman times. How could it have been different? After all they were *the* pre-Indo-European people. They were there when all the newcomers started to arrive. The Carthaginians must have displaced them from Sardinia. The Greeks founded colonies in southern Italy. Invaders came from the North, among them Sabines and Latins. Still, during the first four centuries of Roman expansion they were powerful enough to retain northern Italy (Fig. 4).

Besides the warring know-how they transmitted to the Roman legions, they were, as good Euzkos, master seafarers.

The Greeks feared their famed plundering ships and recognized them as a maritime power (*thalassocracy*).

Pliny the Elder attributed to them the invention of the prow ram. Sailors of other nations recognized them as deadly experts in its tactical use.

The Greeks learned how to use the prow rams from the experienced Etruscans. So the Greek fleet was able to beat the Persian ships at Salamis.

The Romans, who were not sea people, speedily formed fleets to fight their rival Carthage. For shipbuilding and sailing tradition they had the Etruscans, under their dominion at that time.

Rome had conquered southern Etruria completely by 351 B.C. Little more than a century later all Etruria had been dominated. The Etruscan cities did not join invading Hannibal in 205 B.C., and their fleets and marine expertise were decisive in the final defeat of the Carthaginians. They did not participate either in the social rebellion at the beginning of the first century B.C.

For all that, they were accepted as Roman citizens gradually after 91 B.C. Then disaster came.

A decade later, after betting on the wrong side in the civil war, Sulla stripped the Etruscans of all rights. Due to his harsh measures, Etruscan peasants could not own small pieces of land any more. Small farmers and tenants, sharecroppers, and laborers, they all became slaves.

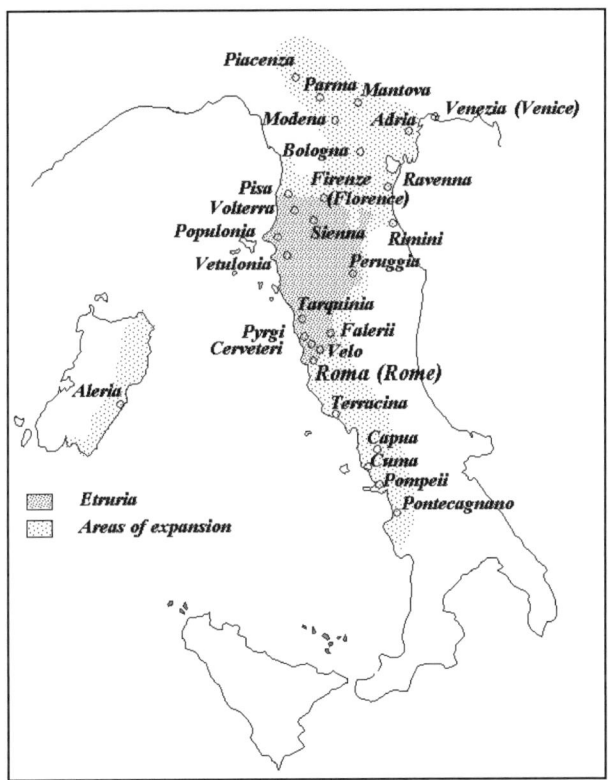

Fig. 4. Etruscan lands before Roman expansion

That brought social disruption, paving the way for Spartacus' rebellion and other revolts.

In spite of these disasters, the Etruscan culture continued influencing religion, engineering and many social and political customs.

These ancient Europeans were *bonvivants*. The Etruscans appreciated a good table, with varied foods and wines. Their standard of life was opulent.

They knew how to exploit farming on a massive scale. This was attained by a carefully studied irrigation system.

The Romans learned road building and water diversion from the Etruscan engineers. Their expertise was so incredible that one of their engineering marvels, the *Tagliata Etrusca*, built to avoid Lake Burano becoming a marsh, an ingenious self-cleaning channel designed to work with tidal flux and reflux, is still working, unattended, *more than two millennia later.*

They drained and dried marshes and bogs, irrigating at the same time arid lands, allowing an increasing population density. Later, in times of the Roman Empire, due to social and political decay, the drainage systems were disregarded and fell into disuse. Then marshes appeared everywhere. With them, malaria and other diseases spread. The poorly administered farms were unable to maintain their high production. Malnutrition and plagues were the outcome. The ensuing depopulation prognosticated the end of Rome as a power.

As good Euzkos, Etruscans knew how to tend sheep. A delicious sheep's cheese, *pecorino*, became internationally famous. It still keeps its worldwide renown.

They skillfully cultivated grains and raised all kinds of animals. Olive oil and wine were two of the many products they exported. The Greeks called Italy *Oenotria*, the land of wine. Gaul chieftains became addicted to Etruscan wine, which was also famous.

Horace tells us that Falernian wine was superb. One vintage year (42 B.C., *consule Planco*, during the consulate of L. Munatius Plancus) was of great fame and became the first one registered in wine history. Falerii was one of the twelve cities of the Etruscan league, sometimes a leading member. So, part of the present fondness of the French for good wines came to be through these ancient Europeans. No wonder Italy is still the largest maker and consumer of wine in the world.

The love of a good meal continued in Tuscany even under Roman dominion, and even a thousand of years after the fall of Rome. When Catherine de Medici abandoned Florence to marry who would become Henry II of France, both the cooking and table manners in the Paris court horrified her. She sent for her own cooks and started the tradition of the famed French *grande cuisine*. The use of the fork was another of her innovations.

Present Italian shoe exporters are just following a famed Etruscan tradition of nearly three millennia. No other ancient people exhibited such devotion for so many varieties of shoes. All types were produced. Elegant, sophisticated, luxury shoes or cheap, simple ones for mass consumption, all were exported to any Mediterranean port.

They became master artisans. Their *bucchero*, a black lustrous pottery, is found along the entire Mediterranean coast and also in Britain, Switzerland, Germany and Hungary.

Luxury loving Etruscans inspired superb goldsmiths, some of whose techniques have not been explained even today, and whose masterpieces found buyers all over the ancient world. Their bronze works were much admired and played an important role in the development of metallurgy among the Celts.

Etruscan furnaces in Populonia processed some 10,000 tons of iron ore a year, for more than four centuries, providing another boost to their formidable commercial power. They became amazingly rich—due to all those export items. As a logical counterpart, their imports were also enormous. So, *more decorated Greek pottery has been recovered in Etruscan lands than in all the Hellenic territories.*

Etruscans were not only noted by their love of a good table but also by their appreciation of the arts and entertainment. "The Etruscans so love music that they knead their bread, practice boxing and whip their slaves to the sound of pipes," marveled Greek writer Athenaus. It was their favorite instrument. They were just like the Basques, who even hunted to the tune of pipes. Roman called their piper *subuli*, the Etruscan name, in acknowledgment of their mastery.

The birth of the symphony is attributed to their double pipes.

Their mastery of the lyre and of trumpets was recognized everywhere. They had a great fame as actors too. Actually, good at histrionics would be a more proper way of saying it, as the Roman word *histrio*, actor, is just the Etruscan word. At the beginning the *histrio* seems to have been a religious dancer.

Fig. 5. Etruscan sarcophagus from Cerveteri (600 B.C.)

Women and men are shown dancing in the frescoes of many tombs.

The world famous annual Palio Race in Siena seems just a copy of those depicted in many tomb paintings. Competitions, hunting, fishing, celebrations, it all showed they knew how to enjoy life.

It is very difficult to estimate the influence of Etruscan art. When Italian Renaissance masters were looking for models they never had to go far. Their favorite painting theme, the Virgin and the Child, was also the most appreciated Etruscan motif, the seated Mother and Child. Paintings where an emaciated Lucifer is depicted blue or green, with pointed ears, long fangs, horns, wings and a proper tail come straight from the paintings in the tombs in Tuscany.

The angels of Fra Angelico, with their many colored wings, are the heavenly brothers of those depicted in the tombs. Famed Michelangelo owned an Etruscan alabaster urn. A relief in the urn is similar to his wonderful *Pietá*. Did the inspiration for the sculpture come from the Etruscan relief? Some experts are now wondering...

The Etruscan passion for music and dance, which astounded both Romans and Greeks, has never abandoned the Tuscans.

The region has consistently produced master musicians, singers and composers during all ages. The remarkable influence of Etruscan art and culture did not limit itself to its main legacy, Rome, but also reached the modern world through the Tuscan people. Their taste, tradition and millenarian culture were the adequate cradle for the Renaissance.

The modern impact of the Tuscan cities is unequaled by any other region in the world. Bologna, Padova, Piacenza, Mantova, Perugia, Siena, Modena, Parma, Ravenna, Pisa. Their universities and art workshops revolutionized the world, not to mention a city placed deep in the heart of Tuscany, Florence.

The cloth guild of Florence commissioned Ghiberti to make the splendid doors of the Baptistery. Art critics usually select that point—at the beginning of the fifteenth century—as marking the birth of the Renaissance in Europe. The doors were more than a masterpiece. They were tradition. The mixture of mercantile wisdom and sensibility, of its resulting opulence finding expression in an art with religious symbolism, was also more than a happy coincidence. It was an old life-style giving its best again, as the existing conditions allowed it, but that had never been really lost in that Euzko region, in spite of Romans and barbarians.

What about the Etruscan language? It has been considered a mystery. In spite of their many accomplishments, no heroic poems, no histories, no literature has reached us. About 13,000 samples of Etruscan writings are known. Most are very short. The majority of the terms are just proper names from tomb or vase inscriptions. Larger inscriptions are so scarce, and so relatively short, that they are all well known by any specialist. If not many they are, at least, really peculiar.

Three golden bilingual tablets were one of the latest discoveries. They were found in Pyrgi, the port of Cerveteri, in 1964. They contain a few dozen words. Another celebrated find is the Magliano lead, a circular calendar of offerings to the gods, with some 70 words forming a spiral. Some fifty words come from a strange source: the cover of a sarcophagus—an image of the deceased is shown with an open, legible scroll in his hands.

Among all those rarities, the most extraordinary text is also the longest script found until now. An Egyptian mummy, of uncertain origin, was donated to the National Museum of Zagreb, at the end of the 19th century. A surprise followed. There was a sacred ritual book written in the linen cloth used to wrap the mummy. The language was Etruscan. Only 500 of its 1,200 words are not repetitions. Not all of them are known.

With only one exception, there is no other ancient writing in languages that could be considered related to the Etruscan. Yet modern methods, applied to linguistic analysis, aided by computer power, are allowing present scholars new approaches in their attempt to build a human-language tree. The extinct Etruscan language has been postulated in the last decade, as an example of the Sino-Caucasian group of languages, a branch of the Dene-Caucasian superfamily of languages (Fig. 6).

To have an idea of what this means, let's just say that Japanese, Eskimo or Hebrew are much, much closer to any Indo-European language than those Sino-Caucasian ones. Are there any other European languages in that peculiar, so far away Sino-Caucasian branch? There is just one, and not so extinct: Basque.

So, Arana-Goiri, was right one more time. Etruscans were Euzkos.

Considering their relationship, we must not overlook another aspect. Between Basque and Etruscan the linguistic differences are greater than among Indo-European languages. They are farther apart, for instance than German and Spanish. In a certain way, that is only reasonable, they are expected to be related and, at the same time, far, far apart. Why this? In languages, as in chromosomes, the differences between the subjects submitted

The Italian Euzkos 61

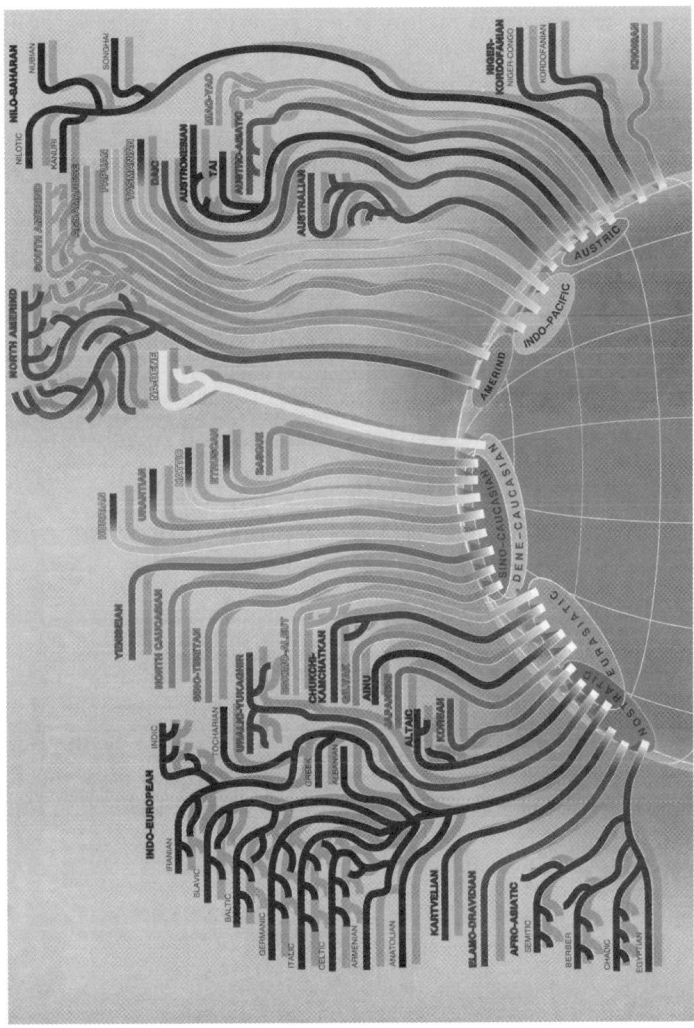

Fig. 6. "GENEALOGICAL CHART relates entire families of languages to proposed superfamilies. The Indo-European family, for example, includes English in its Germanic branch (top left). Some soviet linguists group the family with six others in the controversial Nostratic superfamily (bottom left). An alternative superfamiliy, Eurasiatic, has been also proposed. None of the superfamilies and not all the families are accepted as proved by the majority of linguists." (from Hard Words, by P.E. Ross, Illustration Ian Worpole, Scientific American, April 1991)

to study tell us for how long they have been separated. Given the long permanence of the Euzkos in the continent, a greater difference can be expected.

If the antiquity of Basques attributed by some archaeologists is true, it can only be surprising that they are even remotely connected to any living language.

There is one curious point. The Sino-Caucasian family is part of the Dene-Caucasian superfamily. There are other living languages within that superfamily: the Na-Dene ones. They are all in North America. The tribes that still speak them live in two regions. Some of them are inhabit in western Canada and eastern Alaska. The rest of them are in South-West U.S.A. and Northern, Central Mexico. One example: the Apache. It is fascinating to see that these people American had produced on both sides of the Atlantic famous, legendary warriors. Cyrano and d'Artagnan would have been proud also of an Apache Mescalero whose name was Geronimo.

As was mentioned before, there was also another example of an old written language that was close to Etruscan too. It also corresponded to Arana Goiri's claims: there were other Euzkos. Nobody would dare to consider this other branch of the Euzkos unimportant. Their presence marked one of the pinnacles of civilization. Their cataclysmic disappearance has also marked us all, in all aspects of communal and private life, indelibly until the present.

5

The Greek Euzkos

Just as the Italian Euzkos played a primordial role in the civilization of the Latin and Sabine tribes, the Greek Euzkos, at their time, exerted a formidable civilizing influence over the incoming Aryan tribes.

Compared to what happened in Italy, the process that took place in Greece, during that conflictive cultural encounter, offers an additional interest. Being more richly recorded, it is an unparalleled window to the past, to the origin of many present customs and traditions, to the essence of the European soul.

The difficult merging of the Aryans and Euzkans forged present Europe. Indo-European and non-Indo-European cultures clashed and gave birth to the present.

The invasion of Europe by the Aryan tribes did not happen all at once, it took thousands of years. All that has been revealed by archaeology, myth, lore, tradition and history. Linguistic and genetic analyses tell almost the same story.

Few elements allow us to understand cultures as the contrasts between them.

The comparison of the well documented traits of both the Euzkan and Indo-European populations in Greece, the many stories of the opinions and strong emotions that each ethnic group provoked in the other one, during the more than three-millennium period in which the two cultures interacted, not only allows us to appreciate in detail the extraordinary differences between the two cultures, but also to visualize something that is usually forgotten or ignored—the deep, unequivocal mark left by the Euzkos on the modern Europeans.

The religious-political wars between Euzkos and Indo-Europeans left a social inheritance that still weighs heavily on the present social, religious, economical and political structures.

Thanks to the remarkable Euzkan women, the reader will recognize immediately some of the peculiar traits of the modern European society and of their offshoots in other continents.

The displacement of the Euzkan religious hierarchies is felt even today. In many aspects, Europe is still recovering from the many reciprocal wounds inflicted during that long process, which was sometimes ruthless.

There is also another aspect concerning the displacement of the Greek Euzkos. The abundant chronicles allow us, for the first time, to know the individuals of antiquity, their physical descriptions and their habits. Even their families, friends and lovers are well described.

The prolonged ethnic conflict in Hellenic lands made famous some of the main actors on both sides. It left scars and remembrances collected in Greek history and art. It is through all that that we are allowed, for the first time, to meet our ancestors from both sides face to face, to distinguish the individual, to recognize the name.

Many of those names, of both males and females, are still famous and surprisingly recognizable. Many of them are heard many times a day from TV screens. They are familiar not only to historians but to children throughout most of the world.

In trying to grasp the complex process of the Aryan invasions, it is important to realize that it did not happen at once.

The Greek Euzkos

When the first of the four successive waves of Indo-European tribes—Ionians, Eolians, Acheans, Dorians—started to pour down from the North into what is now Greece, about 4,000 years ago, they encountered different populations which spoke non-Indo-European languages—Caucones, Carians, Lysians, Leleges, Maeonians, Mysians, Paeonians, Pelasgians, Phrygians, Thracians, Thessalians, Eteo-Cretans. Gradually, those Aryan tribes started to call all of them Pelasgians. That was the only name they were using for any pre-Aryan population in the 5th century B.C., in Herodotus times.

Pelasgian is the name and the meaning to be used in this book for the Greek Euzkos.

To call all members of a group by the name of just one of its components is a generalization. A common process, we still do the same with the Greeks. They call themselves Hellenes, and their country Hellas, but everybody else calls them Greeks, the name the Romans used for them. It is all because the first Greeks the Romans met were the *Graeci*, a small tribe on the Adriatic coast.

Similarly, the name Euzko, a word originally meaning Basque, is applied in this book to Basques, Scots, Scandinavians, Etruscans, and Pelasgians, following Arana Goiri's intuition and extending it to the rest of the Celts.

It is widely believed that Pelasgians stands for Pelak-skoi or Pelag-skoi. Pelag means "the sea." So, Skoi or Euzkos from the sea was Arana Goiri interpretation. Being Euzkos that was a redundant name.

The incoming Indo-Europeans considered the Pelasgians very ancient people. Very old stone constructions were attributed to them—the prehistoric walls of Athens, the fortress of Mycenae, the acropolis of Tiryns, among many others. All these had a characteristic in common: they had been built with enormous, gigantic stones, put together without any binding agent, forming perfect joints. Sometimes small stones in the interstices evened them out. They were called cyclopean, built by the mythic Cyclops. Today scientists call them megalithic constructions (from the Greek megalithos, big stone).

Long, narrow skulls were common among the Pelasgians, as among the Basques. As we see, Pelasgians also exhibited many of the Euzko features: stone builders, navigators, and fierce warriors.

The former inhabitants were seafaring people. The coming Indo-European tribes did not know the sea and had not a word for it. They took from the Pelasgians a word, *thalassa*, to name the sea.

The root *tala*, in Basque, is linked to water, to humidity. It appears in many words connected with water: *talapastu* (to agitate a liquid in a glass), *tala-tala* (to drink water). Thalassa is a typical Pelasgian word, ending with the suffix *-assos* or *-essos* (*Halikarnassos*). Other common ending in the pre-Greek language is *-inthos*: *Korynthos, labyrinthos*. Quite a few other names are also Pelasgic: *Athens, Argos*. Residual Pelasgic names are most common in Thessaly, in Asia Minor and, above all, in Crete.

When the first Greek-speaking, Aryan nomadic shepherds, invaded Greece, they met a strong, splendid Aegean civilization. Maybe it had been prompted by Egypt, maybe by Anatolian and Palestinian influences, but it was surprisingly independent. It was already more than two millennia old but still flowering. It had successively passed from a Neolithic stage, until copper appeared. Then the bronze became the new technology, marking the beginning of what is called the Minoan civilization.

It would still last more than a millennium, until the third wave of Indo-European invaders, the Acheans, crushed it and the fourth and last wave, the Dorians, totally erased it. It reached its highest development in a beautiful, sunny island, Crete—most appropriate for Euzkos from the sea.

Until the end of the 19th century almost everybody took Homer, Herodotus and other Greek chroniclers as very creative writers but with very scarce links to reality. Then Heinrich Schliemann arrived. He was an extraordinary, self-educated German who had had a complete trust in Homer since he was a child.

Following the *Iliad*, Schliemann discovered the legendary Mycenae and proved that Troy was not a myth. He then tried to locate the palace of legendary King Minos in Crete. The rapacity of the local functionaries, and the inconveniences they caused, forced him to leave the excavations, begun in the hill of Hissarlik, where he had found promising remains.

It was a Briton, Sir Arthur Evans, who succeeded in fully revealing the Minoan culture, in the same place Schliemane had wisely chosen. So, the unbelievable palace of Knossos came to dazzle the new visitors, as it must have done everyone until some 3,500 years ago.

The splendor of the ruins shook the British archaeologists. They had never expected *that*—four-storied, polychromatic buildings whose doors had modern-looking locks.

All palaces were decorated with beautiful frescoes of remarkable lines. Its luminosity was startling.

The central palace covered 5,5 acres (2,5 hectares). To say that their architectural conceptions were strikingly modern would be an understatement. They did things even modern architects do not usually dare. They ingeniously exploited the irregularities of Cretan sites (not only in Knossos) and wide flights of steps, conceived as *decorative* features, led to a multilevel design. Their solution for air, light and space was brilliant. They refrigerated their splendid residences through a clever channeling of the breeze. Their use of running water anticipated the Roman innovations by much more than a millennium.

The drainage of the large series of open courts and terraced roofs was solved by stone-built conduits and clay water pipes, which were also used for sanitation. To get an idea of what the latter means, it is necessary to remember that *these uses were not rediscovered by western civilization until a few centuries ago, and that Knossos sanitation engineers' ideas were not surpassed until the last century.*

All those were no small achievements for people living on an island in the Mediterranean at 1,500 B.C.. It has been estimated that, at its height, some 100,000 persons dwelled in Knossos. It was the largest city in Europe.

Cretan art showed a passion for life. Their frescoes had a surprisingly modern style. They were mostly landscapes and seascapes enlivened with animals and fish: cats stalking pheasants, deer leaping, monkeys prowling over rocks, birds in flight, plenty of fish swimming—all painted with bright colors, with a superb composition, in a highly naturalistic style. Delightful, gaily-colored dolphins, as those portrayed by those long gone Euzkan artists, have had no match in the past or in the present. Their frescoes, paintings and ceramics, show us another side of their lives: like the Etruscans, they loved public festivals. Scenes of elaborately well-dressed women, boys and girls carrying or receiving ritual instruments are abundant.

Like the Basques and Etruscans, Minoan people were famous for their deep religiousness. The double ax (*labrys*), identical to the *bipennis* that was at the center of the Etruscan *fasci*, was profusely present in frescoes, ceramics, jewels in Crete, Thera and other places of the Minoan civilization. The horns of the consecration can be seen in the tops of their buildings and in altars. It was the civilization of the Bull.

Athletic young men and women appear in their frescoes leaping over bulls, during what is believed a religious ceremony, reminding us of one of the few places on Earth where young people still traditionally defy those powerful animals: the annual run of San Fermin, in Pamplona. That famed Basque festivity is celebrated close to the summer solstice.

The Aryans mocked the Pelasgian, Cretan warriors. They believed them effeminate because they grew among women until puberty. The incoming Indo-European hordes might have mocked them, but rarely to their face. They must have been formidable, frightening warriors, even by the remarkable Euzkan standards. How can we know that? Easily, just by taking a good look at the palace of Knossos. It was really a palace, *not a fortress, not a castle. None of the many Cretan cities had walls.* Athens, Mycenae, Tiryns, all did, as it was current among most of the mainland cities.

The absence of walls in Cretan palaces points to a notable good relationship between rulers and people. Something that was not common at those times for other peoples. Cretan cities showed, according to archaeologists, a surprising independence among them. They were convivial, civilized people.

To value them within a proper perspective, it must be remembered that no city lacked walls on the mainland, except in Lacedemonia. More than a millennium later, Spartans boasted that the chests of their citizens would be the best of walls. It was so. The Spartan legislators intentionally banned all kind of public or personal riches—in order not to invite marauders. That deliberate poverty, combined with the fighting ability of their hoplites, recognized as the best Hellenic troops, kept even the Spartan villages free from invaders for centuries.

Cretan cities might have no walls, but were far from poor. Knossos in particular was full of everything that could attract looters. It was a golden city, replete with gold, silver, precious stones and stored goods. All of it was very easy to transport after a nice sacking. Spartans were also smartly located in mountains.

Any tourist can appreciate today, when traveling through those charming but difficult mountain roads of Laconia, the advantages that the natural defenses presented for the Spartans. On the other hand, Knossos, Phaistos, Palaiokastrons, Zakros, all the main Cretan cities were *ports, or near to the sea*. At that time that was the most accessible kind of target any looter could have dreamed of—easy to get in, easy to leave.

The lack of walls show that, anticipating the Spartans, in the middle of a sea famed at all times by the audacity of its pirates, somehow the Cretan warriors must have been a kind of wall much more frightening and discouraging in itself than anything that could have been built with stones—the frightening Euzkos, the *feroces vascones* all over again. Herodotus wrote that king Minos was the first ever to have a fleet and that he freed the sea from pirates. An awesome thalassocracy, just like the Etruscans, they really were the Euzkos from the sea.

Their system must have worked. Occasional, strong earthquakes, frequent on the island, destroyed their cities, but invaders rarely did so. On the very few occasions when it happened, the Cretans seem to have rebuilt their cities without walls again. It was a magnificent, continuous show of self-confidence. They were decidedly against changing what was more than a philosophy and constituted a whole life-style. They lasted more than three millennia. That is a formidable epitaph in itself.

It was an affluent civilization. Like the Etruscans, they showed an appreciation for good food. The word we use for wine it is still theirs: *oinos*. Except in Scandinavia and Scotia, where the climate did not allow vines to grow, all Euzkos showed a remarkable appreciation for wine. They associated it with their myths and cults.

They had *zatricchion*—their chess. Being merchants, they could boast of *registered trademarks* and a central system of weights and measures. Their calendar was based on careful astronomic observations. Crete was a commercial center for all the Aegean area. In the depots of Knossos only, the rows of huge, richly ornamented, oil containers were judged to have a 79,000 gallons capacity. No wonder that their discoverers were marveled at the opulence of their finds. Not surprising either that they used *locks* to protect their riches.

The sophistication of their economy can also be seen in its bulls.

Fig 7a. Long-horn fighting bull. Notice the difference of bodies with the one in 7b. This sketch of a famous fresco, from the East wing of the Palace of Knossos has been interpreted as a ritual scene. Both women and men are shown. Archaeologists believe that it was an important religious ceremony carried on in the central court (all the Palace was built around it). The other Cretan cities also had similar central courts.

Two types of bulls appear in their frescoes, pottery or jewelry, and they are noticeably different. One, the enormous, long-horned, agile, aggressive bulls that appear in ritual objects or in religious frescoes with bull-leapers, which could be easily recognized by Spanish lovers of *corridas de toros* or bullfights. It is the well-known *toro de lidia*, the fighting bull (Fig. 7a).

It is the other kind of bull that surprises us by its presence: the typical, highly domesticated breed (Fig. 7b). The statuette represents a high-quality beef-producer, never to be mistaken for a fighting animal. Its characteristically rounded forms reveal not only a long experience in breeding but also skillful know-how on feeding and raising such splendid animals.

Nineteen-century cowboys from the North American Plains could have easily recognized the two types of bulls. They mark a transition to rational exploitation of land resources. The Pelasgian civilization of Crete was astonishingly high-tech in many areas.

Fig. 7b. A typical beef-producer bull (Sketch of a terracotta statuette, ca. 1500 B.C.)

Their hieroglyphic writing (Linear A) has not been deciphered yet. When the waves of Eolian and Ionian invaders arrived, the two cultures were probably associated and merged. Legends, myth and history tend to point that Pelasgians and those first Aryan visitors, Eolians and Ionians, intermarried, creating an interbred society. The Aryans accepted the Pelasgians' religious preeminence, and the Indo-European gods found a niche in the Euzkan spiritual sphere and rituals.

There was no marked change in cultural patterns at that time, except for a faster impulse to reach their best in the arts. No brusque, sudden cultural alterations appear to be connected with the arrival of those first two waves of Indo-European settlers. Nevertheless, scriptures from the 15th century B.C. (Linear B), which were deciphered, brought a surprise: they were written in ancient Greek. Maybe what happened there was a remake of the Celtic story: a minority of newcomers imposing their language. Or maybe they were just coincident with the third Indo-European wave, the Achean invasion. Perhaps it occurred in famed Theseus' times.

General destruction took place in the island during that period.

Since all the towns and palaces of Crete were destroyed or damaged by fire at the time, scholars concluded that the destruction was caused by enemy action, attributed mainly to groups from the mainland.

Through a careful reading of ancient authors and Greek myths, together with archaeological evidence, most scholars have come to believe that the Acheans were responsible for the turmoil.

Minoan prosperity continued for a while but the island was reduced to a seemingly subordinate position in the Aegean world. Then the fourth and last wave of Indo-European invaders, the Dorians, hit them. Loss of population and desertion of urban sites followed, particularly of coastal towns. The Dorians established in Crete a social system that was judged more Spartan than that of Sparta. Fortified cities grew, continually warring among themselves. A mercantile, highly civilized society disappeared. It was replaced by a highly stratified, rigid and war-prone culture. As a result, art and economy decayed.

Crete never recovered.

Evans found evidence of a great earthquake, and thought it had caused the extinction of the civilization.

Other centers survived a little longer. In the times of the maximum splendor of Crete, about the 15th and 16th centuries B.C., cities had already grown prosperous on the mainland. The main centers of development were those which controlled trade routes, like Tyrins on the coast. Mycenae dominated the passage to Korynthos, the northern Peloponnese and mainland Greece.

Under Mycenaean rule, as far back as the 15th and especially in the 16th centuries B.C., the Argival plain became the springhead of Greek development, displacing Crete. In times of the Trojan War, Mycenae was already the leading power, under Achean rule. It was brief. Soon the Dorians overcame most regions and a dark age followed. Scripture was lost, commerce decayed and the arts suffered a regression.

The Greek Euzkos 73

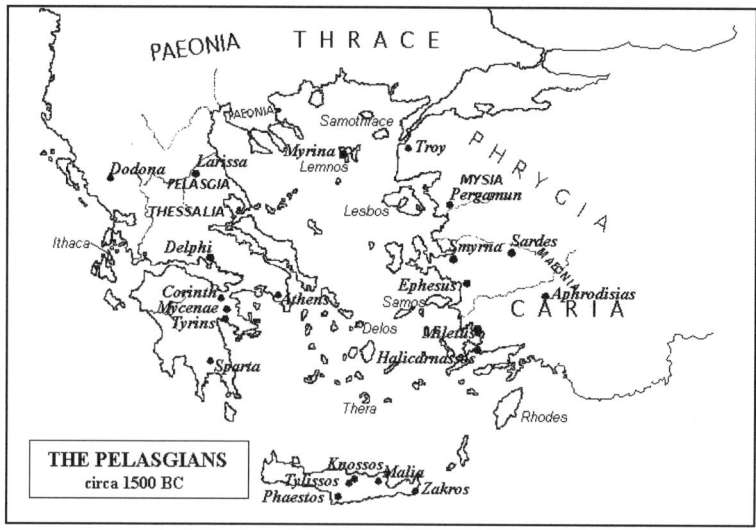

Fig. 8. THE PELASGIAN WORLD: The Pelasgians, which gave their name to the whole group, appear in Larissa at the north of Thessaly. They seemed to have been also in Dodona, in Argos, in the islands (Crete, Lemnos and Imbros, for instance) and in many more places in the mainland and in Asia Minor. That widespread distribution was similar for the other groups. The Leleges, for instance, which do not appear in the map, founded wealthy Smyrna (name of their Amazon queen), which has stubbornly retained both its name (Izmir, in modern Turkey) and its prosperity, still being one of the busiest ports of the area. However, the main Lelege's region was outside the map in southwest Turkey. They were also in the islands, in the Peloponnese and some authors put them in some regions of Thrace and Illyria. The names of some of the cities do not necessarily coincide with its ancient ones. When the old name is unknown or controversial, the above name only point to places which were affluent or religiously important in the past. How to know if the ancient Minoan ruins of Malia in Crete were known by that name? Most probably not. Most of those cities reassumed their prosperity after the Dorian crash. Caria became one of the richest satrapies in Persia. Its satrap Mausolus' tomb in Halicarnassos was considered one of the Seven Wonders of the world. Ephesus, founded by an Amazon, queen of the Leleges, became the second richest city in the Roman Empire. Its temple to Artemis (Diana), another of the Seven Wonders, was the largest building of the Hellenistic world (four times larger than the Parthenon). The difficulties of the map can be appreciated considering that some authors also put the Carians and the Pelasgians at Ephesus. Not improbable, given the great lapse involved and the mobility of those cultures (Rome, just in this century was under both German and American dominion). Aphrodisias was the opulent capital of golden-touch King Midas. The Pelasgian World was a rich, commercial one and its cities fought to maintain that wealthy tradition through the ages.

Between 1100 and 1075 B.C., the once prosperous and powerful Mycenae reverted to a phase of limited rural production, and never recovered from it. Its decadence was so complete, that three thousand years later, Homer's description of its former power was taken, until Schliemann rediscovered its ancient splendor, as a poetical overstatement, conceived just to confer some grandeur to Agamemnon, its most famous ruler.

So, at about the 10th century B.C., the Indo-Europeans, a millennium after their arrival, were triumphant over most of the Greek-Euzkan societies. Crete and Mycenae had irremissibly lost their power. The magnificent Pelasgian world (Fig. 7, see page 82) disintegrated. The new society produced mostly dull, slow farmers with scarce aptitude for the arts, the politics and the commerce.

But the new world, with a marked Indo-European or Aryan supremacy, was far from homogeneous. And the once splendid civilization that the Pelasgians had achieved started slowly to emerge again.

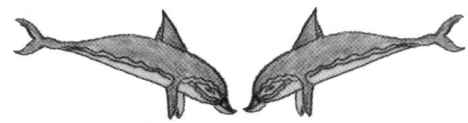

6

Rebirth

It is fascinating to see how certain historical, cultural processes tend to repeat themselves. In Italy, the Renaissance would spring up in Tuscany, the Euzkan region. Antedating them, the Euzkan civilization in Greece, finally crushed by Acheans and Dorians, would have a rebirth precisely in those regions where the residual Pelasgian influence was stronger.

Greece was not uniform. There was an extraordinary disparity among the peoples of the distinct regions. To understand it, it is necessary to observe that dominance of the most modern invaders, the Dorians, was stronger in the mainland (Sparta) and in Crete. In the coastal cities in Asia Minor (modern Turkey) and the islands near them, their influence was less (Fig. 9, See page 76). That entire region had been considered Pelasgian by Homer, at the time of the Trojan conflict, and had sided with Troy, as did the rest of the Euzkan cities.

In Herodotus' times, in the 5th century B.C., the Greek cities on the western coast of Turkey were denominated Ionians, as many of the islands of the Aegean. The Ionian dialect of Greek was closely related to the Attic spoken on the Greek mainland, like the Athenian, for instance.

Fig. 9: INDO-EUROPEAN GREECE: It should be compared to the preceding map. The usual ethnic mixture in those zones did not make it easier to draw the map. Take Sparta in the Dorian region. There the class of the Perioeci was constituted, according to Ephorus (as quoted by Strabo), by the original Acheans, which were allowed to commerce and a certain freedom but were not considered citizens and were forbidden to marry Spartans. So, there were Acheans in Dorian regions. To add to the confusion the term Perioeci was a political designation and could mean other ethnia with similar rights in other regions. In some zones the Dorians were the Perioeci (Kythera). In Sparta the Achean Perioeci were in an intermediate situation between the Spartans and the much more numerous Helots, who were the slaves (most probably the residual Pelasgians from Lacedemonia). The regions in the map point out the distribution of the four Greek dialects or at least the dialect spoken by the dominant group, but for some authors the Achean is so close to the Dorian that they consider them identical. Most authors do coincide that in the regions where the Eolian or Ionian dialect was spoken there was a strong Pelasgian influence. On the other hand the Dorian regions exhibited the strictest Aryan customs.

Similarly the cities on the eastern coast of Turkey were considered Eolians.

Those first Indo-Europeans, Eolians and Ionians, showed a marked difference when they were compared to the latecomers, the Dorians. That disparity turned often into an open confrontation. That almost permanent conflict dominated Greek history for more than a millennium. Why? Some three centuries after Homer, about the 6th century B.C., the Spartans, who were Dorians, still deemed Pelasgians the Ionian and the Eolians, as the Acheans had done before them.

Why Pelasgians? Thucydides wrote that the Spartans judged the Ionians not-true Greeks, but to be mostly pre-Greeks or people of mixed breed at most. What those Dorians really meant was that both the Ionians and Eolians were not pure Aryans anymore. According to the Dorians they had gone native.

They had reasons to think so. *Both the Ionians and the Eolians seemed to have intermarried with the Pelasgians. That was exactly the accusation that, according to Herodotus, Thucydides and other authors, the Spartans laid on them.*

The Ionians, on their side, according to both Thucydides and Herodotus, judged the Dorians newcomers, accusing them of being non-Greek, northern invaders.

They were right too. The first two Aryan waves, Ionian and Eolian, had properly intermarried with the Pelasgian dominant families, becoming the male military aristocracy without having to fight much their way into it, accepting the Pelasgian religion and customs. The old rituals were slightly modified to incorporate them but not essentially changed. They had adapted and were now considered locals.

The third wave, the Acheans, was not so compliant and simply crushed the old inhabitants.

The final invaders, the fourth Indo-European wave, the Dorians, made quite a point of avoiding crossbreeding and excluding as much of the old Pelasgian traditions and culture as their situation allowed. In that sense, they kept being alien to the local culture, so both Ionians and Eolians were right in calling them foreigners.

The Hellenic world was heterogeneus. Two ethnias were the main strugglers. If that is not understood, it is impossible to appreciate the later development of the Greek world and the extraordinary influence the Pelasgians had in it.

Whenever the Spartan or Dorians made those accusations of racial purity to other peoples, they were never considering *all* the population, *just the ruling classes*. Spartans were a ruling minority; they reached only 8,000 male citizens at their prime. The rest of the original Pelasgians and part of the former three Aryan waves constituted the dominated majority. Trade and manufacture was in the hands of the *perioeci*, who had no political rights. Agriculture was left to *helots*, who were not considered citizens and lived in a perilous status under the Dorian domination. Their rights were scarce if not inexistent.

The Spartan was a typical, Aryan, four-chaste system, with priests and warriors at the top. Any Hindu would have recognized it. Spartan despotic and frequently unjust rule was famous in all Greece.

A case illustrates their ruthlessness. The despised *Helots* could neither have weapons nor receive military training. Nevertheless once they had to fight to help the Spartans resist an invasion. They did so and distinguished themselves. Their only reward was an obscure and unmerciful annihilation after attaining victory.

The root of the continual conflict between Athens and Sparta was not merely a matter of commercial interests or differences between political systems. *The breach was much deeper than that. The Spartans also considered that the Athenians were Pelasgians*, or half-breeds at best.

They were right again. From the names of the four original Athenian tribes it has been inferred that they had Ionian roots, mixed with Pelasgic ancestors. Theseus, an Achean, through cunning and force had unified them under his control. From what Plutarchus wrote, Theseus seems to have respected the local Athenian aristocracy, incorporating them into new rituals and into a new social structure, dealing harshly only with those who had dared to oppose him. So, many of the Pelasgian rituals, customs and people were surviving in them.

The democratic parties in Athens had their influence *because* of that ethnic composition. The oligarchic minority was not just rich people who wanted power only for themselves. Many of them also considered themselves fully Indo-Europeans as the Dorians. They thought that it gave them a historical right to govern. That is also the reason why oligarchies all through Greece sided with the Spartans.

It was not just ideology. *It was an ethnic conflict.*

It also explains why the zones where the old Pelasgian traditions predominated, thanks to the intermarrying of the leading Euzkan families with Ionians and Eolians, were all to ally with Athens. The Peloponnesian War, in the 5th century B.C., which ended the power of Athens and paved the way for Alexander's Macedonian troops, just detonated an old antipathy between descendants of the last wave of invaders and the residual Pelasgians, which had incorporated the tribes of the first waves.

The chronicles of all those conflicts allow us a clearer vision of the former Euzkan societies. Their mutual accusations are precious, because they illuminate clearly their ethnic tensions and rivalries. Above all, they show the considerable difference in family structure and other social and political aspects between Euzkans and Indo-Europeans.

Some six centuries after the Cretan debacle a vigorous civilizing revival had started. It must be noticed that most scholars have always considered it a revival, not a birth. There was even a time, recently, when everything was considered to have started in Ionia, where the ancient, remaining Pelasgian influence was greater, thanks to the mixed ancestry of their leaders. There were reasons for it. Even if some of the most famous philosophers—Socrates, Plato, and Aristotle, for instance—were from Athens, the beginnings of what is known today as Greek philosophy happened across the Mediterranean Sea, some two hundred years before, in the coastal cities and islands of what is now Turkey, the Ionian region.

The Ionian cities were already energetic, thriving and opulent at that time. If a seer had told their citizens that Athens would be considered the richest and most influential city two centuries later, they would have laughed at what they could only consider a joke. The old Euzkan trade in the Aegean was prosperous once more. Their cultural influence was initially overwhelming.

One of the particularities of the Ionian school of philosophy was that its first philosophers were tied not only geographically but also in their methods and aims. They aspired to explain the material universe in terms of matter, movement, and force. Their unity of view was extremely rare in Greece.

Thales was the first philosopher to achieve fame. Anaximander and Anaximenes gained recognition after him. Heraclitus followed. Parmenides and Zeno were the first who left Thales' original approach. Then a long list followed, where the most prominent were Anaxagoras, Diogenes of Apollonia, Archelaus and Hippo. Some scholars also consider Empedocles, Leucipus and Democritus as belonging to the Ionian school.

They were the most representative among the thinkers that started the philosophical tradition in Greece. Their style influenced all other currents of thought.

The powerful Ionian, or Pelasgian, intellectual influence, was not limited to philosophy. Ionian literary prestige was immense. Homer was Ionian. Scholars have often pointed that the *Iliad* seems anti-Achean, in spite of being apparently written by the winners. Achean invaders are shown as wild savages, fighting among themselves—arrogant, unruly and unfaithful. In a startling contrast, the defeated Trojans show a certain degree of civilized manners and attitudes. The sympathy of the author for the Trojans is so obvious that it has confused readers throughout the ages.

Homer is supposed to have compiled traditions and songs that were treasured in Ionia. It all came from a region that had backed Troy during the conflict. All the Pelasgians had sided with Troy, as the same Homer tells us. Why were Aryan names present on both sides? The reason is that apparently many Ionians and Eolians had been fighting the Acheans, defending the Pelasgian life-style they had adopted. The Trojan War was an ethnic confrontation. For that reason Thucydides quoted it as one of the causes of Peloponnesian War. The cultural antagonism persisted through the centuries, bursting out in the war between Sparta and Athens a millennium later.

The deep cultural disparity was shown in literature. Ionian poetry deals with persons and personal matters. Their poems were light and rarely political. The contrary happened in Sparta. Ionians were famous for their festivals where poetry and, especially, music were important. They were not only identical to the Etruscans and Minoans in that but also in their hedonistic lifestyle. The more conservative Dorians considered their music too sensuous.

Herodotus was able to leave his wonderful history books partly because he came from a region that, in spite of Dorian dominance, was Ionian in customs. Herodotus' intellectual curiosity was typical of the Ionian culture. That is also the reason why he had access to so many different sources of information, concerning the oldest inhabitants of all those regions. He wrote in the Ionian dialect from his home city, Halikarnassos. It was one of the two main cities of a region, Caria, which had been entirely Pelasgian, and where many of the most important features of their religion and customs still survived. Halikarnassos was a formidable commercial and cultural center. The monumental tomb of Mausolus, satrap of Caria under the Persians, was considered one of the Seven Wonders of the World.

The considerable Ionian attainments were also of technical character. The island of Samos not only produced the sage Pythagoras but also had, according to Herodotus, the world's first modern harbor. Its breakwater was a quarter of mile long and built in water 120 feet deep. It became the prototype in harbor planning, followed by naval architects all through ancient and also well into modern times. Thanks to it the Samos' navy was able to rule the waves and successfully blockaded the mainland subjects of Persia during the Medic Wars.

The Ionians could boast not only of the Samos harbor but also of one of the most extraordinary undertakings of ancient times: their water supply and pipe lines. Both Greeks and Romans used open lines and normally sought a hydraulic gradient to carry water. They carried water from a high source to a lower city using what was just a covered channel. Surprisingly, in

Patara and Pergamon, the Ionians used *pressure* lines. The one at Pergamon, for instance, was almost two miles long and at one point crossed a valley 780 feet deep. They must have used pipes able to withstand a water pressure of no less than 300 pounds per square inch—an engineering marvel for the time.

Miletus, the opulent Ionian trading city, was not only the cradle of Thales and his theorem. It also gave birth to Hippodamus, the physician, and father of city planning. His innovations were designed in order to secure a maximum of healthy light and air, something that ancient Pelasgians in neighbor Crete already knew. Hippodamus created a style still in use nowadays—rectangular blocks with straight streets and the avenues running at right angles to one another.

The cultural revival reached its climax in Athens. Like Rome, it was a hybrid city where the best from the Indo-Europeans and the Pelasgians, and also part of the worst, found its expression. The Attica, where Athens reigned, was also the traditional Ionian-Pelasgian region in the mainland.

When the Persians invaded Greece, they started by the Ionian and Eolian cities, which were an easy prey, located in the Asia Minor. The Ionians immediately claimed, and obtained, Athenian support. The revolt of the Ionian cities led to their destruction and occupation by the Persians. When the Ionians migrated, to escape the invaders, the last Pelasgian political influence was lost. Even when some of them returned it was never the same.

Following the Persian defeat, the power of Athens reached its maximum. It aroused the envy of the Spartans, and a new suicidal, ethnic war started in 431 B.C., masterfully described by Thucydides in *The Peloponnesian War*.

Soon the Macedonians, under Alexander, would profit from the debilitating conflict and take over all Greece, and from there expand to the neighboring regions. That expansion of Hellenic culture was relatively brief. The Roman legions shortly ended it.

The Pelasgian or Euzkan influence throughout all Greek cultural development was remarkable. Even theater came from those Euzkos. The ancient, religious, mimic ceremony accompanying the Dionysian festivities was its origin—like those performed by *histrios* among the Etruscans.

Dionysus was a Pelasgian fertility god or myth, related to the culture of vine and wine production and consumption. Mimic rituals were common in the ancient Euzkan cults. It is believed that, at the beginning, a priest was the actor.

Those wonderful pieces of Aeschylus, Sophocles, Euripides and Aristophanes, were later represented as part of a ritual. The plays, together with a sacrifice and procession, constituted the Great Dionysia—the annual spring festival dedicated to Dionysos.

How do we know that the Pelasgians were Euzkans? Apart from their striking likeness in culture and life-style there is another significant point. Earlier it was pointed out that *there was another example of a non-Indo-European language linked to Etruscan.*

Where? The sacred island of Lemnos, which had a fully Pelasgian population even until the second half of the 6th century B.C., when the Athenians, following orders from their tyrant Pisistratus and commanded by Miltiades, conquered them.

The Lemnians spoke the ancient language. The similarity of the few examples left of their ancient tongue with the Etruscan is impressive. There is also an extraordinary affinity between names of cities and places in Italy and the corresponding Pelasgian ones in Greece. Herodotus tells about Pelasgians in Italy, speaking the same tongue. Ancient writers identified Etruscans with Pelasgians. Some present scholars are of the opinion that if not identical they belonged to the same ancestral group. So, Arana Goiri was right in considering them Euzkos.

Even if the fall of Athens, and the destruction and occupation of the Ionian and Eolian cities, seemed the end of the residual Pelasgian influence, it continued culturally expressing itself. After all, most of the population, through interbreeding and cultural exchange was already carrying some Euzkan character. How can we know this? In order to recognize that influence, it is not even necessary to study Greek history after Roman occupation. To verify the Euzko influence it is enough to take a look at *modern* Europeans.

Actually, it is enough to ask what makes Europeans to be considered Europeans. It is a trait wholly inherited from the Euzkos. The only trait shared by *all* Euzkos. It has not been considered in this book yet, in spite of being the most important. It is the trait that makes it easier to recognize Euzkos through history. It is the one that marks the Europeans apart.

7

Cherchez la Femme...

What makes the Europeans different?

It is something apparently easy to see. They are big, hyperactive, bearded, white men. Wrong. There are other big, hyperactive, bearded, white men. They do not qualify. After all, many Muslim invaders in the 16th century, for instance, fitted that description quite well. On the other hand, many Mediterranean Europeans are considerably darker, quieter and smaller than those oriental invaders and nevertheless they *are* Europeans.

It is a cultural, more than a physical trait that makes them different and, most important of all; it is not actually about men. *It is their women that make Europeans different from practically the rest of the world, more than their men.*

It is the independent, self-assertive European woman that distinguishes the European culture from most others in the globe.

Non-Europeans easily spot European men, and are usually not much at ease with their habits, but what really shock them are the European women.

Nowhere in the world are they used to them. How many cultures are there where women eat and can mingle freely with men?

The cultural shock between most non-Europeans and Europeans starts at the couple level. Any executive traveling to Africa or Asia can tell lots about that. Women's status is quite different almost everywhere.

The distinctive European male-female relationship is rare. The most common Asiatic anti-European propaganda before World War II was centered on the European women—taking them as an ominous symptom of the present decadence of their continent. European men should all be going down the drain to allow it, that was what all that meant. They were wrong, totally wrong.

The independence and other remarkable traits of European women are not modern. It all comes from ancient, very ancient times.

Actually, *it is not now that they are more independent.* They have not gained independence during the last millennia, but have almost completely lost it. European women were not merely independent in the past. They seem to have enjoyed a remarkable high status. They were practically in command.

That was the most important and distinctive trait among all Euzkos, what distinguished them—the only one common cultural mark among all the Old Europeans—their women.

Did that remarkable characteristic of independence come with the Indo-European tribes? Did the Latins bring it? Were the Greek newcomers responsible for all those independent, self-assured women? The answer is a complete, total no. None of them had anything to do with it.

Among Indo-Europeans the woman's position was clear—well down on the social scale. For Latins and Greeks, women were just a little above, never much, over other reproductive animals. Their only advantage and utility were that they were indispensable for producing other men. Apart from that, they scarcely counted. They had no social rights. They were transferred from their father's authority, or possession, to that of their husbands. From them, if they survived their spouses, which was very unlikely, to their children. Male children, of course; females never counted. An exaggeration? We have only to read Roman and Greek writers—especially *moral* writers. Those who intended to better their customs (*mores*).

Greek writers, as Theopompus and Hesiod, and their Roman colleagues, as Cato, showed a total agreement on what was expected from a woman: only to provide legitimate children. Not even pleasure was expected from them. Nobody considered them good company. They also agreed on what should be their education—none, excepting weaving and cooking. They never doubted their place—just at home. They never expected any woman to appear in public, neither outside *nor even inside their homes.*

In civilized, lawful Rome, well until Empire times, women could not have any property. They could not own. They *belonged*—to a father, brother, husband, son, to the next male kin. They were such nonentities that *they had no names*. Whenever we meet in literature some Emilia or Claudia, those were not their names. Those were *family* names. It just meant they belonged to any of the Emilii or Claudii men. It meant just a Miss or Mrs. Jones. To distinguish them they were just *numbered*, according to their birth order.

Were an ancient Latin to be invited to dinner to a present-day, traditional Arab family, he would have enjoyed his fare and would have never been surprised that the females who prepared it did not join the guests. Neither he nor a Greek invader would have ever expected *that*. After all, there were certain things like manners always to be observed. Male power, *patria potestad*, was overwhelming.

An understanding judge absolved a Roman husband who had killed his wife because he had caught her *drinking*. Writers chanted and celebrated his very moral conduct for generations.

The Greeks we find celebrating in Plato's *Symposium* (The Banquet,) are all men. Considering the amazing sophistication of the participants, the absence of women is astonishing. Women were excluded even among philosophers. Exactly the same happened in Roman families. All Roman and Greek families? No, not all. Both conservative Romans and Greeks were scandalized by the utterly disgusting, unashamed misconduct of both Etruscan and Ionian ladies. Actually, they never called *them* ladies. That old Euzko trait again...

It was the main Euzko trait—*the* Euzko trait.

Ionian women, who were of Euzkan extraction, and Etruscan ones, who were the same, incurred always in upsetting violations of the morals of the time. Conservative Greeks and Romans heartily hated them.

What did these depraved, insolent Euzko women do? Well, they all had this degrading habit of joining their husbands at their meals and celebrations, which put most Roman and Greek males upside down, a most peculiar habit any present European couple would recognize. They, this was very difficult for poor Greeks and Romans to believe, even joined their husbands at their *businesses*.

Worst of all, unbelievable, they even had their *own* businesses! They *owned*. They *inherited* and *passed on* property. They interacted freely with men.

Modern archaeologists tend to think, backed by inscriptions and dedications, that these remarkable Etruscan ladies *knew how to read*.

Inscriptions also show that they were of a competitive nature. They enjoyed beating their husbands. Not that those Euzko hubbies complained. Nowhere is the connubial theme better treated than in Etruscan frescoes, statues, jewelry or ceramics.

Love in the couple was common, apparently, in the old Euzko family. It was an exclusivity of the Euzkos. Nobody else in the Aryan Europe showed such singular, upsetting habits.

Many modern etruscologists also tend to believe that most modern Italians, and also most of the rest of the Europeans, would have felt much more comfortable among the Etruscans than among the Latins. To reach such a peculiar conclusion they only have to compare past habits and present habits, old life-styles and new life-styles.

If we want to know what would have been the destiny of European women, had they not been contaminated by those terrible, anarchic Euzkan customs, it is only necessary to look around and search for other present, surviving branches of our paternal Indo-European tree. Take Persia, or Iran as it is now called. There the population has straight Indo-European roots. Nobody would have ever accused the Shah's country of being a paradise for women. What after the ayatolahs' revolution? Care about to question any ayatolah on the subject? Women's rights? Who's kidding? Let's not blame them. They are not even traditionalist Indo-Europeans. Latins or Dorians would have complained sarcastically about their heresy: why do these Muslims teach their women to write?

Another example? A trip to India would suffice. There, among the conservative, in the best Indo-European style, *in spite of present civil law*, many widows still burn themselves, or are forcibly burnt by their families, at their husbands funerals.

That is happening *today*.

It is neither the past century nor generations ago. It is strict Aryan law.

They are saying to us that, according to their old customs, a woman has no right to an independent existence. Her husband is the only justification for her right to live. Similarly, Greek women counted their age only from the moment they married. Another way to tell us their society considered these women inexistent by themselves. If not married, they were not even considered alive by their Indo-European contemporaries. No wonder that both Etruscan and Ionian women shocked both Latins and Greeks.

When present day Europe, and also its offshoots in America and other continents, exhibits such distinctive women it is not because of the little time that patriarchal Indo-Europeans, in spite of leaving us their languages and genes, have spent on the western side of the Urals. It is because the astoundingly long occupation by Euzkos that European society has such peculiar aspects, and most of its civilization. European women, their unusual man-woman relationship, are the Euzkos deepest and far-reaching legacy.

Where, among present-day, European women, are those who according to the U.N. enjoy the best rights? All research, all statistics point to one region that Arana Goiri classified, almost a century ago, to be of Euzko roots: Scandinavia—one country above all: Norway. Is it also a coincidence that it also shows off one of the greatest percentages of Rh-? In his magnificent *The Golden Bough*, Sir James Frazer found one strange reason to enter both Scots and Scandinavians together in the subject index. It was about a certain matter that, at first, had had him definitely puzzled. It seemed, he pointed out, that not many generations ago, Scot and Scandinavian kings had acceded to their thrones, in a very queer way, *by marrying queens and then displacing them*. In the *Heimskringla* or *Sagas of the Norwegian kings*, for instance, the males of the Ynglingar family are shown obtaining at least six provinces in Norway through marriage with princesses. No prince appears getting a share of the land. This is the most cherished Euzko tradition, the high status of their women—*only women inherited kingdoms*.

Frazer has also left us a rare description of the taboos restricting the *Flamen Dialis*, the successor of the sacred king of Rome as Jupiter's priest. The twin consuls in Republican times had inherited their war leadership from him. It is a most precious description because the Romans seem to have modeled their kingship after the Etruscan one. It is the *only* description about the Etruscan kingship itself, even if a second hand one, just as we know about the Etruscan royal togas and scepters mostly through Roman customs. It is known that the Etruscans had an amphictyonic king, chosen yearly in Veltumna. A look at the Roman kingship can be illuminating.

How was that Roman kingship? First, on account of many historical peculiarities and a lot of surviving traditions, Sir James Frazer pointed out that Roman kings were probably *ritually killed*. Second, a noticeable point: *in spite of having sons and grandsons, no king was ever succeeded by a son*. Tatius, Tarquin the Elder and Servius Tullius, for instance, were all succeeded by foreigners who married their *daughters*. In other words, it was plainly a matrilineal and matrilocal political system. It was marriage to a royal *princess* that conferred the Roman scepter. The Flamen Dialis, *the religious successor of the Roman kings*, could accede to the throne only through his marriage to the *Flaminica*. He could not divorce her and had to resign his kingship if she died. So, *politi-*

cal power among the Etruscans also came from a matrilineal source, just as among Scandinavians and Scots. An all-Euzko trait, it seems.

Anteceding two thousand years the Scandinavians and one thousand years the Romans, Cecrops and Amphictyon had won their way to the kingship in Athens *marrying their predecessors' daughters*. That was not a new political maneuver in the region. Cecrops and Amphictyon had been themselves anteceded by the Ionian and Eolian male aristocracies, who seem to have used, many centuries before them, this marriage approach to integrate themselves into the Pelasgian power structure (that gave origin to the famous Dorian accusations of going native).

Some of the frescoes and paintings in Etruscan tombs also show a meaningful subject: first, the scene of a festival. Second a banquet with a woman, which has been interpreted as an ingestion of hallucinogens. Third, the common scene of Kharun carrying his precious cargo in his boat, with winged beings. All point to a sacrificed priest-king. Everything indicates a typically Euzkan, religious-political institution.

So, 2,500 years ago, Etruscan ladies had some equality of rights. How had they gained this? First of all, they had not gained it. They had simply inherited it. To be more objective it must be said that they had not improved their position at all at that time, but had been continuously losing their rights, from ancient times, when they not only had equal rights but also probably had a far more important role in the control of society—*if not the control*.

What was one of the most impressive finds of Evans' expedition when they started their excavations at Knossos? *Frescoes*. Not for the frescoes themselves, not that the painting style was revolutionary, even if they resulted strikingly modern, not for the luxury and comfort, so rare at all other places in Minoan times, a rarity even at Evans' times. No, its impact on the discoverers came from other source. *It was the women depicted in the frescoes. It was their air.*

They were beautiful women, splendidly dressed. Another aspect of those singular females was really shocking in that old Minoan, Euzkan culture. It was not necessary to be a specialist in body language to see that they were not just pretty *femmes* and royally dressed. *They were in charge.* Not only for the ceremonial dresses. It was their attitude. These were not simple, ornamental women. Everybody immediately took them for what they are still considered, goddesses or priestesses. The sophistication was such that one particular woman, depicted in a fresco, was aptly called *La Parisienne* (Fig. 10). That was at the time when Paris women had the lead in the continent.

Fig 10. Sketch of La Parisienne, from a fresco found at Knossos. The knot at her back, common in many Minoan figures, has been interpreted as signaling a ritual role of the user.

Only the women were richly dressed. *Mostly women* appeared to be *leading* the ceremonies. That did not happen only in Knossos. Frescoes in the island of Thera or Santorini show the same trait. It is a remarkable characteristic also in the frescoes of Mycenae and Tyrins. On the word of one of the present experts in Minoan culture, we have no reason at all to doubt that the priestesses and the nobility were one. *They were the nobility*. It is convenient to remember that religious and political power were the same at those times. Soon in academic circles, a strange concept became to be heard and debated: matriarchy.

The main characteristic of all Euzko societies was that they showed matriarchal influences. They were matrilineal, matrifocal societies. The top in the henpecking order was not the king. It was the *queen*. Kings were such *only because they were married to queens*. If the queen died the king was automatically off his job. It was the daughter of the queen, or other ladies of noble stock, who inherited the right to the *queendom*. In some cases, it was the youngest nubile woman in the tribe.

The new king would *never* be the *son* of the former king. He was the least likely in the whole queendom, not being allowed to marry inside the family. In many cases royal sons were not even allowed to survive. The new king would be the one who *married the youngest nubile daughter* of the queen, or some other young noble woman.

In a certain way, *we all have known that since our childhood*. All those ancient, traditional, children's fairytales, where the king promised the hand of his daughter *and his kingdom* to anyone who could perform a great service, namely killing an ogre or something similar, probably are *Euzko tales*, prehistoric stories reaching us through the ears of many generations. They are thousands of years old, and still carry the matrilineal mark.

Only one thing was wrong.

The king needed only to offer his daughter in marriage. The *queendom* went along with her, without any need to say so. The king could never offer *his* realm. *It had never been his*. Most probably, in the most traditional tribes in ancient times, his charge was brief, mostly ritual and had a tragic end. He was sacrificed.

Then a new king was chosen. He lasted usually six months or a year before giving way to the new, transient king.

This custom, which is thought to have lasted for thousands and thousands of years, (there are many good reasons to think so) has deeply influenced even our most modern institutions. It constituted one of the oldest and most durable social and political systems.

Before discussing it, before discussing the underlying religious beliefs, before analyzing how it was all superseded, first gradually and later catastrophically, by the Indo-Europeans or Aryans, who were not really Europeans in those times, as the Ionians justly complained, let's go back to an old subject. After all, this book started with those oldest Europeans, the Basques. What about *them*? What about *their* women?

For a long, long time, specialists in the Basque tongue have pointed to one of their many language peculiarities. There is a strange, residual characteristic in the family relationship, according to linguists. It is alien to present family ties. *Brotherhood and sisterhood seem to have been different.* In the Basque language, children are named according to a surprising system. All children, when named in reference to a sister carry the suffixes *ba* or *pa* (*arreba*: sister of a man, *neba*: brother of a woman, *aizpa*: sister of a woman). That ending *ba* means the family attachment. This rule does not apply to male brothers among themselves. *Anae, anaya* mean brother of a man. A family suffix *ba* is not found in any male-male relationship. It is a little startling; it has been interpreted as if men, among them, were a little isolated. There was a lesser bond, no family attachment. *Brothers were just considered only a little more than men living together.* Their family status came not by their relationship to any men but *only according to their nexus to the women.*

As by its stone roots, Basque family still shows in its language an old, prehistoric arrangement. If their tools speak about the stone, the names for family ties remind us of an ancient matrilineal organization.

What about Basque women's status? Since medieval times at least, another strange characteristic was typical among Basques: inheritance. The first child inherits house and lands. That is one of the reasons why Basques have been emigrating everywhere all through history. Basque traditions did not permit parceling. The first-born inherited all. But, this was the real difference, *first male or female.*

Women have always had equal rights of inheritance among the Basques since medieval times.

This was something absolutely shocking for medieval and Renaissance attorneys everywhere else. For Basques it was plainly normal. In the 17th century, Jacques de Béla, for instance, found the matter totally just and clear: if men and women had to work equally in the fields, they had to have equal inheritance rights.

It was obvious only for Basque lawyers. What was being denied, at that time, to none less than all ladies of the French and Spaniard nobility, not even princesses escaped the rule, what would be denied to all women even *after* the French Revolution, had been a regular, common right for any Basque peasant girl for centuries, millennia, not because of some social revolution or some militant feminist campaign, but because they were Euzko women, because they had been raised in the deeply rooted, common law of Euzko usage.

But maybe it had been just evolution, maybe Basques had just anticipated the feminine revolution. Maybe in the past they had been more inclined to the macho tradition, like Indo-Europeans.

Really? Quite the contrary, if we believe what ancient writers tell us over and over. Strabo, the well-known Latin writer from the first century B.C., was comprehensibly shocked by their customs. He wrote that some of their obnoxious uses included that "husbands had to pay a dowry to their wives" and, much worst, "*inheritance goes to the woman*". Wow! But what must really have astonished him was that, even at those times, "*the marriage of the brothers was decided by the sisters*".

Linguists were right, ancient Basques were a female structured society, with men at the side. Paleolithic Europeans seem to have lived in a woman-centered society.

Strabo commented, "their uses imply a certain matriarchy". Of course he realized that this was revolutionary and revolting. We know that he felt the need to clarify to his males companions where his feelings and opinions were, for he added immediately a self righteous remark: "this is in no way civilization". All Indo-European males, who decided the marriage of their sisters and daughters and had the exclusivity on property rights, and who even had the right of life or death on the family women would have agreed. Indeed.

Through many different writings we know that the customs that had shocked Strabo were still being respected at least until the 10th and 11th centuries A.D.

The *Roll of Benasque*, for instance, contains more than seventy property scriptures during those centuries, all concerning lands from a woman of name Sanza and her two successive husbands. It shows a *matrilineal* right of inheritance. The people in the Benazque valley were still using *maternal* names. Almost all mentioned persons, excepting some foreigners, *were known by the name of their mothers*, well in accord with the Basque tradition. Royal houses and the nobility of the region were adopting the paternal names typical of the Indo-Europeans, but the common people, especially in the country, still observed the ancient proper social regulations of the Euzkans.

Even when their rights were finally shortened, women still managed to maintain a certain equality in the Basque lands well into modern times. Let's not forget that it was not an improvement. Their society was matrilineal, matrilocal, and matrifocal until some centuries ago. Only a millennium back *women were the sole inheritors of any property*. Family clans were organized around sisters and women kin. Men had to pay a dowry and to leave their families to live within their wives clan or family, in a marriage arranged by their sisters or mothers. Yet it is still common to hear those who argue that women's rights are of recent data, a present offshoot of the modern economic development.

In an Euzko society there could not be patriots. There were only *matriots*. In Crete they used a feminine word, meaning *matria* instead of the *patria* inherited from Latin in many modern languages. It was really the *motherland*.

The female influence went beyond those matters. There was a particular field where their influence seems to have been overwhelming.

8

The Old Religion

Fig.11. Venus of Willemdorf

They have been there for such a long time. Archaeologists wonder at them. It is always them, just them and so, so long. They were made from stone, antlers, ivory. They are called the Venus figurines—tiny, sensuous carvings representing female torsos (Fig. 11). Most of them are small, steatopygous dolls, where the emphasis was laid on breasts, buttocks and paunch, with slender arms and thighs.

They are undeniable sexual.

Many are evident representations of a pregnant woman. They can be found from Siberia to the Basque country. They seem to appear almost everywhere in Europe.

For nearly thirty thousand years thousands of generations seem to have been under their spell. They point to some irrefutable African origin.

Only in hot climates steatopygous women are common. Their steatopygia allows them to accumulate most of their fat in breasts, buttocks and paunch. Almost no fat is stored neither in their arms nor in their legs. That way these women can attain a more efficient heat transfer through the skin of their limbs, resulting in a better refrigeration of their bodies.

In hot central Africa, being able to dissipate heat efficiently is a decisive survival factor. Women carrying those genes would have had a biological competitive advantage. Not in the much colder regions of Europe, where heat conservation is biologically favored and fat, a good isolating agent, tend to be stocked uniformly distributed under the skin of body and extremities.

The steatopygous statuettes must have imitated some human model. So, the cult most probably originated in Africa and spread to Europe. Some migrants wandered up north with their religious beliefs and their statuettes.

Some of the dolls are highly stylized representations. The majority of the human figurines, whether carved or modeled, were naturalistic—at least where the trunk was concerned. Not only their continuity though the ages is remarkable, but their presence is also enhanced by a noticeable absence: *practically no male dolls are found.*

No wonder some traditions lasted so long.

The Venus figurines are taken, almost unanimously, for fertility goddesses. Later they suffered transformations. After many thousand years of remarkable continuity, they started to evolve, very slowly and, in the terms of its vast time scale, very recently. In the beautiful Cyclad islands of the Aegean Sea, for instance, some Neolithic, pre-Greek artists started to sculpt them in marble. The statuettes were not steatopygous any more but slender. It is astounding how the Cycladic figurines started to show a distinct personality, even if they all fall with the general type of the naked goddess. From them, in a leap, in a few thousand years, nearby artists began to show us those beautiful, wonderful, ivory figurines of richly dressed goddesses or priestesses of delicate features, their breasts naked, and holding snakes (Fig. 12). They already are in the category of realistic sculptures.

Fig. 12. Sketch of a Cretan priestess or goddess holding snakes (faience statuette, c. 1500 B.C.)

They resemble and are contemporaries with the also beautiful, imposing women represented in the frescoes of Crete, Mycenae and Thera more than three thousand years ago (Fig. 13-17). That tradition is continued in the severe, majestic, impressive lines of the Ladies found in Elche, Albacete and other places of Spain and dated around six or seven centuries B.C. It culminated with the erotic beauty of the sinuous and delightful Aphrodites of the Classic Greece, with the imposing glare of the giant statue of Athena by Phidias in the Parthenon, that we know only from a small reproduction, and with the also impressive statue dedicated to Diana in her temple of Ephesus, considered one of the Seven Wonders of the ancient world.

Diana, Aphrodite and Athena were then the theme of some of the best sculptors in the history of mankind. Their statues

Fig 13. Sketch of a woman holding wheat stalks. From a fresco found at Mycenae (c. 1300 B.C.)

and temples became of unheard size. But even if sang by inspired poets, their cults and power were a mere shadow of what they had enjoyed until a few centuries before, when they had reigned supreme and uncontested, together with a constellation of other goddesses.

During more than a millennium, Indo-European, Aryan tribes had been invading Greece from the north. They had left their mark as they passed, that strange novelty that archaeologists would later unearth, almost absent until then, male statuettes all along their way.

The gods had arrived.

These gods would dispute the realm of the goddesses and finally reduce them from their ancient, all-powerful role to that of subservient, secondary figures, with only a feigned semblance of command. It was happening—as we are allowed to know by archaeology, myth, lore and history—a heavenly repetition of the displacement that was already taking place at a more earthly level among men and women. As the Scriptures say, just in Earth as in Heaven.

What was Her name? She had many names— the Goddess, the Great Mother of all Gods, the Mother of All Livings, the Mother Goddess, the Triple Goddess, the Lady, the Queen of

Fig. 14. Sketch from a fresco found in the palace at Knossos (c. 1400 B.C.)

Heaven, the Mother. She had many more names—in many different languages, but always the same goddess. Let's call Her the Mother Goddess or just the Goddess.

For tribes in the Ice Age, weather and seasons were all important. Religion was linked to it. The beginning of agriculture did not make man independent of seasons but increased his dependence. Fertility gods were linked to rain and water all over the world. Paleolithic man seemed to recognize just three seasons—an annual cycle of three phases. The Mother Goddess was also the Moon Goddess. The moon is linked to femininity, the menstrual cycle coincides with lunations, as many other cycles in nature. Triads of goddesses were common in Her cult.

Fig. 15. Sketch from a fresco found in Thera (Santorini) c.1500 B.C.

Fig 16. Sketch of a ring with feminine figures. The scene has been interpreted as part of a ritual. Labrys (double ax) at center. From Mycenae.

She appears as the hunting virgin *Artemis* (Roman *Diana*), the sexy and promiscuous *Aphrodite* (*Venus*) and matronal *Hera* (*Juno*)—symbolizing the pre-nubile, nubile and post-nubile stages in woman. It coincides with waxing, full moon and waning. The White Goddess, the Red Goddess and the Blue (or Black) Goddess. In good accord with the three then acknowledged seasons of the year.

Another trinal expression was as Queen of Heaven (Selene), of Water and Earth (Aphrodite) and of the Underworld

(Hecate). The number three was commonly associated with Her. Three were the Furies or *Erinyes*, goddesses of vengeance. So the three Fates, goddesses that controlled human life, called the *Moirai* by the Greeks, *Norns* by the Germans. Some times, in order to enhance her divinity, each member of the sacred triad was also split into three, so *nine muses,* goddesses of the arts, exist. It emphasized that all artistic inspiration was Hers.

Her cult was extremely ancient. Some creation myths make scholars think that they evolved *before* the relationship between coition and pregnancy was established.

She had many symbols. We know them mainly through the Greek myths; most of them were originally Pelasgians. In ancient times Her followers knew them well and also their significance. The Chimera was one. A mythological being, it was made from *three* animals: a lion's head, a goat's body and a snake's tail. It symbolized the three seasons of the year, the three phases of the moon, the Triple Goddess herself. Each animal was an usual symbol of one of the aspects of the trinity. It has been thought that each animal had also an astronomical meaning, hosting the sun in its corresponding constellation while some seasonal or heavenly event was taking place. In some regions the important seasons for agriculture or the chase were just two—a rainy and a dry season, for instance. In that case, a composite of just two animals was the symbol of Her cult.

Fig 17. Two goddesses (according to some interpretations Demeter and Kore) and the "divine child." Sketch from a terracotta statuette found in Mycenae. (c. 1400 B.C.)

Thirteen was also one of Her sacred numbers—or twelve plus one, which is the same. It is the number of the moon months in a year. Those ancient astronomers knew there were two kinds of months. The synodic month, the time taken by the moon to complete a cycle of phases is 29,5 days. According to this, the year has 12 months and eleven days. On the other hand, the time the moon needs to reach its same position on a fixed zodiacal constellation, the sidereal month, is 27,32 days. For many peoples the sidereal month was taken as 28 days. So, a week of seven days was possible. The seven was also the number of the celestial bodies: the sun, the moon and the then five known planets. The year was thirteen months (13 x 28 = 364) plus one day.

Examples of the sacred number, thirteen, or more precisely, twelve plus one, were found everywhere. Good examples were the confederation of the twelve Etruscan cities and their sanctuary or the Greek Amphictyonic League of twelve cities and their sanctuary at Delphi. We also find remembrances of the number in King Arthur and his twelve knights. The judge and the twelve jurors are still in use, inherited through the Scandinavians.

Thirteen is also the number of nights between the first crescent and the full moon. Whenever that number is found, we are also listening to an old echo of the Goddess.

There were other numbers with sacred resonances. Planet Venus, with her elongation-conjunction, 72-day season proportionated that number and also the number 5 (because there were five of those seasons in a year). Pythagoreans felt special veneration for the numbers 8 and 9. Eight is the numbers of years of the Earth-Venus Cycle (eight Earth years=five Venus years). Pythian Games were celebrated at first on a eight-year basis. Then it became a 4-year celebration (a Venus Hemicycle). It indicated to whom they were paying respect. The Olympic Games probably suffered a similar transformation. The fact that the product of the sacred number 8 and the sacred number 9 (the triple triad of the Goddess) gave 72 added to their magic.

For ancient Europeans, all spirits seemed to be feminine. For the Greeks, for instance, there were spirits (*nymphs*) of mountains (*ore-*

ads), of waters (*naiads*), of trees (*hamadryads*). It has been postulated that nymphs were priestesses in charge of sacred trees. Each type of tree in the wood had its own spirit or nymph: oak (*dryad*), ash (*melia*), nut (*caryatid*), willow (*helice*). The Goddess was pervasive. Ancient Europeans considered She influenced everything. Animate or inanimate, all was under Her spell and control.

Her dominance extended to the sciences. It seems that the oldest symbolic scripture left is a lunar calendar. It is the first astronomic record in human past: the bone found at Blanchard, France. It has tiny incisions that may mark—according to the top expert on the field—the phases of the moon over a period of more than two months. Some anonymous astronomer carefully engraved the marks more than 30,000 years ago. The engraver was probably also one of the Goddess' followers. Festivities in Her honor were linked to the phases of the moon.

She might have induced both agriculture and cities. Some scientists now believe that the first use for cultivated cereals was not to *feed* people. Those first crops apparently were fermented and transformed into beer, to be consumed during Her festivities. A brewer recently revived one beer from antiquity—using an ancient recipe found in Sumerian clay tablets, attributed to the Middle-East goddess Ninkasi.

Cereals also provided hallucinogens (details on the religious use of ergot fungus, corroborated by archaeology, can be found in Chapter 14). Hallucinogens seem to have been all important in ancient rituals. It is not difficult to see that rye and other cereals were in high demand for those uses before becoming a basic dietary item. Her priesthood probably acquired the know-how to grow cereals for religious uses. Then it must have found a later use—feeding the ever-increasing number of dwellers of that other momentous invention, cities. With the concentrated produce of agriculture the transition from villages to cities was made possible.

What was Her cult? Sir James G. Frazer asked that same question in the last century. He asked himself what had been the cult offered to the goddess Diana, at her temple in the island of the lake Nemi, in Italy. He wrote *The Golden Bough* as a result. It was the birth of anthropology. His answer was shocking. His research showed that the priest of Diana was always a slave, who had had to kill the former priest. That ritual murder turned him legally free. It also invested him as the new priest of the temple of Diana at Nemi. The image of the self-instated priest of Diana wandering through the island, fearsome of the next, self-postulated candidate anxious to succeed *him*, haunted many generations of readers.

What it is conjectured today, through the accumulated evidence of myths, lore and history, and also from what has been known from certain Mother Goddess cults in Africa, professed by tribes which were genetically and culturally linked to Mediterranean people and religions, is that Her cult evolved greatly over time.

First, let's remember that European tribes in ancient times had animal totems, protected by taboos, except from the yearly chase and sacrifice of a single specimen (or of many on a single day). Just like the people of the region of Cocullo in Italy have been doing for thousands of years—the whole town of Luco still chases snakes on May Day. Then they take an image of San Domenico of Foligno in procession, covered with the snakes they caught. Their ancestors did the same in ancient times in honor of their goddess Angitia or Ankisia. They do not kill the reptiles anymore—an innovation of the last decade—complying with the conservationist wave, but set them free after the ceremonies and processions.

Each tribe or group had his totem in the Stone Age and even later, when metal came. When they fused together to make greater conglomerations, the totem of the dominant group was usually adopted. Athenians also had a yearly owl hunt. The owl was their totem. It became the symbol of the goddess Athena, and also their state city symbol. It still is. The city has changed owners and religions many times, but the owl, the ancient Goddess' bird, abides, its former meaning now lost in the fumes of cars and industries.

Many European cities still keep emblems from the past, which might have come from some Goddess cult. Animals, birds, fish, trees and plants formed part of the cryptic languages of Her cult, linked in a system of calendars and symbols. They allowed travelers in the past to know immediately the nature of the local cult, in spite of different languages.

Instead of beginning with what Her cult was in the far past, well into the Ice Age, let's start a few thousand years ago, in Greece. Before any of the first Indo-European invaders—the Ionians and Eolians—had arrived. At the time the Pelasgians still called Hera the Mother Goddess (Uni among the Etruscans). A college of priestesses served Her. The Goddess' consort was a pastoral sacred king, not exactly an incorporeal deity, but a flesh and blood man. He achieved instant sanctity, and his royal status, by marrying the representative of the Goddess, the priestess of the tribe or clan.

On their marriage, it was believed, depended the welfare of the tribe. He was supposedly wedding Hera, so in ancient times he was commonly called a *Hero* everywhere in Greece. Yes, that is where our word hero comes from—one married to the Goddess.

In later times the Goddess assumed many different names, but the priestly king was still being called a Hero.

That is one of the reasons that many ancient gods appeared frequently in couples: Tin and Tina among the Etruscans, Dio and Dia among the Romans. It was always the Goddess and Her human consort, who at the end of his reign achieved divinity at the cost of his life.

Let's start with the most famous Hero of all times: Herakles, the one the Roman called Hercules, as we do today, and the Etruscans Erkles. He was the Melquart of the Phoenicians, the Dagdá of the Irish and the Txomin Chendo of the Basques. Herakles means *Glory of Hera* or *Glorious gift of Hera*. He was the only mortal who was taken to the Mount Olympus, the residence of the gods, to be deified.

Master historian Herodotus felt confused about Herakles. He thought that there had been two Herakles. One, who might be called the historical one, had supposedly taken part in the expedition of the Argonauts in the 13th century B.C., the celebrated voyage of the ship Argos. The other Herakles seemed to have been a god, whose cult was much, much older than that.

Herodotus was right. There had been those two Herakles. Actually there had been *hundreds, thousands and thousands* of Herakles, with the same or many different names, all over Greece and all over Europe, all along the Mediterranean coast, both in the Asian and the African part.

Now, how is all that possible at the same time? Which is the true story? One, two or many Herakles?

First, it seems *there was a historic* Herakles who traveled in the Argos. Second, Herakles was a *title*, not a name. It was a title conferred to the man chosen to reign as *sacred king, as consort of Hera*. It was one of the royal titles of the Hero. The historical Herakles, an Achean warrior whose real, or more mortal name was Palemon, the son of Alcmene and Amphitryon, ascended once to the high status of sacred king, consort of Hera. Actually, according to the chronicles, he did it more than once. How he dealt with his kingships constitutes one of the most precious narratives left by Herodotus. They were dramatic episodes marking social upheaval, catastrophic times and a turning point in history. They meant the end of the goddesses' power or, to put it in undisguised terms, the end of almost all Euzkan or Pelasgian religious and political predominance in Greece.

Herodotus knew well that the Herakles tradition was much older than Palemon, who had lived only some eight centuries before him. Herodotus was aware that Egyptian priests attributed the institution of that Herakles sacred-kingship at some 17,000 years before the reign of Pharaoh Amasis—nearly 19,600 years from us. His Egyptian name had been *Shu*, not Herakles. Just as in Britain one of his names had been *Bran*. Probably, at the beginning, one of his Pelasgian names (or titles) had been *Cronos*, and many more names were adopted as the cult of the Goddess evolved. It is important to remember that, even if he attained godship, he was always only the consort of the Goddess. The final power was always Hers.

Whatever his name, in many distant places, in many different tribes, during thousands of years, a pastoral sacred-king was chosen. At the beginning it happened probably twice a year. Each king was probably sacrificed, in some places, at the winter and summer solstices respectively. That was probably the custom among Nordic Europeans.

In other regions, like Greece, the ceremonies may have taken place during the equinoxes. That is known because until classical times the year in Athens began in spring. Two Dionysian feasts marked the beginning of the Spring in Athens. The Anthesteria was the first one—a festival of the dead and of resurrection. Dionysus was the god of *wine and ecstasy*. His cult had arrived from Thrace and Phrygia. The strange legends of his birth and death and his marriage to Ariadne, in origin a Cretan goddess, suggest that his cult represented a reversion to pre-Hellenic Minoan nature religion.

The second day of the Anthesteria was a time of popular merrymaking in Athens, but the state performed a *secret ceremony* in a sanctuary of Dionysus in the Lenaeum, in which the *wife of the Archon Basileus married to Dionysus.*

The Archon Basileus was one of the nine principal magistrates of ancient Athens. Most historians believe that features of an ancient kingship had survived in the Archon Basileus, who, as chief religious officer, presided over the Areopagus (aristocratic council) when it sat as a homicide court.

The most important feature is the wedding. Specialists have also recognized in it the traces of that old institution—the *Hyeros Gamos* or *Sacred Wedding*. It was the most important ceremony in ancient times—the King publicly copulating wiht the Queen—ensuring the survival and prosperity of the realm.

The Sacred Wedding marked always the crowning of the king (or his renewal or rebirth) and the beginning of the year.

The Great Dionysia followed the Anthesteria. The Aryan invaders separated the state from the old religion but kept respecting the rituals. So it is possible to suppose what happened during those rituals in the Paleolithic thanks to theater evolution.

It is known that it started with an actor improvising the religious *dithyramb* songs and a fifty-member chorus. Like the Etruscan *histrio,* the actor had a religious role—a *priest* role.

As the king was the main priest in pre-Indo-European times, it probably was his responsibility and privilege to perform those improvised song and dance rituals. According to Archilochus, the leader was *"wit-stricken by the thunderbolt of wine"*. It is not hard to presume that kings were in some kind of hallucinogenic trance that supposedly gave them prophetic powers.

Palemon must have danced his part, when he became the Herakles of the city. He must mimically have battled against the twelve constellations (his *Twelve Labors*) —fighting the stations of the year to secure the all important harvests and other tribal activities.

The fifty members of the Chorus probably originated in the king's companions. Sacred bands of fifty or a hundred members were common among totem fraternities, e.g. the mythical Hekatontocheiroi—the one hundred hands. So they must have accompanied him in his song and dance, mimically battling the natural or supernatural enemies of the city or village while the king-priest danced and sung about the life, death and return of Dionysus.

Euripides described in the *Bacchae* the frantic religious dance of Athenian women (called *bacchantes* or *maenads*). It opened the representation. They stamped the ground and whirled about in rhythmic convulsions—froth at their mouths. According to ancient authors, they were duly intoxicated.

The Chorus sung and danced in the disguise of lecherous satyrs, following the wild dance of the women. The goat skins that dressed them may have originated the name tragedy (from Greek *tragoidia*: *tragos*, goat + *oidé*, song). Or maybe the name originated in the goat sacrificed in the festivity. Given the importance of the feast and of the ritual, it is not hard to presume that in older times a person was ritually killed, dressed with a skin goat.

Gradually the priest became an actor. According to Greek tradition, the genial actor and playwright Thespis invented the drama when he expanded the chorus of the dithyramb giving different masks to a single actor (formerly the king) to portray several different characters. With the increased possibility of dialogue between the actor and the chorus, more complex themes and modes of storytelling soon were developed. In 534 BC, at Athens' first dramatic festival, one of Thespis' tragedies won the prize. Years later Aeschylus added a second actor and reduced the chorus from 50 to 12. Sophocles brought the chorus up to 15 and added a third actor. So modern theater started.

In spite of all theatrical changes and evolution, the traditional Sacred Wedding kept taking place in the Anthesteria celebration. *The Archon Basileus also kept his* prerogative *of choosing the poets who were to compete with their plays in the Great Dionysia.* It was another telling sign of *who had been the original actor* in the pre-Indo-European times. As it was an important religious attribution, it meant that he had inherited or retained the ancient priest-king power, so he could delegate or confer his old privilege into others. The feast was celebrated until the 4th century A.D.

Hercules iconography is well known—tall and muscular, covered by a lion skin. The lion was a symbol of the Goddess—the Lady of the Lions. Herakles is always seen carrying an oak club. The oak was the sacred tree that attracted lightning, whose place in the wood was sacred too. Ancient Germans who made the foolish mistake to just scratch an oak were reminded of its sanctity by being deprived of enough of their skins as to cover the damaged tree surface. Death was the penalty for any severe damage to any sacred oak.

Among Herakles' symbols were the acorn, the rock dove, the serpent and the mistletoe—the same mistletoe that grows in the oak branch (the motive of one of Turner's wonderful paintings, *The Golden Bough,* which Frazer chose as title of his book). The place under the oak, right below the mistletoe, was the most sacred in all the wood for druids. The same mistletoe which is still hung, honoring the now already forgotten priest-king sacrifice, in most houses at Christmas time, as that date superimposes itself upon that old pagan celebration, the winter solstice. For some Nordic tribes it was the time when the sacred king died and the new king was invested, meaning the resurrection of nature, the return of the sun, the renewal of fertility, the coming of the New Year. The same mistletoe than druids cut with their golden sickles for their ceremonies, a ritual symbolism of the Hero's emasculation by his successor.

Through the mistletoes hanged near Christmas time, a vague resonance of the ancient Mother Goddess cult is reaching deep into present homes—well installed in the most respected traditions, reminder of the antiquity of the birth of many beliefs and creeds and of their permanent evolution.

The chosen sacred king was healthy. He had to be free from any mark or deformation. Strong, at the height of his sexual power, he symbolized fertility. Even today the words for seeding and reproduction are the same in Greek. He was the chosen companion of the Goddess, at that time Queen of the Woods. Their sacred coupling restored order, making sure that the seasons would follow the right sequence. He was the Rain Maker, who with his sperm insured the growth and greening of vegetation, the return of the annually migrating species of birds, fish, animals, upon whom the community depended. He was offering himself for the good of the community, of his tribe, to be transformed into a god. Our word hero still conserves that ancient meaning: one ready to die for the good of others.

The day of his death, he was given some hallucinogenic brew, which induced an altered state of consciousness. That and later coupling within a ritual was considered to induce the deification, which was only attained upon his death. Probably the hallucinogens also helped him to go along with the rules and die without complaining (even if we are told by Herodotus that the historic Hercules, the former Palemon, when his time arrived was not that compliant and had really a thing or two to say about all these procedures).

At the proper astronomical celebration the sacred king was killed. Sometimes, beaten first by priestesses, his successor or his companions. Then, unconscious but still alive, flayed, blinded, emasculated and then hacked to pieces on a stone altar. His blood was collected, and the whole tribe, or some chosen members, sprinkled with it. His successor, sometimes also the priestesses, or sometimes the whole tribe, drank his blood and ritually ate part or all of his body. Usually the genitals, the brain, or part of the shoulder or the thighs were chosen.

All these particulars varied from tribe to tribe, from region to region, and much with the passing of time. Written in such a short space, in just a few lines, it might seem that the differences or possibilities mentioned, as well as the many names of the

Goddess or of Her husband, were somehow irrelevant. The practitioners did not believe so. The cults were much more varied and complex than these lines imply. Any small difference implied between them is the kind of subject that today makes anthropologists contend in any congress. At those times, those apparently slight differences in cult were more severely dealt with. They were among the main alleged reasons of most tribal wars and social revolts.

Each kind of cult marked who was in command, which group had power, whose totem was reigning.

In the Greek creation myths, for instance, many inherited from the Pelasgians, we found Cronos emasculated and then killed by Zeus, his son, who thus gained his high post among the gods. Modern mythologists believe it marks the succession of one type of cult by another.

Gods ascended and descended, in that way, in the celestial rank, following closely the success or failure of the tribes, or confederation of tribes, which had adopted their cult.

The same Zeus started—even if no one can be sure of his real original name—if myth, legends and traditions, and the comments of ancient writers are to be believed, just like one more Hero or Herakles in a dark cavern in Crete. In some regions he was just a minor god, below Apollo and others, denoting the scarcity and weakness of his followers. In others, he fought for power with many other gods and goddesses. At the end of all the Indo-European invasions he was reigning supreme in the Olympic court. The real meaning of his ascent to the celestial sovereignty was the advent and supremacy of patrilineal tribes, when a new, patrilineal college of priests, backed by Indo-European clans, had completely displaced old, matrilineal colleges of priestesses of Euzkan origin.

The sacred king was the male leader in ceremonies and rituals, accompanied by priestesses and, sometimes, other males. His conduct was all-important. He was, as Frazer denominated him, a priestly king. From the moment he was invested every one of his acts had a symbolic, prophetic virtue. The sacred rainmaker was expected to attract rains by rattling his club in a hollow oak and stirring a pond with an oak branch. The Goddess conceded Her powers through the Sacred Marriage and his sperm brought the beasts to be hunted and the fruits to be gathered and harvested. He also had to observe many taboos.

One interesting point is that some part of the cult of the Goddess remained mostly an all-female one. There were ceremonies and secret rituals where only women took part. That custom continued even when the goddesses had been deposed and totally lost their real power. A few festivals and some old cults like Demeter (Roman *Ceres*) remained in the sphere of women in some regions of Greece, no men were ever admitted to them. The men played a part only in some of the rituals. That characteristic of women's ritual secret societies has been found in tribes in Africa; they tend to protect women and to restrict male power.

In Italy, for instance, *only women* attended the Bacchanalia at first. It was the equivalent of the Greek Dionysian feast. They held it in *secret* on three days of the year. They admitted men later and the celebrations started to take place more often.

The Heroes became gods at the cost of their lives. Once dead, cannibalized, their bones were often brought to a sepulchral island, be it in a river, lake or sea. This ritual probably gave birth to the legend of *Charon* (*Kharun* among the Etruscans)—the ferryman in the ritual—who originally floated the sacred remains off to its last home. Later, when the sacrifice of the sacred kings was abolished, Charon became more democratic, and in Indo-European times he was transporting everybody's corpse down the river Styx to Pluto's dead kingdom—for just a coin. This time it was just a story; the real transportation had faded away with time. It can be seen that status seeking was not confined to our modern times, even a post-mortem one. Nobody seemed to feel bad about the possibility that at least the final transportation was godlike. In the Goddess' times it was real and the sole prerogative of the Hero, who had also had to pay dearly for the toll.

Sometimes the tribes kept just the skull, sometimes more bones, on occasions the whole body. These remains were always considered sacred—invested with the power the Goddess had conferred on the Hero.

Neglect of the worship of these Hero remains meant—in their religious viewpoint—pestilence, poor harvests and other misfortunes. They believed that honoring the sacrificed Hero brought prosperity. So the Heroes—now totally turned into fertility gods—continued doing their work.

The islands where they were buried or kept also acquired a sacred character. They were truly famous in the antiquity, becoming sites of veneration and pilgrimage—Lemnos, Delos, Pharos, Samothrace, in the Mediterranean, Leuce, off the mouth of the Danube, Iona, off the coast of Scotland. In all of them temples dedicated to the Goddess existed, under some of Her many names.

There were also some cults where the Heroes' bones were laid or buried in a cave or in the top of a mountain instead of ferried to a lake.

The same tradition was kept in the Middle East and Egypt. In later times kings were interred with ships or miniature ships to provide transportation of their souls to the sacred island, or to some place with supposed supernatural characteristics. At least, the kings' souls would be carried to the afterworld.

The sacrifice and burial rituals seem to have been the most important public celebrations. We can even guess how they sounded. In Etruscan tomb murals, for instance, a variety of horns can be seen, carried by white-robbed officials at burial processions. Romans inherited the instruments and traditions; the members of the guild of *liticines* and *cornicines*, players of *lituus* and horns accompanied the funerals of emperors. The *tubae* is the only one of them that left a legacy. Sacrificial tubas, for instance, were different from those played by the *tubicines* of the Roman legions–which had no drums–during exercises or at battles. Strident pipes were also employed, as it happened in Egypt, when the sacred boats transported the Pharaoh's mummy to his tomb.

The cults kept always on the move, always changing, at the same pace as the societies where they were professed. The coming of agriculture, also with its cyclical times of clearing, plowing, seeding, tilling and the final harvest, implied new festivities and novel theological implications. The Heroes were not pastoral anymore; the Queen of the Woods became Queen of the Fields, presiding now over the ceremonies of communities of farmers. Among the Baltic people, for instance, Laima, the goddess of the woods, kept her old reign but ceded the agricultural domain to Mara.

These kinds of celebrations kept demanding the sacrifice of the sacred king, but under new rituals, and his powers and expectations became also more complex. Arts and crafts were emerging, professions and specialists. All that led to increasing heavenly rearrangements. A smith, Hephaestus (the Roman Vulcanus) appeared consonantly in Mount Olympus, a show of the high standing of that new technology. Hera became many goddesses, each with her own field of influence, in good accordance with the increasing specialization of humans at ground level. Artemis at Iolcus, for instance, was the patroness of fishers and sailors. The differences became notable.

Nevertheless, in spite of the geographical distances and the cultural differences, people knew about the identity of the different goddesses. For instance, those previously mentioned three golden Etruscan tablets, found at the port of Cerveteri, informed that their temple was dedicated to Uni-Astarte. We can learn through it that they considered their goddess Uni identical to Phoenician Astarte.

All these sacrificial rituals were common in ancient times. Not only the devotees of the Goddess institutionalized ritual killings. Human sacrifice was a constant, widespread social characteristic not so long ago, as it is believed, or wished.

In Central America and Mexico, babies were sacrificed when corn was seeded, youths were offered when the first plants appeared and adults were the price of the full-grown cob. These practices continued for centuries, in spite of Spanish occupation, in some remote regions.

Ritual deifying sacrifices were also common among Mayas, Aztecs and other peoples. The victims were given hallucinogens and deified while being opened alive, their beating hearts were extracted and their blood collected to be ceremonially drunk. They were finally eaten as an eucharistic meal by the whole community or by just part of it. Their sanctified crania were also collected in sacred places, chosen as the favorite supernatural adornment of many temples, which any tourist can now easily visit.

In practically all continents, all cultures, ritual killing seems to have had a place, occasional or continually.

The Bible is a magnificent repository of these cultural practices, marking not only their kind but also their evolution or ending. The offering of the first born, for instance, when it was demanded from every kind, vegetal, animal and even human. The clans used to ritually murder the entire population of rival tribes—including their animals—when they were declared an anathema.

Archaeology has confirmed the existence of ritual sacrifice in the Pelasgian world. It was one of the most moving discoveries in the second half of the twentieth century. Among the ruins of a Minoan temple in Crete, brought down by an earthquake 3,700 years ago, archaeologists discovered some human remains. The noteworthy investigation that followed produced an unprecedented verdict: a man and a woman had been offering an 18-year-old male, whose blood had been collected. The earthquake froze the scene in time, leaving the first evidence of a human ritual killing while it was going on.

They offered human victims after a victory, after a long voyage, after a good crop, at the dedication of a building, in gratitude for almost anything, and whenever any peril was considered important enough to demand it. Many people will find hard to believe that they are still being carried out in many places in Africa, Asia and America.

Which was the kind of sacrifice the Mother Goddess was offered in the Ice Age?

A British expert in myth and lore, the late Robert Graves, had a hint of it. He thought that there was a probable clue both in the caves of Altamira, Spain, and of Trois Frères, in France. Both places have paintings of stag-men, dating at least 20,000 years. The male figure in Trois Frères, with an erect phallus (at all times taken as a fertility symbol), is wearing a stag mask (Fig. 18a).

The Old Religion   117

Graves pointed that both the stag and the bull were sacred to the Goddess, and to traditions, still alive in writer Pausanias times, of *men dressed in deer skins who were chased and eaten in the Lycaean precinct of Arcadia*, a region so conservative that all the Goddess' temples there were still dedicated to Hera. He saw a not casual similitude between those Ice-Age stag-men with a Bronze-Age figurine from Sardinia. It was a stag-man whose horns resembled oak branches. He had a short tail and an arrow in one hand—in the other a bow-serpent.

Fig. 18a. Sketch of the stag-man of Trois Freres

Was Graves right? If he was, in those stag-men, the oldest Heroes ever recalled can be seen.

He included in that same interpretation a Dordogne (France) cave painting of a bull-man dancing and playing a musical instrument shaped like a bow. Graves considered him another sacred king, an apparent ancestor of the Cretan Minotaur, half bull, and half man. It is fascinating to observe that Ice-Age carved animal bones, worn down by long handling, apparently made to be used for a long time, with some specific purpose, for this reason thought to be of ritual use (not other one could be guessed), show flora and fauna which were obviously connected with the advent of the seasons, also one of the Goddess most powerful domains.

There was an African connection, too.

Graves was impressed by the likeness with stag-men and bull-men in the caves of Domboshawa and other places of Southern Rhodesia. A stag-man was shown there dying, ejaculating and forming with his seed a heap of corn, with an old priestess lying naked besides a cauldron. Close to it, young women were shown dancing, surrounded by clouds of fruit and heaped baskets. Graves interpreted it as another Hero.

Fig. 18b. Sketch of the only human figure in the Lascaux cave. Do the laying position and the erect phallus point to a sacrificial king?

Only one question can be asked. It is difficult to assert which were the real cults at such an ancient time. Everything must be inferred—all is conjecture. It is an open field to many theories and interpretations.

Somehow, there is a certain point that is disquieting.

Whenever the cave painters are depicted by artists, to illustrate books, scientific or divulgation magazines, or museum paintings, some priests and acolytes are always shown in the Ice-

Age caves, reclining or squatting, laboriously drawing and painting ceilings and murals with fingers, sticks and pads, at the lights of the many fat lamps that have been recovered in those places.

Now, how can anyone be that sure? What authorizes anybody to think that way? Which facts are backing it? What kind of arrogant reasoning can justify that in a continent where for nearly three dozen thousand years the Goddess enjoyed an almost total command of the scene, *priests* are shown doing that job? Is there any reason not to think that maybe *priestesses* had a hand at it? Could at least a few women artists have painted some of them too? It is amazing to see that the old Indo-European customs keep playing tricks even in scientific fields.

How did the Hero gain his kingship and his right to die for the Goddess? It is thought that competitions took place. At the beginning a foot race must have been common—maybe a wrestling match.

Did the Olympic Games originate this way? It has been thought so. According to Pausanias, they originated in a *girls'* foot race—the *Heraia*, the oldest event of the celebration. These young females probably competed to become *Hera's High Priestess—the Queen*. Let's remember that, due to what was expected for a woman in such position at ancient times, the winner should have been the one destined to marry the Hero. It kept being run all through history, always before the Olympic Games started, which, at the beginning, were also only a men's foot race.

As Herakles instituted the games, knowing what that title means makes it very significant. It seems that the winners of both foot races became the Moon Queen and the Sun King. It became the most important *religious* celebration of all Greece. So important, than even wars were stopped whenever the games started. That way everybody could take part or be a spectator. A sort of commemoration of the original way the divine couple, Sun and Moon, was chosen.

There is another eloquent clue to the original regal status of the foot-race winner in the Olympic Games. *The Greeks gave the winner's name to that game and the four-year period following it. That was one of the most common traditions in ancient times: to name a regal period by the name of the king.*

When the lists of Olympic winners started, in 776 B.C., the Pelasgian ritual killing of the sacred king was not much remembered, except by priests and members of leading families, and the Olympics already resembled very much any Indo-European games. The earliest extant building known is a temple to *Hera*. It is very revealing what successive archaeologists have pointed out about the splendid ruins that were then dedicated to Olympian Zeus: there are traces of an altar near the Heraeum—Hera's own zone—*much older than the great altar of Zeus and considered the original center of worship.*

In Pelasgian times it is difficult to see a more important civic and religious event, concerning Hera, which could not mean the Hero. So everything points to an original Pelasgian religious ritual and tradition superseded by later Indo-European ones.

It is interesting to notice that what had probably been once an amphictyonic, that is interstate, tradition, kept that character and became Panhellenic later. It is also interesting because the presence of those rituals in an amphictyonic religious center suggests that not only villages and cities had Heroes, but that the whole league had their chosen Priestess and Hero.

Another telling point: in classical times, when priestesses had been displaced and women were not allowed to witness the men's competitions, the sole stone seat on the northern side of the stadium was still reserved for the priestess of Demeter, a clear signal of deference toward the Goddess. An old tradition was being respected, even when the Goddess had already fallen in disgrace.

Did all those famous bull games in Crete have the same purpose? Did they mean the election of both the Goddess' Priestess and the Hero? Some scholars have also thought so.

What is beyond any present discussion is that bull games were extraordinarily important in Cretan cities. The palaces in Knossos, Phaistos and Mallia, had the same general plan, with the most magnificent buildings surrounding large, rectangular courts of practically identical shape and size. Two sides of the central court of Mallia, at least one in Phaistos and probably at Knossos were bordered with colonnades. They seem to have been fenced with timber between the pillars. It has been considered obvious, by most archaeologists, that all these central courts had been destined for a common, traditional purpose, as the arena of a religious bull-leaping ceremony.

Frescoes, rings and statuettes show splendid young men and women leaping on the bulls. As these cities were the domain of the Goddess, it seems difficult, with so many concurrent clues, to point to any other meaning, apart from the election of the Priestess and the Hero, which could have made that ceremony all important. Plutarch has let us know that Knossos was the center of an amphictyonic league too. So, the youths coming from Athens and other cities, each nine years, were probably competing to be the next sacred royal couple of the league.

Later, at the times of the *Iliad*, probably due to Indo-European influences, we find princes competing in horse and chariot races and in archery, to gain this time the hand of a princess and become sacred kings.

Some kingships were gained in a much more complex way. It is known that Atreus, father of Agamemnon and Menelaus, won his kingship in Mycenae, over his brother Thyestes, through the prediction of some sort of celestial phenomenon, probably an eclipse. That astronomic phenomenon must have been momentous, because another myth says that Palemon—destined to be the most renowned Herakles—was illegally generated that same unusual day at Thebes, not by his nominal father Amphytrion, who recognized him in spite of that.

Oedipus is believed to have won his sacred kingship (and the right to his mother's bed, including the unavoidable duty to kill the former king, his father) in some sort of wisdom test, as it is indicated by the Sphinx's riddle.

The transition in Greece between the oldest traditions and the new ones was marked probably by the arrival of the first two Indo-European waves.

It has been suggested that Indo-European chieftains could have married the Goddess' priestesses, incorporating themselves into the power circle without damaging its structure. After all, sacred kings were always expected to be of foreign origin, as the matrilocal customs required. Examples of intermarriage between matrilineal and patrilineal tribes have been found in Africa. It seems that when that happened concordant couples of male and female gods of different types appeared at the same time in the celestial sphere. As this was also a feature of the Greek Pantheon, some scholars did not think unreasonable to deduce that a similar intermarriage took place between the followers of both goddesses and gods during the Bronze Age.

There are also historical arguments, seen in preceding chapters, which testify the extended belief, among Greeks from the classical period, that such intermarriage had taken place.

What are even more interesting, some Greek sacred scriptures show hints of a matrilineal system surviving well until the third Indo-European wave—the Acheans—ended the system. Those sacred writings cryptically tell us about the sudden, dramatic abolition of both the matrilineal system and the Goddess' Hero cults.

This time the events happened at a very fast pace. The final displacement occurred in the short time of about two generations.

The events and the protagonists are astonishingly well known, not only for scholars.

＃ 9

The Founding Fathers

History, as such, started with the Greeks. Herodotus is considered its father. He begot it by writing his Nine Books of History—dedicating one to each of the Muses. They chiefly concerned the Persian Wars (499-479 B.C.). On doing that he had to confront an annoying problem. He was trying to explain the origin of the Greek people. Their language at that time was almost universally Greek, Pelasgian tongues were still spoken in a few regions. Herodotus' trouble was that for him, as for all his contemporaries from the 5th century B.C. as well, the names and deeds of most of their forefathers were almost totally unknown.

Herodotus, as any educated Greek of his time, knew about the names of his predecessors for just a few generations back. He could identify leaders from his father's times. But he could reach only to his grandparents' time. Then a long, empty space followed.

Why that void? Indo-Europeans had been penetrating Greece since millennia and half before. Ionian and Eolian invaders had established themselves, settling and merging with the Pelasgians, but practically neither their leader's names nor their deeds are left. In surprising contrast the names of the leaders of some four generations of the third wave of Indo-European invaders, the Acheans, some seven centuries before Herodotus, were remarkably well known. Not only for Herodotus, they were famous all through Greece. *They are well known and famous today.*

Hercules, Theseus, Jason, Achilles, Agamemnon, Menelaus, Odysseus or Ulysses. Not only is their extraordinary fame conspicuous, contrasting with the obscurity concerning their predecessors, but also another fantastic void follows: the name of their *successors* is also lost. Even more: the *last* wave of invaders who came after them, the Dorians, in spite of their influence, in spite of becoming the *dominant* ethnic group, also shared the general anonymity.

From those four generations of famed Acheans to Herodotus' ancestors another blackout follows—almost nobody known.

Why all this? This singular darkness can be partly attributed to the lack of history books. After all, the first ones were just Herodotus'. Nevertheless, the main names of those four generations of Acheans were widely recognized by all Greeks. What made those men so famous? What did they do to achieve such spectacular recognizance *among all generations*, to have been chosen by the fame over both the *preceding* and the *succeeding* leaders?

Perhaps a more modern example could explain that inconsistency. When U.S.A. citizens are asked about their presidents of the past centuries two names immediately come out: George Washington and Abraham Lincoln. The two of them are not only famous in the U.S.A. but also abroad. Easily recognized by any educated person of any country.

On the other hand, pollsters are keenly aware that even educated people in the U.S.A. show a terrible vacuum when asked about the other presidents of the 18th and 19th centuries. An embarrassing silence is the most frequent answer to that kind of question—not to mention some remarkable blunders.

What made Washington and Lincoln so eminent among all the U.S.A. presidents? Easy. Washington was the *independence war leader* and also the *first* president. He is permanently associated with the *birth of the nation*. Lincoln is associated with a *traumatic civil war* and a deep change in the *social structure* or social rights. Both the independence process and the civil war meant a considerable *social transformation*. So the two names more prominent at those convulsed times are well remembered.

All that gives us a clue about Herodotus' troubles.

It is telling us that, in spite of the continuous invasion of Indo-Europeans, no major, traumatic change in the government structure or social rights took place at first. That during the Ionian and Eolian invasions or settlings the Pelasgians structures survived more or less intact. We can guess that by the scarcity of news. On the other hand, *social structures must have been submitted to some kind of cataclysm by those four generations of Acheans.* It is the only explanation for their astounding degree of recognizance. Those four generations of Acheans were considered some kind of founding fathers.

What happened in Greece at those times? If all those names are linked to the birth of a nation or the reshaping of a community, what actually happened there? First, at those times the concept of nation as it is presently understood was practically inexistent. In spite of that, the Greeks recognized among them a kind of national, cultural identity.

An Athenian would consider himself with duties and responsibilities just toward Athens. Everybody was a citizen of just his mother city, nothing else. Nevertheless, they all knew they had a certain common cultural identity that linked all the Greeks in the mainland, the islands, the Near East and in every colony in the Mediterranean.

Apart from a more or less common language, common cultural habits, there existed another kind of ties of a strong nature—*a religious relationship.*

Religion is a word that comes from the Latin, *re-ligare*, reunite. It did just that. It linked, or reunited, all of them. Religious ties bounded the Pelasgian and Etruscan cities. Among them amphictyonic leagues of cities provided an intercity cohesion.

The Indo-Europeans inherited the amphictyonies. The leagues were always organized around a sanctuary.

The League of Delphi became the most famous and powerful in Greece. Based in the ancient sanctuary of Delphi, near the foot of Mt. Parnassus in Phocis. It became the meeting place of the most influential of the Amphictyonic leagues. Also the site of the quadrennial Pythian Games, instituted to celebrate the dethronement of Pytho by Apollo.

What was the role of the sanctuary at Delphi? The oracle's messages given at the shrine were an important political guide. They gave its accord about the convenience or not of the placement of a colony. The oracle also pointed the deity to whom the colony was to be dedicated. Most wars were started *only after consulting the oracle*. Alliances were also decided. The influence of the oracle prevailed throughout Greece until Hellenistic times.

There were other sanctuaries and other leagues, like the Achean and Aetolian ones. In order to defend themselves against the Persians, for instance, the Delos League was created, under Athenian hegemony. The center was the sanctuary at Delos, an island with a long religious tradition. It had been a former sepulchral island for Heroes.

So, if that was the structure of their supposed nationality, and if those amphictyonic leagues came from older times, what did those founding fathers actually do?

The change involved much more than a mere transference of power. It was a complete social, economical, religious and political turnover.

First, it was an ethnic dethronement. The Pelasgians had absorbed without great apparent shocks the Ionian and Eolian invaders. The myths are full of gods seducing nymphs. As it happened in other patrilineal-matrilineal tribe mixings in Africa, the male aristocracy of the patrilineal invaders became the next line of Heroes. Apparently a longer period for the sacred kingship was negotiated, coinciding with the adoption of longer astronomical periods. That change was gradual. It meant first the adoption of a nearly 100-lunation cycle, a little over seven years, when a near coincidence of the lunar and solar cycles takes place. The sacred king could survive all that time, but as a yearly sacrifice was necessary for fertility and the welfare of the community, substitutes were offered. Male adults or mostly royal male children died in the place of the sacred king.

A nearby example of that kind of arrangement was the Babylonian kingship: a mock king was chosen for a day and then was sacrificed. Then the king reassumed his functions in a ceremony that marked the New Year.

More modernly, some African tribes had *okrafo* priests, who died yearly instead of the king.

It seems that the period of survival of the sacred king was extended even more, first about to nine years, and finally, based in a longer coincidence of the lunar and solar cycles, to some 325 lunations (very close to 19 years). Yet, in spite of the yearly sacrifice of the substitutes, most probably the sacred king still had to die. Those four generations of Acheans, the founding fathers, probably became the last wave of Heroes. Greek poets always pointed that theirs was "the Heroic age." Adding cleverly, "men like them do not exist anymore." Why were they the last Heroes? The tempting answer is that they simply refused to die. If power came not from Hera anymore, the Hero institution simply ended. They rebelled.

On doing that they became a historical turning point. Even more, they gave the final coup to the old Euzko matrilineal system. Power was not granted anymore through the marriage with a *queen* or *princess*. From then on it was inherited directly by the *prince, who could only be the son of the king*. Farewell to the *mother* system. They really were the founding *fathers*.

They did not accomplish that revolutionary displacement acting separately, in an individual impulse. It was a shrewdly conceived, well-concerted and organized team maneuver. They were not acting on their own either. They were told to. The displacement of the queens was not the only change. It was a much deeper structural transformation. It was a *sacred* war. It meant an abrupt turn and simultaneous displacement in the religious hierarchical system—a dramatic break with the past.

The narratives left of some of the final moments of that confrontation had been hailed as two of the literary monuments of mankind.

10

The Beginning of the End

For the first time, the names appear—names from both Indo-Europeans and Euzkans. Names that gained fame some 3,300 years ago.

The Greeks, in Herodotus' times, were familiar with the names of those four generations of Acheans who caused such social upheaval.

Their names? The earliest were, for instance, the renowned generation of Heroes that ended many mythological beasts. Bellerophon killed the frightening *Chimera*. Hercules or Herakles freed the world from many monsters while accomplishing *The Twelve Labors*—theme of a vast number of artistic pieces. Theseus killed the *Minotaur* and founded Athens.

Modern mythologists have a new approach. The Chimera was one of the symbols of a Mother Goddess cult. So, we know that Bellerophon eradicated it, probably at the cost of killing most of the priestesses of the region. He used Pegasus, the winged horse, to liquidate the Chimera.

Remarkably, Pegasus was a chimera in itself, being a composite animal. It was a Goddess' symbol. The horse was one of Her favorite animals, its hooves leaving another of Her symbols, the moon, whenever they hit the ground. As Pegasus was made from two animals, a horse and a bird, it probably represented a Goddess cult that maybe recognized only a two-season year. The Chimera logo involved three animals, maybe representing a cult with a three-season year.

We are being told that Bellerophon exploited in some way the rivalry between two Goddess cults. He ended controlling one and annihilating the other. It was not an easy task. How can we know that? Because, the myth also tells (in one of its many versions) that he fell from Pegasus and died. That meant revolt. Maybe he could not control the cult that well. Maybe he finally was duly sacrificed.

The killing of the Minotaur by Theseus is presently believed, by most of the specialists in that period and region, to mean an Achean invasion of Crete.

Hercules or Herakles or, let's remember his former name, Palemon, was trusted with many jobs of the same nature. His Second Labor was the killing of the Hydra of Lerna—a many-headed monster. It probably meant the elimination of a whole college of priestesses at that place. Greek writers described some traditions of the ancient Lerna. They left record of a very suggestive one—all men being ritually killed annually. Palemon surely turned it the other way—all priestesses were killed.

Another labor, the suppression of a Goddess cult at Stymphaly, is the most probable origin of one of Herakles' myths: the shooting of the Stymphalian birds with his arrows—his Sixth Labor.

The religious importance of Herakles' deeds was well rewarded—the only mortal deified. In doing that, another weapon was being used in that religious war. One common in any kind of war: misinformation. All Heroes were deified at their death, in the Euzkan Goddess' cults. All that was transformed, the stories of all those Heroes were erased and only one Herakles remained, Palemon.

The new Hercules or Herakles myth had hints of the ancient ones, but was cleverly distorted.

He worked for Hera in the new myth. A cruel deception, as Hercules (Palemon) gained recognition by extirpating the most prominent Goddess cults—or at least the most rebellious ones. He played an important role using the most effective Achean weapon—marriage.

By marrying a sacred queen these generations of Heroes achieved instant political and religious status. Somehow this was not always possible. From myth we know that Palemon commanded an expedition to obtain the Golden Girdle from Hippolyte, the Queen of the Amazons, the warrior women—his Ninth Labor.

That expression, to take the girdle, had a very clear meaning for the Greeks. Maidens used a girdle over their tunic. To take their girdle was a phrase symbolizing deflowering. So, the myth is telling that Palemon was ordered to marry the Queen, as a way to become the Hero-King of that Euzkan region. Theseus, Iolcus, Peleus and many others accompanied him.

The myth tells that Hippolyte fell for Palemon. It also tells that Hera spread a rumor among the Amazons that the Acheans planned to abduct Hippolyte. This clearly means that the Amazons knew the real intentions of Palemon and his gang. They were aware of the treacherous nature of their marrying attempt. Probably they had learned what had happened to other tribes in other regions. There was a battle. The Amazons were killed.

One of the modern currents interprets the Amazons' land as the sacred island of Lemnos—a sepulchral island where, according to some traditions, all men were yearly killed (yes, notice the similitude with Lerna. Those traditions were common in other regions too). Both the names of one of the island queens (Hypsipyle) and one of the chief towns (Myrina) were Amazon names.

The marriage approach was not always rejected. Sometimes it was successful. How did Palemon behave through one of them is one of the most interesting pieces in Herodotus' History.

Herodotus wrote that story about Palemon a little reluctantly. In the region where it had happened human sacrifices were no longer tolerated, so Herodotus questioned the truth of what he had learned. He did not know that until a few centuries before him the Pelasgians, the Indo-European invaders and also practically everybody in the Mediterranean area—and in the rest of the world as well—ritually killed humans. Historian as he was, the story was transmitted, in spite of his doubts. No wonder he is considered the Father of History.

Herakles, says Herodotus, "was crowned and then carried in procession to be sacrificed to Zeus; he remained quiet for a time, but when they started the sacrificial ceremony beside the altar he recurred to the use of the force and killed all them by knife."

Herodotus could not understand either how "Herakles alone and yet mortal" could have ended so many people. It is well recorded, as part of the myth that Palemon seldom traveled or fought alone. Other fearsome warriors usually accompanied him. The secret of the Achean's success was just that. His expedition to the Amazons, for instance, could have well been just part of the voyage of the Argos. They passed a time in Lemnos. A generation later, the Lacedemonians gave asylum to the Minyans, thrown out of Lemnos by the Pelasgians. The Minyans claimed to be sons of the Argos' sailors with Lemnos women. The Lacedemonian recognized them as such, says Herodotus, and allowed them to settle in their land.

Through Herodotus, it can be learned that the Amazons were right when they chose to fight. After all, death would have fallen upon them, or at least their rulers, even if the marriage had taken place.

The Acheans' moves were cunning, conceived to gain some legitimacy through marriage. Then they attempted to stamp the ruling class off if they insisted in preserving their age-old habit, the Hero sacrificial death. An uncomplicated and highly efficient policy, but it worked mainly for one reason: they acted together.

Palemon and the other Achean warriors of his generation did more than gain political and military bastions through Greece. After suffering the Achean invasion, Crete's maritime empire must have been in disarray. The Acheans sent two missions to explore trading routes.

One went to the east. The famous trip of the Argos, under Jason's command, apparently was a probe on the Black Sea possibilities for both military expansion and commerce or, no less attractive, for piracy. Palemon was part of the enterprise.

The visit to the island of Lemnos, and the frustrated attempt to dominate the Amazons through the Sacred-Marriage tactics, shows that the objectives of the expedition and their methods were rather loose.

They continued their travel to the East. Palemon, famous for his ill temper, is said to have killed two of his companions. Probably in part for his crankiness, and maybe on account of some leadership disputes with Jason, of which no few hints are left, poor Palemon was slyly marooned. Someone with his manners and irascibility, whose physical power and warrior skills were legendary, must have been evaluated as an uncomfortable partner in the reduced space of a ship for such a long journey—good company in case of a war but far too dangerous as a close neighbor. Risks must have been weighed and he was left while he was in a forest.

Palemon must have felt bad when he returned to the beach and discovered the Argos had parted. Tradition says he had originally ceded the leadership of the trip to Jason, who had planned and organized it—not an easy accord. Palemon was recognized as the strongest man of his time, a well-known warrior compared to the inexpert Jason. Maybe that was the root of his bad mood, but perhaps he did not need much of an excuse, it seems that no one ever accused him of being an easy fellow. Nevertheless, he must not have complained for long. Soon the other Achean expedition was trusted to his command.

This time the ship went west. Where? There is no clear report. That silence was not unusual. Even millennia later, until modern times, trade routes were considered a most valuable secret. Those who dared to give them away were usually killed—some elaborated torture session was almost unavoidable. Phoenician traders preferred to sink their ships if followed, rather than reveal their route. Palemon, alias Herakles, went searching for the apples from the Hesperides' garden, in their father Atlas' dominion.

He had some trouble finding his way. He had to fight old Proteus in Italy to learn it. As Proteus was an old Euzkan myth, it probably meant that he bribed, or rather coerced some Euzkan sailors to disclose the adequate course. According to his *résumé*, it is a sure bet that Palemon could be terribly convincing. For many reasons it can be supposed he reached the Atlantic Ocean. Nothing is said about its fruits, but at least it is a good guess that Palemon returned. Because it is well known how he died.

Not only from the Amazons' episode but also through many instances, it can be inferred that after some initial heartaches, the sacred queens and the colleges of priestesses began to understand what was happening.

It must have taken a time, especially in those places where the sacred king had extended his survival period. In some cases that meant nearly twenty years, until the sacred king could not postpone his death any longer and had to fight if he was not much used to the self-sacrifice idea. The first cases must have been considered isolated, not part of a long-range strategy. After a while, it was finally understood. The pattern of the Achean takeover became evident.

After all, it was a gross violation of religious traditions, the most callous way of impiety to Pelasgian eyes. It was big news, quite a scoop any time it happened, and the first report any traveler would spread. Besides, one of the first techniques the Acheans craftily developed was to leave the kingdom at the time they were expected to die.

After marooning his difficult friend Palemon, Jason did exactly that with Medea. He married her, a sacred queen. When his time arrived he sweet-talked her and both left.

On leaving the kingdom, not accepting his death, he created chaos. At the same time, even if incurring in sacrilege, he kept some kind of royal rights.

Medea learned the hard way what Jason's real intentions had been. It is known that she could not return to her kingdom.

Abandoning a priestess' post, running away with the intended sacrificial victim, must have probably meant a terrible sacrilege. At that time much more minor sins meant the death penalty.

Destitute and rejected, it is understandable then that Medea tried to help King Aegeus of Athens when young Theseus appeared, obviously sent to win the Athenian throne. Medea must have advised Aegeus, out of her hardly won experience. She tried to poison Theseus, but failed. Theseus went to Crete, where he played up to Ariadne (the princess who helped him through the Minotaur's labyrinth) the same trick than Jason used with Medea. On his return to Athens, Theseus killed Aegeus and succeeded him to the throne. Then he banished gloomy Medea. Ariadne, Medea and all the manipulated queens must have also contributed a lot to make it known that the Acheans were trying to destroy the matrilineal system. Queens started to fight back. Medea failed with Theseus' diet, but Palemon was not that lucky.

On account of the myths, it can be conjectured that Palemon married sacred queens no less than three times, probably many, many more. He seems to have killed at least one of them, Megara. One of his last wives, Deianeira, avenged all her wronged colleagues.

In preceding lines it was pointed that a favorite Achean trick was to take a leave during the kingship, an unexpected behavior in a Hero. That way a king could marry many queens in different kingdoms. It was a clever move that could help to unify or control a wide region. From all the stories, Palemon seemed to love that part. Not much of a problem from his viewpoint, since he did not intend to die at the end of the term of any of his multiple acquired compromises, and anyway, could die only in no more than one kingdom.

On the Euzkan side, it can be guessed that such misbehavior was considered a more than annoying informality.

In theory it deprived all the kingdoms but one of the right to sacrifice the Hero and collect the expected supernatural benefits.

The Euzkan system was a remarkable way to replace the head of state after his fixed period. On the social side, it can be guessed that families, who were in the cue, waiting for their own candidates to ascend the throne, must have felt disdained when this happened.

There are hints that the rupture of the old, well accepted system, brought problems even into Achean families, as we learn of the tragic saga of the rulers of influential Mycenae, where the misfortunes of the House of Atreus gave splendid material for so many tragedies. It also explains why most of the tragedies were based in the stories of that agitated period. A change of social, religious structures always mean disorder and anguish. The social psychic instability continued for centuries, as historians registered the confrontations of the different ethnic groups. The tragedies served a clarification purpose, and to vent some of the internal turmoil of the citizens.

As these were the first bets in that multistage power game, the players did not know yet the ruses and feints each side could use. We have the right to think that Palemon incurred in that kind of whim often, because after marrying Deianeira he continued with his usual myth-making toil. He must have been a real hyperactive, type-A guy. The dangerous thing was that his partly compulsive, partly ill advised behavior took him frequently abroad.

Deianeira, relates the myth, became jealous of his many mistresses. Palemon must have thought his escapades would go unnoticed. This is a risky notion in any kind of marriage, but in his case, he was proved deadly wrong. Queens at that time were anything but tamed kittens. Medea, Clytemnestra had left quite a mark in history. Deianeira seems to have been of the same kind.

When she conjectured that her matrimony was not destined to a happy end she must have asked wisely for some marriage counselor. Surely she got more than a little advice. Such marital differences were a typical case of cultural shock. Many people were involved on both sides and trying to interfere—as in many marriages.

From myth, it is safe to suppose that the chief advice came from Euzkan people, who had had an earlier and rather traumatic experience with Palemon. Not an unlikely assumption, his main problem was that even his best friends usually had severe, traumatic experiences with him. This time the discontented was the tribe of the Centaurs—Pelasgian horsemen. Their well-known symbol, or tribal logo, probably denoted a two-season Goddess cult. Palemon was generally credited with killing their king, Cheiron, and not a few others. It was bad manners, since Centaur Cheiron had politely trained him well in archery and also in the difficult art of the use of hallucinogens.

Deianeira must have carefully considered their resentful warnings. She anointed one of Palemon's shirts with a swift, potent poison gladly supplied by Centaur Nessus (Nessus' blood in the myth).

Liposoluble drugs can penetrate the skin as fast as a hypodermic shot. Ointments were the most common type of medicine until the last century. Today we use "patches." The description of Palemon being consumed by a high fever, complaining in his delirium of being burnt, is a well-known part of the Herakles' myth, where flames supposedly devoured him.

In all likelihood—in order to avoid Herakles temper tantrums—heedful Deianeira neither allowed him to guess the surprise nor waited until the end of his regal period.

It might have not been a proper Hero's death, full of preceding ritual and celebrations at the right astronomical moment, with a nice festival where the whole tribe or at least the most prominent citizens had a chance to participate, but it was, unquestionably, an apt execution. Deianeira must have felt considerably safer after that. Most probably some kind of adequate funeral celebrations took place later.

The posthumous satisfaction of being deified was reserved for Palemon. He was neither the last Hero nor the last Herakles. For a time at least, Pelasgian rites went on in the cities, and Heroes kept ritually dying in many places in Greece. For a much longer period, more than two millennia, well into our time, they continued in other parts of Europe. But the misinformation war had started.

For Indo-Europeans, Palemon soon became the *only* Herakles—the only Hero to become a god. The remaining myriad of Herakles in Greece disappeared. Even if the traditions and cults continued, they were mixed and reshaped into the new, Indo-European myth. All that gave occasion to Herodotus' perplexity some centuries later.

Maybe Deianeira felt much better after getting rid of Palemon. Her alleviation could have been short. For her and all the other queens, time was ending. For all Pelasgian women doom was at the door. Their millennial rights were condemned. Indo-European men had no place for them in their social conceptions. The Pelasgians were fully aware now of the Achean scheme. It was a lost cause.

The Acheans knew how to act *en masse*. It was something that for Euzkos, at all times, in all places, seemed very hard to attain. The final coup in the confrontation was given by the next generation of Acheans. It was not easy. It took them at least a decade of hard, gory efforts to succeed. The crucial points of the story of the conflict were narrated by one of the all-time best storytellers, if not the best. It became the subject of two of the most exquisite jewels of universal literature.

11

The Fall

"Sing, oh Goddess, the anger of Achilles son of Peleus, that brought countless ills upon the Acheans. Many a brave soul did it send hurrying to Hades, and many a Hero did it yield a prey to dogs and vutures, for so were the counsels of Jove fulfilled from the day on which the son of Atreus, king of men, and great Achilles, first fell out with one another."

Homer, *Iliad, first Book*

A new generation of Achean warriors took the lead. Jason and Palemon had commanded famous expeditions to the east and west. The ambition for political dominance and the control of commerce and trade routes continued. The sons of the Argonauts were many of the main actors of the last stage in the war between the last powerful Pelasgians and the Acheans.

Peleus, Telamon and Laertes were among the sailors of the Argos. Their respective sons, Achilles, Ajax and Odysseus, soon dedicated themselves to the same task that their fathers had attempted, the control of the eastern trade. This time they were trying to subdue a city named Ilion.

It became more famous by another name—Troy.

The city was located in a strategic point from where a certain control of the trade routes with the Black Sea could be exerted. The siege is described in some of the most memorable pages ever written, the most beautiful piece of epic poetry, the *Iliad*.

That wonderful book was taken for a long time as some kind of masterful nursery rhyme. When Schliemann discovered Troy and Mycenae that conception went sour. The archaeologists discovered that Homer's narrative was real. All the finds from the times of Troy correspond more or less exactly with what the blind poet described.

Things had changed since the Trojan War when Homer composed his beautiful song. Some of the opulent cities that took part in the war at Troy had ceased to exist at Herodotus times, or were mere villages, like Mycenae and Troy. On the other hand, cities like Athens had been just minor towns at the time of the war. What the dumbfounded diggers discovered was that there was a surprising correlation between the Homeric descriptions and the power of the cities as shown by the excavations.

The remains of those cities described as powerful, that contributed the greater numbers of ships, and whose kings had apparently enjoyed the greater prestige, showed that they had been rich, important cities in the past. Except for a few details, the poem proved true in its descriptions of places and social customs. The economical and political world was confirmed too. There are some discrepancies, warriors are seen using iron weapons in the *Iliad*, in spite the war been fought in the Bronze Age. In general terms, the credibility of the two books has increased, earning another laurel for immortal Homer.

What caused the war? Paris, son of Priam, King of Troy, kidnapped Helen, the Queen of Lacedemonia. Homer and other poets blamed it for originating the war. An army was raised to rescue her, commanded by powerful Agamemnon, King of Mycenae and brother of Helen's husband, Menelaus, King of Sparta.

Most historians, from Herodotus to present ones, have doubted that such a conflict could have its origins in an episode of that kind. As it will be seen, most probably that was the real cause. Many considerations suggest that the abduction of Helen truly triggered the siege. So, in that aspect the tradition and the *Iliad* can be true.

In a deeper sense the *Iliad* also tells us what was the real nature of the conflict and what had been at stake. To understand it, it is necessary to take a close look at both the *Iliad* and the *Odyssey*. The two are peculiar books. Wonderful epics, they have elicited the admiration of later poets and have inspired generations of artists. Operas, paintings, literary masterpieces, uncountable works of art found their birth in some passage of those two splendid poems. Any educated Greek at Herodotus times knew them by heart. Still, to look at them only from a literary, artistic viewpoint would be totally wrong. They were intended to be of a high narrative quality. Nevertheless, that was not the point. Their main value was *religious*.

They were religious, sacred books.

Their recitation was the *central event* in the Panathenea, the quadrennial religious festival celebrated in Athens by the Ionian cities.

An idea of their relevance is given by their astonishing power of survival: of the nearly 1,500 extant papyri whose authors are certifiably known, about 600 are copies of the *Iliad* and of the *Odyssey*. For an adequate comparison: only 6 copies are left from Aristotle's writings. It constitutes an enlightening hint of which two titles must have had the greatest number of copies in the great Library of Alexandria, set on fire by the Romans.

Why were they so important? As religious books, both have various levels. On the economic side, both describe the new attempts of that Achean generation to control both the commercial routes of the east (the *Iliad* describes a chapter of the war for the control of Troy) and west (the described travels of Odysseus in the *Odyssey*). They also describe the raise and splendor of the powerful House of Atreus, commanding rich Mycenae, which represented the most accomplished Achean union of Greek states, as close to an empire as it was possible in those times. Many other meanings have been attributed to both, but the key to what really it was all about can be found in that first paragraph of the *Iliad*. A seemingly simple, artless line: "*...so were the counsels of Jove fulfilled...*"

That sentence sums up not only the whole book but also the total conflict—its roots, its outcome, and its consequences. It is an undisguised, naked truth advisedly told by an inspired poet who really knew. He had to, in order to write a sacred book in the cryptic language it required. Now, *who* was this Jove? Or lets call him by his other name, Zeus. Just his name tells the whole story.

When the Indo-European tribes arrived they carried with them a trinity of gods. Indra, Varuna (the Greek *Ouranos*) and Agni. Apparently, an obscure deity also came with them—a thunder god, whose name was Djeus Pitar. Was that the same name of the Hero that the Cretans had been sacrificing and burying yearly for eons? Or had the Cretan thunder god another name? Ancient people recognized gods in spite of the names, anyway.

That god's peculiar name suffered a dramatic development. The Romans transformed the Djeus Pitar into Jupiter. Pitar meant father, that way Djeus Pitar, Father Djeus, became Father Zeus for the Greeks. That word Djeus... It still had another evolution and meaning both among the Romans and the Greeks—a meaning it conserves until today. The word Djeus in Latin also became *Deus*. In Greek there was a word that was its equivalent—*Theos*. No wonder that Deus and Theos have the same translation: *God*.

So, it is possible to understand the real meaning of Djeus Pitar: *Father God*.

Knowing that, is there really any trouble to understand what was His will?

That is the central, real meaning of both the Iliad and the Odyssey: the final displacement of the Mother Goddess cult—the end of the matrilineally structured societies. It is the description of a sacred war. The story of how the colleges of priests overcame the colleges of priestesses—Mother Goddess Amphictyonies being defeated and replaced by Father God Amphictyonies. That is why both books were religious books.

They both mean, hello Father God. Bye, bye Mother Goddess.

All those warring Heroes were acting on priests' advice— *"for so were the counsels of Jove fulfilled."* They were carrying on their God's will. They were being given oracles. From their own viewpoint, those Heroes were not merely warriors but *pious* men— who obediently put into practice the guidance they received from the priesthood.

They were considered *sacred warriors.*

Tradition has it that Herophile, the Pythia, had predicted the war. The seer must have done a little more. People came to the oracle mainly to know if a war was convenient. We are being told that the Delphic oracle had advised to start the siege. The male priesthood of Apollo, the Olympic newcomer, wanted blood.

The Trojan War *was* a sacred war—*a religious war.*

That is one of the many reasons those Heroes were chosen as *examples* for posterity. One of the reasons why their names were not allowed to disappear into oblivion like both their ancestors' and their descendants' had.

In ancient times, official poets and priests were almost the same. The cryptic language of poetry used religious symbols, which were kept secret from the uninitiated. That is *the* reason why songs and verses dedicated to celebrate those Heroes constituted an important part of countless religious festivities for so many centuries.

Due to their obeisance, the priests considered them models to be imitated. Many generations later, when the underlying causes of the war had deliberately been forgotten, the Greeks would start to doubt the convenience of such peculiar models.

At Socrates' times they were questioning the existence of such animals as the Chimera, the Hydra or Pegasus, ignoring that they had been mere symbols, or logos, of some cults no longer extant. Achean Heroes started to be seen as too cruel, ruthless and merciless, characteristics that had been exalted by the priesthood of their times. Above all, eight centuries after the conflict, they could not understand anymore how such a war could have started on account of just a woman—unthinkable.

Modern specialists doubt that the twelve hundred ships mentioned in the *Iliad* were in Troy all at a time. There would not be place enough for them on the beach. How did they keep all those men there during the ten years that supposedly the siege took? The modern view is that the number of ships and people sent was correct—only that they were not there all the time, neither at the time of the *Iliad,* after nine years of war, with a whole year yet to go. They probably took turns at the siege.

The book was recognizing not only the individual contribution but also the help from the cities. It was a way to mention the support given—a kind of literary trick, just as one of the famous scenes where Priam, the King of Troy, asks Helen about the identities of various Achean chiefs that he was seeing from the citadel. Helen answered, consigning to posterity the description of many Achean warriors. Thus we came to know that the imposing Agamemnon was tall, and that his tricky companion, red-haired, wide-chested Odysseus, had short legs. It was, obviously, another literary trick. After nine years of conflict, that question should not have been necessary. Homer just wanted to depict the combatants, being commissioned to reward with fame their participation and efforts.

In the same scene, Priam tells Helen not to consider herself guilty, "*I lay no blame upon you, it is the gods, not you who are to blame. It is they that have brought about this terrible war with the Acheans.*" That is Homer telling again the real roots of the war.

Probably Priam had many reasons not to blame Helen. Yet *she was the true cause of the war*, in more than one sense.

12

Orea Eleni

"Small wonder that Trojans and Acheans should endure so much and so long for the sake of a woman so marvelously and divinely lovely."
                    Homer, *Iliad, Book II*

Fig. 19. Sketch from a fresco found in Thera (c. 1500 B.C.)

"Beautiful Helen"—"*Orea Eleni*"—so the immortal Homer called her. People of her time and poets of all ages sung her incomparable beauty.

Fig 20. Sketch from a fresco from Thera (c. 1500 B.C.)

Helen of Troy has fueled the imagination of many generations of artists as few women before or after her.

From all traditions she seems to have been a stunning blonde. Even during her childhood her beauty appears to have marveled all those around her. The Euzkan woman described by Homer seems to have had few other charms apart from her splendid shape.

In the *Iliad* she appears as a shy, docile creature, quite repentant of having produced such a conflict and being comforted by Priam.

In the *Odyssey*, years after the fall of Troy, she is presented back in Lacedemonia, again at the side of sacred-king Menelaus. She gives the impression of a quiet, repentant woman, contented to be back home, horrified of the destruction she had brought on so many people, still a striking *belle*.

Fig 21. Sketch from a fresco from Thera (c. 1500 B.C.)

The real Helen probably could not have been more different, except for her dazzling charms.

Helen of Troy seemed to have been kidnap-prone. Paris was not the first to carry her off. Theseus, the founder of Athens, killer of the Minotaur, kidnapped her when she was a child.

At what age? Scholars have long debated on that. Some of them think she was no older than five at the time. There is a general agreement that she must have been at least under twelve, because impetuous Theseus could not marry her, which was his intention.

Theseus was forced to entrust her to other hands until his involuntary fiancée reached the appropriate age.

How she got back is an obscure episode. Myth generally attributes the feat to her brothers, the Dioscuri. Maybe. Maybe Theseus died first. Will we ever know? But why all that?

Why all those kidnapping frenzies about her?

She had been recognized as a dream girl, *"the most beautiful woman in Greece,"* but even if Greeks in general, and Theseus in particular, were not much given to continence and were famous by their use of not only women but also young men and children of both sexes, this case seems excessive even for the father of Athens.

Why abduct such a young girl with all the risks it implied? Of one thing we can be sure. *Theseus really intended to marry her.* At her tender age? It was not a matter of age or of sexual attraction. *She was going to be the Queen of Lacedemonia by right of birth*—the youngest royal daughter.

Marrying her meant, according to the old Euzkan, matrilineal custom, the access to the throne. It also explains why Theseus had no choice but to wait for her coming of age. The throne went to the youngest *nubile* Queen's daughter. She had to be able to conceive.

Theseus unified politically the region of Attica, around Athens. According to legend the four Ionian tribes of the Attica were made a single state by him. From the Achean record we can bet which was the method followed by Theseus, who, Plutarch tells us, obeyed completely the priests in political matters. He must have married the Queens, becoming the Hero and King of the tribes and achieving an instant unity through his person among tribes that were traditionally rivals. Maybe some people disagreed with that social innovation and aberration, an insult to the Goddess, a polygamous king, but Theseus and his followers convinced by force the unbelievers, as Plutarch discreetly informs us.

Until that time Athens was almost unknown. After that, and some social changes he instituted, it kept growing. The attempt on Helen seems to have been part of a wider scheme to gain control of the whole Peloponnese. It tells us a lot about Theseus' unifying technique. It failed this time, but poor Helen seems to have spent quite a time far from home. We can be sure she was an uncommon girl.

Helen was, almost certainly, not her real name. It was most probably a title. *Most of the names in the Iliad and the Odyssey must have been titles—Heroes and Queens.* Far from the Hollywood silly blonde image, Helen must have had quite a character.

Fig. 22. Sketch from a gold ring from Isopata with a representation of a dance of worship (c. 1400 B.C.)

Queens were not merely women seating on a throne. They all came from a long chain of women trained to exercise power, used to a high social standing.

She was not only a Queen but also a priestess. Let's not forget: *the* Priestess—the supreme representative of the Moon Goddess among her people. As such, she must have been submitted to an intensive and careful training.

When Telemachus, Odysseus' son, visits her and Menelaus at Lacedemonia, Homer tells us that *"she cast a drug into the wine whereof they drank, a drug to lull all pain and anger, and bring forgetfulness of every sorrow."* Concerning that aspect of her abilities there can be few doubts. In the *Odyssey* she gets the drugs from Polydamna, a woman of Egypt.

Priestesses seem to have been the depositaries of the medical and pharmaceutical know-how in those times. Helen's training must have been the equivalent of modern college coed's. It meant that she knew about herbs and their properties—when

Fig 23. Sketch from a fresco found in Thera (c. 1500 B.C.)

and where to collect them—and was familiar with the subsequent processing and the required dosages.

Archaeologists have long deduced that the Pelasgian priesthood was in charge of the storage and distribution of foods, which implies she received a practical training in the complex problems of transport, storage and commerce. She must have had a more than elementary knowledge in astronomy, indispensable for establishing the dates of the all-important public festivities.

Helen must have enjoyed that gift that few women—and not many men—would possess for thousands of years: the then rare art of reading and writing.

In antiquity, all that knowledge meant power. It was carefully transmitted and kept secret.

Above all they must have trained her well in the religious rituals and taught all the traditions and history of her people. The women in charge must have trained her in many skills from childhood, probably merely from contact with them—to be the center of her city religious, artistic, economic and political life.

There was an area where her expertise must have been unrivaled: hallucinogens and their use. A powerful Goddess' domain, they were used in religious ceremonies. Most probably, this must have been the priestesses' main secret. Their consumption was only ceremonial, never intended for other uses. Production of hallucinogens and the very complex art of their ever-dangerous use was a priestess' craft.

We can even guess what she looked like. For a modern observer, not used to Euzkan rituals, to witness Helen while at state's duty in a procession, during one of the many religious festivities, would have been a jolt—quite unusual for present values.

Most present bishops or cardinals are old men, well past their prime. Let's imagine a bishop or cardinal (that was her equivalent religious status, if not a Pope) leading the solemn state procession of her times and *looking just like a very seductive Marilyn Monroe.*

In addition, *especially* for these occasions, Helen's breasts were not only bare but sustained and enhanced by the older version of a modern wonder-bra. The Hollywood star never dared, or was never allowed, to exhibit her bosom in any movie.

Fig. 24. Sketch of a scene from a gold ring. It has been interpreted as a fertility ritual. Mother Goddess at left (Tyrins, c. 1500 B.C.)

Fig. 25. Sketch from a fresco found in Thera (c. 1500 B.C.)

The comparison or image linking Helen of Troy with the Monroe is not casual. Both were celebrated blondes, both were beautiful, both, above all, were fully determined to represent (practically had no other choice, due to solid professional reasons in both cases) the embodiment of a fertility goddess. From the many frescoes, paintings and statuettes of women left from Helen times, we are not allowed any other expectations (Fig. 21-28).

Some of the women in them are young. Others denote maturity. The hair of some is dark, in others fair. Their hairstyles and dresses might differ, but all, absolutely all, young or mature, are extraordinarily attractive and extremely sensual.

If artists were representing goddesses or priestesses is a present matter of study, discussion and dissent among scientists.

What cannot ever be put into doubt is that the artists must have been copying earthly models.

Actually, some of the representations are so alive, so personalized, their expression so vivid, that they must have had some human models.

Fig. 26. Sketch from a fresco from the Queen Apartments in the Palace of Knossos (c. 1500 B.C.)

Theories aside, men of her time must have suffered a breath-taking effect whenever they contemplated Helen's insinuating walk in full regalia at any official parade or presentation. As Paris must have felt, when he first contemplated her in Amyklae. She surely headed the celebration of the Hyakinthae, the most important Lacedemonian ritual. No wonder that poets remembered where he saw her first. No surprise. Her beauty was considered quite high above the standard, a vision for friends and foes alike. She was expected, for both theological and state reasons, to excite all men and inspire their wonder. She did.

Her fair hair was probably long—rouge in her cheeks and lips, her eyes and eyebrows carefully delineated and painted. She probably had a complete make-up job and, like *coquette* ladies during the last century, maybe a few moles—some of these taking the shape of some religious, multicolored symbol. Unlike ladies of the last century some of these symbolic moles could have decorated not only her beautiful face but also her breasts. A strategic device to call the attention on her charms and also on some theological point, concerning the festivity and its meaning. After all, it was all interlinked, her many charms *were* theological tenets in themselves.

Her coiffure must have been, from the examples left, a masterpiece, with some casual locks (quite like modern fashion photographers have learned, or relearned to show) hanging in a suggestive

Fig. 27. Sketch of a gold brooch from a tomb at Mycenae (c. 1500 B.C.)

way. To top it, artists' renderings from her times have left us many options: weighty golden crowns resembling gigantic flowers (Fig. 29), or a high tiara topped by the statuette of some animal or snake (Fig. 30). Sometimes she possibly styled a similarly decorated bonnet. Could these vary according to the celebration? On other occasions, maybe she wore just a profusion of strings of gems, gold pieces and pearls, graciously interwoven with her curls (Fig. 31). Could it have been just her hair free, hanging in well-brushed waves? She surely used richly elaborated headbands most of days, or bands around carefully separated bunches. Bangs, ponytails, braids, chignons, all of them and many others were in use.

Her dress? Sometimes it must have been a skin-tight corset, just a laced jacket open at the front, supporting and shaping her nude breasts, pushing them up, also restricting her waistline and emphasizing her hips, that were covered by a long dress, and sometimes with an apron over it (Fig. 30). On other occasions a loose fitting robe, always with a deep, generous *décolletage* to allow the exhibition of the boasting emblems of the Goddess, the erect breasts of a nubile woman (Fig. 29). Whose nipples, less some dumb man had failed to notice them, had been adequately colored.

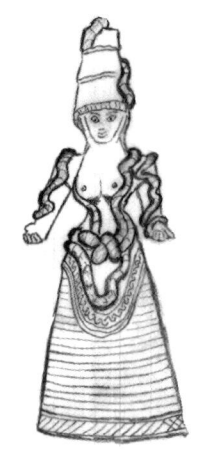

Fig. 28. Sketch of a snake goddess. Faience statuette from the crypt of the central shrine at Knossos (c. 1600 B.C.)

Was she the cause of the war? Most probably. The expurgated version given was the attempt of Menelaus, well backed by his powerful brother Agamemnon, to get her back as being the reason of the conflict. It is totally plausible.

Why? At first sight the opposite was more probable. Among the Acheans, as among all Indo-Europeans, the value of any woman, made it unlikely that her abduction would cause such a conflict—unless some other considerations weighed on the decision. Was Troy a rival?

Fig. 29. Sketch of a fresco from Tyrins (c. 1300 B.C.)

Fig. 30. Sketch of a faience figurine from the central shrine at Knossos (c. 1600 B.C.)

Archaeologists do not concur that Troy was such a great power confronting the invading Acheans. Its position meant a possible menace to the Achean trade routes to the Black Sea. A few lines, by a student of myths from the 5th century A.D., have been interpreted as Laomedon, founder of Troy and father of Priam, obstructing the passage of the Argos. However, Troy did not seem, from archaeological evidence, to have benefited much from the disappearance of the Cretan maritime empire.

Was she the cause then? From myth and legend, from Homer's narrative, Achean warriors did not look like men who would mind that much Menelaus' pain. Actually, not even

Menelaus seems to have been the kind of man to grief much about Helen or any other woman. He appears in all poems as a typical tough guy, too much of a killer, even if possessing a great pride. His companions, however, did not look like a lot given to carry on such a long, arduous and dangerous siege just to quench the pride of a cuckolded man, no matter what his social standing and power. Loot did not seem to have been the motive either.

What was the reason behind such a long and apparently improbable event? It was so implausible, given all the antecedents offered by Homer and other narrators that after a long time people started to think that it had never happened. Many centuries later they began to believe that windy Troy never existed. Classic Greeks, only six centuries later doubted that any woman could produce such havoc. After all, they well knew the low value in which women were held among the Acheans. *But Helen sparked the war.*

Obviously, from all traditions, she was not happy with Menelaus—maybe cultural shock again. Any Euzkan queen, brought up in the matrilineal tradition, was not much prepared for a marriage with an Achean king.

In the *Iliad*, king Agamemnon is seen disposing of women just as if they were cattle. The whole theme of the *Iliad* centers on the struggle between Achilles and Agamemnon, due to the abusive slaving of none other than an Apollo priest's daughter by the latter, done against the precepts and customs of his time.

Let's notice it: her father was a priest of a *male* divinity. Even the hardened Achean warriors found it objectionable. Not because it was a woman that would have been silly, of course, but because of her father's standing.

Making that incident the reason of the temporary Achean failure, the priests, disliking a leader who had disrespected one of their own, made Homer convey to us the image of a despicable man, whose faults delayed the end of the war.

It is difficult to think that his brother Menelaus had been raised with different standards with regard to women.

From the central position a queen could expect in the matrilineal society, to be relegated to an obscure, unprivileged status must have been really demanding. A glamorous queen, dazzling and intelligent, trained for prominence, enjoying the aura of the Goddess and then thrown into the backyard.

Indo-European culture had no place for women, either from the common or from royal houses. Having been taught from childhood that *she* was the fountain of power and then being submitted to a rough Achean warrior, whose ideas on the subject were quite different, must have been far from an ideal situation. From her viewpoint, the king, any king, was only a transitory accident, destined to a fixed period of power, restricted by many taboos, after which he was to be sacrificed. The sun shines only during the day, but the moon, the heavenly symbol of the Goddess, benevolently shows herself both at day and at night. During Helen's life, in the age-old Euzkan tradition, the true, permanent influence in the realm was always expected to be *her*, the ever-reigning queen.

Her disappointment must have grown in a short period, realizing soon which was the new role she was expected to play. An old French saying points that a marriage is such a heavy burden that it can only be born by three. The marriage of Helen and Menelaus seems to fit that malevolent epigram. Enter young, handsome Paris, son of Priam, King of Troy. The fact that she left with him was attributed only to hormonal reasons, common when a *ménage à trois* turns sour and then one of the married couple leaves with the new companion. A lot of circumstances tell a very different story.

Never discarding the love affair between Helen and Paris, the fact that she left and, especially, *with whom*, must have been a devastating blow to Menelaus, who, we are told from all sources, was desperate about getting her back. It was a devious *political* move.

At a time of revolutionary change in the social and political institutions, when everything was menaced, with that swift move she retired instantly from him his only claim of legitimacy: without the queen he had no right to remain on the throne.

She must have really enjoyed that part. She was obliging him to keep his kingdom by the force of arms.

Menelaus, counting on the support of his powerful brother Agamemnon, king of prosperous Mycenae, and with the backing of the rest of Achean kings, also understandably desirous to end the Euzkan institution of the king's sacrifice, could probably maintain his grip on Lacedemonia. The lack of legitimacy, however, must have been irritating. What must have seemed most ominous was the identity of her lover: Paris, scion of the one leader who could menace the eastern trade routes, from the most likely Pelasgian city to attempt defying the growing Achean power. It was too much of a coincidence to be casual.

Maybe it had been her idea, may be Paris'. Maybe he had been sent there with that purpose. Whoever came up with that scheme, she must have had a clear understanding of the political consequences of her eloping. When they absconded a political earthquake followed. Homer presents us a Menelaus desperately visiting other Achean kings to get their aid and recover Helen. He got a most powerful, decisive backing from another interested source: the male religious hierarchy.

Homer tells us many times that the gods had decided the conflict. How else could any Achean leader summon all that assistance during such a long lapse, ten years, with no apparent monetary reward? No due profits were gained, according to the risks the enterprise meant. The priests must have seen in her move not only a political intention but also a serious religious danger as well.

Helen was not just one more wife abandoning her royal husband. She was the Moon Priestess of the realm. Actually, it was *because* she was the chief priestess that she was queen. A clue to the immense prestige of her religious role in the entire Greece is given just from her name. *Greeks call themselves Hellenes even today*. We are told that the name came from king Helen. That can also be true, in a certain sense. *That must have been the title carried by any man who married Helen or any of her predecessors.*

The male religious leaders probably, and rightly, interpreted her departure as a perilous prospect. They probably interpreted it not as a surrendering of her political rights but as a serious challenge. It means that no one took it just like a merely emotional, hormonal affair.

At the time when they were trying to supplant the feminine religious influence, through the simple and lawful method of marrying the queens, the fleeing couple looked like, and most probably was, a concerted action by two of the old Pelasgian, traditional powers, Lacedemonia and Troy. Both regions were influential enough not to be disregarded in the power struggle ahead. The priests went decidedly for the kill. A sacred war began.

A most telling sign of what was behind Helen's abandonment of Menelaus is that never during such a long, terrible war, Priam offered to return her. In the *Iliad* he is shown comforting Helen—putting the blame on the gods. Even if everybody censured Paris, there is no doubt that Priam was the main responsible during it all. He had in his hands the easy way to relieve the dreadful menace on his city, but *he utterly rejected the petition of Achean ambassadors to give her back to Menelaus.*

All the Pelasgian cities aligned themselves with Troy, according to Homer, who gave all their names to posterity.

War began between the matrilineal and patrilineal societies, between Pelasgians and Aryans, between priestesses and priests. However, in spite of their riches and power, the warriors from many of those Pelasgians cities are not much seen in the description of the conflict. Was it because they judged that Priam could stand by himself? Or was it just another example of that exasperating tendency of the Euzkan peoples to almost never act in concert?

One of the stories about the foundation of Troy attributes it to Scamander, who led one third of the Cretans there to escape from a famine. It could have been the aftermath of the terrible Santorini eruption, or maybe some other kind of catastrophe. Was Priam, backed by the descendants of those fleeing Cretans, trying to continue the Cretan traditions of political, commercial and maritime power? Was he trying to displace powerful Mycenae? Did that raise the envy or distrust of other Euzkan cities?

His house was, through the marriage of Paris and Helen, putting some sort of a claim on the Lacedemonian state. Just the same that Menelaus was so anxious to continue doing. It is hard to see how the Trojans could have accomplished it. Maybe, in the best Euzkan traditions, some of the other Pelasgian cities were horrified by the Achean scheme of domination, but not enough to allow one of their own cities to dominate the rest, which would have constituted their objective if they had forcefully backed Priam to sit Paris on the throne of Lacedemonia.

Then, after ten devastating years, Troy fell. Priam and almost all males from the city were put to death. Some eight centuries later, when that wonderful Euripides play, *The Trojan Women*, was represented before Ionian audiences, the actors could be absolutely sure of getting sympathy from the public. The spectators could well appreciate the drama of the captive women. For Ionians, particularly the feminine beholders, *any* woman among the Acheans, no matter if reputedly free, deserved compassion.

Curiously, history has some peculiar revenge. Among the Trojans only Aeneas, Antenor and a few members of their clans survived, and left surreptitiously for some far, safe land. After years of hard pilgrimage, Aeneas and his relatives arrived at the coast of Italy, and established themselves on the banks of the Tiber River. Virgil told us the story in the verses of his precious *Aeneid*. Nearly twelve centuries later, one of Aeneas' descendants avenged the cruel affront of the Acheans, becoming the first man to rule alone over the coasts of all the Mediterranean Sea, including Priam' old citadel and, of course, all Greece. This offspring from that old Trojan stock was also the *Pontifex Maximus* of Rome—better known as Julius Caesar.

Due to that reason, Troy became a favorite of Julius Caesar's nephew and successor, Augustus. This emperor started public works and a renewal of the city. Another emperor, Nero, mistreated the Christians and Rome. But he took good care of Troy, to honor that legendary Aeneas' ancestry, and freed the city from any kind of imperial taxes.

For both Acheans and Pelasgians another revenge, far more contemporary, was evident. Most of the Achean Heroes, or sacred kings, who took Troy, had little time to enjoy their victory. They came to sorrowful ends. Nowhere could it be better appreciated than in the sad fate of the conqueror of Troy, mighty Agamemnon, leader of the Acheans.

His wife Clytemnestra—Helen's elder sister—slaughtered him at his return at Mycenae. Agamemnon's cousin Aegisthus assisted Clytemnestra at the murder, and then became the new king. Everybody must have considered it a terrible revenge of the Goddess. The king being killed with an ax by the queen, who then married another prince of the deceased monarch's house, must have obviously seemed a total reversion to the ancient Euzkan, matrilineal order. The use of the ax, a labrys according to Aeschylus, was a smart touch and probably helped to turn it into some kind of ritual ceremony—a typical sacred-king's end when his ritual time had expired.

Agamemnon was trying to leave his throne to his son, Orestes. The disaster that followed showed clearly the fragility of the patrilineal institution.

The murder of Agamemnon's war trophy, Cassandra, the young Trojan seer, at the hands of Clytemnestra should be seen as a heartless political move—the queen-bee killing a possible rival. Agamemnon's poor captive, Priam's daughter, being younger and of royal blood, whose trances had given her extraordinary fame as a prophetess, must have been seen as a frightening political and religious contender by Clytemnestra, who was not from Mycenae. Agamemnon's choice of Cassandra as booty does not look casual or emotional. He must have intended to keep her in order to assert his rights over defeated Troy. It was the usual Achean move of marrying the youngest royal daughter.

Clytemnestra's revenge was brief. Agamemnon's son Orestes effectively, if sanguinary, returned the succession to the patrilineal order. Well within his notorious family tradition of problem solving, he killed both his uncle Aegisthus and his mother Clytemnestra. We are told he followed an oracle advice—a *priest's* advice. We can be sure of it. No *priestess* would have dared that. He was killing his mother, the queen and the high priestess all at a time. He broke all the matrilineal system in one stroke.

News about his brother's death must have been a frightening blow for Menelaus. With more than enough problems of his own he was losing his stronger supporter. Helen kept being his queen, in spite of her fleeing to Troy, in spite of the brutal murder committed by her sister. No way. He kept her alive.

Paradoxically, Agamemnon's dramatic end made Helen's role as a legitimating argument indispensable. His death confirmed Menelaus the instability of his own rule. After that, more than ever, he could not afford to lose Helen.

Their marriage ranks among the most difficult of all times. Probably, and for the same reasons, it is among the most interesting too.

Menelaus' feeling of triumph in getting her back must have been short-lived.

His brother's death deprived him of his worthiest ally—reminding him his own precariousness. Clytemnestra's reaction to male power must have turned him overwhelmingly conscious of his wife's many gifts as a talented herb doctor.

Fig. 31. Sketch of a fresco found in the acropolis at Mycenae. Their queens, including famous Clytemnestra, must not have looked much different. (c. 1300 B. C.)

It would be absolutely surprising that he had not had mixed, strong emotions on Helen's return. Apart from his wounded pride, all his meals must have been adequately and prudently pretasted. Anyway, in all likelihood, any minor symptom of gastric disarray, or of some unexpected malaise must have given him a lot of food for thought and no little anxiety. To see any of the guys of his entourage longing after her must not have helped either.

All things considered, after all the cataclysmic events, he must have brooded frequently about the convenience of having invested so much time and efforts, coercing so many unwilling confederates, risking his own life, just to get *her* back.

Presumably, Helen had second thoughts too. Homer's information, or intuition, on her feelings when she was forced to return sounds real. She must have seen friends and allies mercilessly killed after her rebellion.

The destruction of Troy pointed irrefutably to the futility of any new attempts on her part to resist the power of the Acheans. Above all, she could appreciate, like no one else, the surging confederate power of the priests that were advising the third Indo-European wave.

Probably, she was the last queen in that entire region who could have made any significant standing in front of the irresistible advance of the new political and social order.

Both from Homer and archaeologists we know that Lacedemonia or Sparta was very important at that time. Her religious-political status was formidable from any viewpoint.

With her, the last influential bastion had fallen.

Her position in history is tragic, not only from her personal situation, but for what must have been her own global view of the evolution of her society.

She was in a privileged, if tragic, historical observatory, located at the crossroads between two powerful social currents. She belonged to a proud line of priestesses, for whom the language of power had been common for many thousand years. Helen had dramatically witnessed a new social order arising where women had not a significant political or social place any more. She could see, as a High Priestess, initiated in the secret religious history, the past. A very ancient one, as her sight extended to the early times when the Goddess had reigned alone. Helen, supreme and conscious representative of the feminine on earth, could realize the new reality taking place around her.

She could also foresee the future for the entire region, the virtual disappearance of the reign of the Goddess, women excluded from power of almost any kind.

Carrying the sad weight of someone who is aware that it will not be possible to transmit in her turn all the inherited knowledge to the following generation, Helen must have realized that she was the last of her kind.

Her appreciation had to have been more terrible because it was not merely intellectual but visceral—not a fruit of thought but of her own devastating experience.

She had lived, experienced, felt the two models of society that were competing and knew, really in her heart, what was going to happen to her fellow women.

An overwhelming social turnover was on the march. The decline of the Goddess' influence, which had been slowly taking place for so many centuries, suddenly was almost total.

The imaginative mythical monsters that symbolized the tribal beliefs and the frescoes of all those splendid, commanding, independent women would soon be gone.

In her loneliness, she surely knew. The entire half of the population would soon share her despair and pain, as their eons-long rights and status were deliberately suppressed.

The meaning of her title, Helen, is associated with light, the dawn of the morning, the aurora. None could better signify her symbolism. With the fall of Troy, the fall of beautiful, orea Eleni, light had gone for the women in the region. For most of them, even if many still did not know it, a dark, long night had started.

Her people would retain her sacred name into their name until today, Hellas. Her sea would still be called the Helesponto, Helen's sea; but her name would loose her ancient, sacred meaning and she would be remembered just as an extraordinary, striking beauty, able to launch a thousand ships full of men trying to get her back.

Experts in Basque language have long since pointed to an ancient and very peculiar link with the Greek tongue. In the Greek language, woman and man are *ghineka* and *andros* respectively. An extraordinary resemblance with Basque, *andre* and *gizon*. They are, as some startled linguists have pointed out, practically the same words. Not only their similitude is remarkable but also a singular difference. *Their meaning is reverted.* The word that means man in Greek is used to design a woman in Basque—and vice versa. All that has baffled specialists for years. Anyway, unable to explain the singularity, they say that the similitude between the words in the two languages is too close for a mere coincidence.

Coincidence? Maybe.

But... Could there be any more apt and concise way to explain what really happened a few thousand years ago?

13

The Wanderer

The control of the eastern trade routes became apparently secure after the fall of Troy. So, the attention fell on the west: a new expedition was sent, following that of Palemon's a generation before. The man chosen to command it was a well-seasoned and famous warrior, Odysseus or Ulysses.

The choice was probably not merely based on his curriculum. The sacred king of Ithaca must have had a very personal interest on its success. He had been reluctant, according to all traditions, to take part in the expedition against Troy.

When Menelaus tried to convince him, wise, tricky Odysseus, always celebrated for his cunning, feigned himself mad to avoid the compromise. He must have seen instantly that his interests were not in that war. It concerned the eastern trade routes. His kingdom, the island of Ithaca, was in the west. Menelaus had asked him to fight just to increase the power, richness and influence of the rival eastern kingdoms. Never considered a fool, he refused. Apparently he was somehow forced. His son's life was used as an argument. Maybe, as we shall see, the future of his son was really at stake.

After Troy, it was not surprising that he was among the most interested in the reopening of any western sea trade. He was trusted with the expedition to the west.

A family tradition was being kept. His father, Laertes, had been one of the famed warriors that had sailed in the Argos with Palemon and Jason.

Where did Odysseus go? Lots of scholars have debated on that for centuries. Many think he never left the Mediterranean. Others believe he went as far as the British Isles. Was he looking for tin to produce bronze weapons? Did he go to Etruria? To Tartessos in the Atlantic?

As in the case of Palemon, his predecessor a generation before, his destination keeps being an enigma—hush-hush again. It has been argued that Homer left us enough clues in his beautiful narrative about the route followed by wise Odysseus. However, let's inspect another side of his problems. Due to his long absence, Odysseus, as many other sailors before and after him, had some marital problems. As in Menelaus' case, there was trouble in the family. This time with a different twist but always with the same root: the traditional matrilineal succession against the new, patrilineal challenge.

Odysseus' marital troubles and his long voyage became the subject of the other Greek religious book, the *Odyssey*.

The plot? While Odysseus tries to get back home, suitors who feast riotously in the house of the absent warrior beset his wife Penelope. Then incongruence starts.

His son Telemachus is worried. It seems that if his father is dead, his prospects are bleak. Why? That seems absolutely crazy.

If his father were dead, *he should inherit the throne*.

Why worry then? He would be the new king—the new master of the house. Instead, he is worried about the suitors devouring all his inheritance.

Worse, his grandpa Laertes is seen around, and like Telemachus, he seems just one more part of the decoration.

Why isn't Laertes the king? Why Odysseus, if Laertes is alive? Lack of character? That would not fit in with what might be expected from a daring old salt from the Argos. No sissies were allowed in that ship.

As the rest of the plot, everything is almost meaningless unless we are witnessing a matrilineal system.

Upset scholars have pointed that in the *Odyssey* everything revolves around loyal Penelope.

The suitors want to replace wandering Odysseus. Why them? What about Laertes and Telemachus? Nobody seems to pay *them* any attention. The suitors, as anybody else, seem to put the delicate question of the king's succession in the strangest place imaginable, in the hands of none less than a *woman*.

Uncomfortable specialists have discreetly pointed that there are "hints of matriarchy" in the entire situation. Hints? It seems that no one apart from Penelope can solve the social problem posed by the sacred king's absence.

She postpones the whole thing by the artful excuse of refusing to treat the question until the completion of a shroud for old Laertes. Maybe that explains Laertes being a zero. She secretly unweaves by night what she weaves by day.

Every reader is witnessing the problems confronted by both queen and king in those difficult days of that transition period.

There were perils for both of them. Like the pressure, well illustrated by Homer, of all those interested in the throne. They found nothing disquieting about sacrificing the king, as long as it was not *their* turn to become the revered heap of bones of a fertility god.

Let's notice that the main problem *was not the absence of Odysseus*. A long time ago, specialists in Homer had identified a singularity. When Penelope and Odysseus secretly met, at the return of the traveler, was *the period in which ancient astronomers considered that the sun cycle and the moon cycle coincided*. The Sun-King and the Moon-Queen were symbolically meeting at the right time. Not a surprise, it belongs to a religious narrative.

As a good storyteller, Homer makes the hero (actually the Hero) appear at the last possible moment. It was the day that ancient Meton called "the meeting of the moon and sun" in his treatise, or near twenty-year cycle (called Metonic Cycle by modern astronomers). It meant that the Ithacan king had reached, by the longest of all possible Pelasgian standards, the limit of his life span. *That* is the central point of the book. Replacement time had arrived.

A new sacred king should be appointed at all costs. All suitors were evidently for the matrilineal thing. No one considered the possibility of Telemachus becoming a king. No place for him in a matrilineal system. Off he has to go.

Telemachus might suffer a worse destiny. As someone has to die, in substitution of the absent king, he and Laertes (had he been in good health) were the obvious candidates for the ritual sacrifice. Both guarantied the royal blood considered necessary for the good of crops, hunting, fishing and any other activity in the realm. Not to mention that the following king would have appreciated a lot to get rid of them. They were unwanted company in those troubled, changing times.

That is the other part of the central plot. Homer is allowing us to contemplate the turbulent transition from matrilineal to patrilineal inheritance. Telemachus is well aware of his father's intention, following the advice of the priesthood. But his father is absent. With him, we are allowed to know, his most trusted men. How is young Telemachus going to make his rights prevail, that deranging patrilineal innovation, against all the noble suitors and the rest of the people? The suitors try to kill him, aware of his revolutionary intentions. Young Telemachus evades their persecution and starts visiting the Achean lords.

He leaves the island, looking for help from his father's old comrades at Troy. Heavenly advice (it must be read: by smart priests) is given to go to Pilos and Lacedemonia.

Telemachus visits Menelaus, apparently to inquire about his father's whereabouts. We can imagine the real dialogue. Okay, Menelaus, Dad backed you when you were in trouble with these crazy matrilineal people, it's now your turn to support me. Menelaus is shown crying a lot on account of Odysseus' fate and politically sympathizes with him—but no help. Has he remembered Odysseus initial refusal to help *him*? Perhaps the problems in Ithaca made him only more sensitive to his own troubles—no need to leave sexy Helen alone. Menelaus was well aware of what her enterprising sister had accomplished during his brother's absence. Telemachus leaves empty handed.

In the first paragraphs of the Odyssey, along with the sensible recommendation to visit his possible allies, he is also given a very strange counsel: *to follow the example of Orestes*.

What had sweet, nice Orestes done? He had defended his right to succeed his father, the king. He killed the king, his uncle, who had replaced his father, and the queen, his mother. None other than Athena gave the advice to Telemachus.

A goddess putting a matricide as an example? That was the worst crime in a matrilineal society. Orestes' victim had not only been his mother but a queen and a priestess as well. Athena advising *that*? Come on, Homer, gotcha in a very big one this time. Impossible.

There can be no doubt about the exhortation. It surely existed; the *Odyssey* was a sacred book. It never tells lies. Adorned, twisted, disguised truths may be found in it—especially in the religious quarter. Just a few centuries later, classic Greeks found that dreadful incitation hideous—totally immoral, even for patrilineal people like them. They were scandalized by the apparent savagery. The religious leaders from some earlier generations evidently had had quite different thoughts about it. That terrible advice came obviously from the supposed emissaries and interpreters of the gods, the priesthood.

It was really a combat of the gods. If a suitor from any matrilineal clan had succeeded crafty Odysseus, the growing patrilineal front would have weakened—one less ally, one more enemy.

Should lovely Penelope choose a successor, the priests were saying—Homer is quite clear on leaving that on record—young Telemachus should not hesitate to do exactly as Orestes did. If Penelope did not play ball, well, then it was just her fault.

It was a risky business being a queen at that time. She had to play along or be terminated. It also tells that Orestes did not act on his own when he settled his family differences. He certainly received a similar abetment as the one Homer retold. Aeschylus was of that opinion in his tragedies.

It was a risky business for all the players. From the queens' viewpoint the priests' attempts were clearly sacrilegious. The penalty was also death. It was a tough, hard play, with death menacing all the participants. Losers died. Winners, anyway, could never look forward to a long, happy life. As Agamemnon had learned the hard way, patrilineal succession had not become established merely by the taking of Troy. Every Hero had to confront at home the same family problems as those faced by the kings of Mycenae and Ithaca.

Homer points out in many ways the powerful influence of the queens. When, after a shipwreck, Odysseus arrives to Phaeacia, he throws himself at the feet of Nausicaa, the princess. A man imploring at the feet of a woman in an Aryan tale was a rarity in itself—but worse follows. She does not counsel him to demand the compassion of her father the king. No, no, nothing of that. Once in the palace, clever Nausicaa advises Odysseus, "*pass thou by him* (her father) *and cast thy hands at my mother's knees.*" Insider's knowledge: don't waste your time with *him*, you dummy, he's nothing, go straight to *her* and state your claim up. Had the king been the top authority that apparently innocent recommendation, if followed by any stranger, would have meant a very difficult situation.

Survivors of any shipwreck had enough trouble to keep alive in a strange surrounding to need any additional complication. They usually ended as slaves, if they were that lucky. Yet goodhearted Nausicaa sent Odysseus to her mother.

Scholars have pointed that Homer significantly underscores the surprising mightiness of queen Arete, Nausicaa's mother. He exalts her good wits and her skill in solving quarrels among men. Wow! That was exactly supposed to be her husband Alcinous' job. The queen is shown as full participant in the feasting that followed—enough to upset any self-respecting Indo-European. Neither Acheans nor classic Greeks were used to that. A few generations later all that would be considered a fairy tale. Except, of course, by the Ionians, and Homer was one of them. He knew.

Who commanded the lotus eaters? Circe got that job. The *Odyssey* shows three far away realms under the powerful political influence of three women. Coincidence?

The fact that Odysseus was chosen as the hero of the second sacred book, points not only at what must have been the successful accomplishment of the expedition he commanded. The energy with which he solved his domestic troubles established him also as a wonderful example of a patrilineal king, a splendid role model, in the eyes of the upcoming priesthood.

He whacked all suitors off, which were obviously for the matrilineal solution. A remake of tricky Palemon's well proven method of dealing with the intended ceremony for the sacrifice of the king—again the unsuspecting crowd being slaughtered by the priestly king, reluctant to become the new member of the pantheon—again a carnage accomplished with the aid of just a few, well determined men.

After such a deliberate, systematic extermination, Odysseus then nicely *killed practically all the household women*. They, above all, must have been all for the old order. Finally he set himself up over the revolting population of the island, which were not Acheans and must have hated him both for the massacre and the sacrilege.

If all that could not gain Odysseus the gratitude of the priests, what would? This unheard of separation between rulers and commoners explains the apparition of the strong walled cities and central palaces. He was chosen and immortalized as the example for all sacred-kings to follow.

On the other hand, what makes the *Odyssey* strikingly different from all antecedents is Penelope's personality and behavior. A queen seems to be inclined to the patrilineal order. Was she a traitor to her gender, to her priesthood? Had she been brain washed by some priests? The Queen of Ithaca has been praised as a paragon of marital loyalty. Maybe *that* was what tilted the balance to make *her* and Odysseus winning candidates for the leading roles in the priest's exaltation of the new lifestyle, which was trusted to Homer's poetical gifts.

Was she really like that? Or was it just Indo-European whitewashing? Whatever course she decided implied many risks.

If Penelope went outspokenly for the matrilineal solution, something which apparently young Telemachus (and the priests!) believed possible, that meant the nasty possibility of later Achean retaliation.

Maybe she was also considering the renowned, recent Orestes' display of unpleasant manners.

On the other hand, if she manifested any inclination for a patrilineal arrangement she could incur the wrath of the ambitious suitors and the people from the island.

The fascinating thing is that never, in the whole book, does she speak publicly for one system or other. Everyone, her husband, her son, the suitors, seems awkwardly unsure of her feelings and thoughts on the royal succession. Everybody demands a definition from her. She is never shown acceding to such understandable petitions—except in private. Maybe she was, as Homer tells, really fond of Odysseus. Maybe she decided that a new husband, after all, would not mean any real improvement. Maybe, not having daughters, she was fond of Telemachus, well aware that a new king, as her son feared, would mean his total displacement, if not his death. Maybe she was just well aware of her husband's resources and expedient mean disposition.

The truth is Homer never really leaves us the impression of a clear definition—only maybes.

She stands in front of the suitors, which demand a prompt solution for the insulting absence of the sacred king. That could bother them, not her. Absent the king, she was free from any eclipsing influence. All those suitors were not bad for her ego either. Why spoil all that and choose a new king, whose unknown habits could be annoying?

Homer pointed the crafty way she delayed the claims until the legal period, the sun-moon cycle, had been properly observed. Most probably Laertes' shroud was a fiction and she just had demanded from all the people to play by the rules. She leaves the situation to solve by itself. Still, she is always the Queen. Everything and everybody are orbiting around her, the central character in the whole story.

In a chaotic age, the wife of the foxiest man described in that whole period seems to have been his more than adequate counterpart. She does not sacrifice herself to any part in the struggle. And becomes the only one who has never been in physical peril at any moment.

This woman, who evidently distressed the priests, who is doubted by everyone, whose own son and husband were unsure of her standing, will be later instituted by the religious hierarchy as the one whom future generations would have no choice but to revere, as a sacred example of someone who could be trusted above all.

The pariah becomes the heroine, who must be admired and venerated as a religious duty.

Homer's brilliant portrait of a queen, which perseveringly minds her words and wisely keeps a low profile—while managing to remain at the same time the evident social and political center—brings to life an interesting example of why the matrilineal institution lasted such a long time.

14

The Witch Hunt Starts

First witch:
"When shall we three meet again?
In thunder, lightning, or in rain?"

William Shakespeare, *Macbeth, Act one, Scene one.*

One of the most remarkable characteristics of religious history in the Western World is the witch-hunt—women being burned at the stake. It happened everywhere.

That name...witch.

It has a bad sound.

It was a terrible word in the past. It still has an ugly resonance. It also presents a noteworthy distinction. Why no one ever speaks of a *wizard* hunt?

Males seem to dominate almost every professional area, except that one. It is a telling sign of the formidable cultural conflict between the old Europeans and the Aryan newcomers.

That other word, witchcraft...

The art or craft of the witch...

Witch has the same root than wise—linked to wit—wise, astute, the one who knows. It has other connotations. Witch comes from Anglo-Saxon *wicca*, related with German *weiks* and Old Norse *vé*, holy, where both words came, respectively, from German *weihen* and Old Norse *vigja*, consecrate—also with Latin *victima*, sacrificial creature. It is linked to *vincere*, to conquer. From there comes *victory*. All that family of words is illuminating. It tells which role witches used to play in the past.

The *witch* was a *wise* woman—someone who had access to a secret knowledge. She was considered holy—in charge of sacrifice, of the offering of the victim. It all adds to just one word—priestesses.

In ancient times they were apparently also in charge of the offering of the victim after victory.

It all agrees. In later iconography the victory for the Greeks (*nikke*) became a winged woman who put a crown of laurels on the head of the victor. Whitewashing, it was just whitewashing. That is precisely what the Achean sacred kings had been desperately trying to avoid when they fought at Troy.

The real story was that in ancient times among the Pelasgians the crown of laurels had signified that the Goddess had just chosen the victim—the person to be sacrificed. Her wings had a well-known connotation at those times—death. Just after a victory or at the end of the term of a sacred kingship. The winners at the Olympic Games were also crowned with leaves, probably because in its beginnings the winner of the annual foot race became the new sacred king of the league.

Post-victory offerings were common. That practice was still in existence in biblical times. Saul, first king of Israel, is seen on the verge of sacrificing his son Jonathan after a victory, but the young man is saved by his popularity among the soldiers. No one saved Jephte's daughter a few centuries before. Victims were common thanksgiving for almost anything of importance—*almost always of royal blood*. Agamemnon sacrificed his daughter Iphigeneia in gratitude for favorable winds. Let's notice the change, not at all insubstantial. As in Jephte's case, now it was a male sacrificing a woman, pointing to an Indo-European rite. A male—the priest Chalcas—advised the sacrifice of Iphigeneia—a terrible political move. It eliminated the legal successor to the throne, the princess. Agamennon's advisers must have believed that the murder of the female inheritor made impossible for aspirants to legally replace the king of Mycenae during his absence.

It failed.

The ruthless episode probably triggered Clytemnestra's reprisal. Agamemnon had also killed her former husband Tantalus and her first born by the latter. It was enough for her. She must have thought it was time to sacrifice the right person.

The words also point to the dramatic reversal. In ancient times witchcraft, or a similar sounding word, should have been the equivalent of modern *wisdom*, carrying with it considerable prestige and power for the lady in question. Later they meant the stake. The one who sacrificed had become the new victim.

It was not an easy fight. After Troy, even in classic times, the Goddess' cult was still strong and going. The Indo-European newcomers kept trying to discredit and suppress it. Sacred burial-islands suffered invasions. Those who resisted changes in their sanctuaries and rites met violent death. In spite of all, the ancient cult refused to die.

Even in the 6th century B.C., some seven centuries after the Trojan War, Athenians—on tyrant Pisistratus' orders—conquered Lemnos, the sacred island. Supposedly to purify the island, all the Hero burials were removed. A similar purification took place in the sacred island of Delos. The Ionians and Eolians bitterly complained of sacrilege. Burials in Delos became forbidden.

Even childbirth, common in fertility islands, was also forbidden. Conquering sacred islands, and submitting them later to harsh rules, gained Pisistratus recognition among the priests, and was probably the main reason why he ended in so many of the then circulating lists of the Seven Sages of Greece.

One of the many historical paradoxes, Pisistratus' hottest political adversary, Solon the lawgiver, Plato's grandfather, also made his way to the lists of the legendary Seven Sages.

Solon and Pisistratus were irreconcilable enemies in politics, but both of them considered central the Panathenean Games, the quadrennial gathering of the Ionian cities. They, along with Pisistratus' son, Hipparcus, made mandatory the recitation of the *Iliad* and the *Odyssey*. It used to take some twenty hours each and constituted the main event of the Games.

Pisistratus is recorded as the first to have given Homer's books a fixed order. He is believed to have produced a politically correct version of both books. He is also believed to have edited some hideous parts that could offend by their brutality the then higher moral sensibility of Hellenes, such as the probable torture of Hector by Achilles.

WHO WAS ON TOP?

Fig. 32. At left, a sketch of the famous Lions' Gate at Mycenae. Three meters tall, they constitute the earliest Greek monumental sculpture. The lions were paying homage to something, now disappeared, on the top of the column. Most probably it was a wooden or stone image of the Goddess. Depictions of her surrounded by lions (like the one at right, a famous Minoan ring print) sphinxes or other symbolic or mythological animals were common. Her stone dethronement may have happened many years after Her institutional and political fall in Agamemnon´s time.

Solon, Pisistratus and Hipparcus were all from the aristocracy (direct descendants of Indo-European conquerors) and as such, as Plutarch narrates, were "instructed in religious matters"—all according to the customs instituted in Athens by Theseus, following the priests' counsel. The three aristocrats clearly knew the importance of what they did and were well aware of the inner meaning of Homer's chants.

No matter how hard they tried to eliminate the ancient fertility cults, women kept flocking to the sacred islands. Many were there just imploring the Goddess to concede them Her most valuable gift—children.

For instance, a few generations after Pisistratus' efforts, there was a princess from Epirus. Her name was Olympias. Not surprisingly, she had certain fame as a witch. Olympias followed the example of her peers and visited the sacred, sepulchral island of Samothrace. The princess wanted a child. She must have considered herself blessed by the Goddess, because in 356 B.C. she gave birth to a son in the city of Pellas. It would not have been surprising either that the ladies of her court might have considered later that the Goddess had benignly awarded Olympias and her son other gifts. Her son became king at twenty and then carried out his father's planned expedition against the Persians—conquering Asia Minor, Syria, Egypt, Babylonia, Persia and even part of India on the side. All that made people add "the Great" whenever they mentioned his name, Alexander.

Slowly, at a pace of generations, the Indo-European, Aryan wave kept expanding to the west. The last fringes were the Atlantic coast and isles. They still exhibit a conspicuously high Rh- percentage. To marry a princess was still the only acceptable way to the throne among them more than two thousand years after Troy, less than a thousand years from us.

Vandals, Goths, Huns all of them kept coming. As in Greece, sometimes they intermarried with the local, matrilineal tribes, adopting the Goddess cult, negotiating the changes in ritual and theology. That seemed to be the case of the Celts, where a minority of newcomers imposed their language; but adopted many of the beliefs and customs of the people they dominated. Sometimes Indo-Europeans overwhelmed the Euzkans and imposed their own patriarchal religion. That happened with the Gotts, who arrived later.

In the eastern zones of the Mediterranean Sea coast, the last Euzkan holy-burial-islands were finally invaded and became Indo-European religious bastions half a millennium before Christ. In the western regions those Euzkan burial traditions continued for long.

Iona, the sacred island, justly called the most intensely publicized three square miles in all Scotland, continued to host the remains of kings almost until modern times. Its chapel and its graveyard, the Reilig Odhrain, were the most revered sites in Scotland until 1200. Then the Roman Catholic Church took over. St. Columba had smartly chosen it as his base in 563 to evangelize the Picts. In a mound of the sacred graveyard lay both Macbeth and murdered Duncan, their differences also allayed, united in a last immemorial rite. According to a 1549 visitor, no fewer than 58 other Scottish, Irish and Norse kings were also in the mound. Those are only the ones recorded by history. It can be guessed that many, many more royal remains lay there.

Even after their triumph, Indo-Europeans kept receiving a strong influence from the Goddess. The philosophers of the Classic Age were all inheritors of an ancient tradition, whose main schools were of Ionian origin. Their ideas have a strong influence even today.

Not only philosophy but also religion was influenced. In old times, philosophy was seldom separated from religion. In Greece, part of the most evolved Mother Goddess cults took refuge in the Mysteries. Secret was common in those rites, not allowing anyone but a few initiates to learn the ancient truths.

Those rich, elaborated rituals, dwelling on internal experience instead of the formalistic, state-centered ceremonies of Greek (and also Roman) religion, exerted a strong attraction on those searching for enlightenment. The Mysteries included ceremonies with offering of bread and wine. Simulated death and resurrection, or rebirth, were central, always reminiscing of the sacred king ritual death and succeeding replacement.

In Crete, according to Diodorus Siculus, Mysteries were open to all and there was nothing hidden. The most probable origin of the *telesterion*, initiation hall at Eleusis, lies in the Minoan-Mycenean constructions.

The most renowned were the Eleusinian, Orphic and Samothracian Mysteries. The last one included a system of confessional. They all included Pelasgian Dionysian rites. Many modern scholars believe that ingestion of hallucinogens was common in all of them and constituted the main event of the initiation. Goddesses Persephone and Kore, mother and daughter, were the leading divinities in the Eleusis Mystery.

Dionysian fraternities or guilds were the seed of many fraternities that had left their mark in the western culture. Some of them later evolved into Orphic fraternities, whose rituals varied much according to the region. In a few cases they involved frenzied ceremonies, with animal sacrifice and wine drinking. In most of them austerity and high ethical standards were the norm. From many ancient writings it is known that they were already old in Crete and Egypt. It has been pointed out that Freemasonry, for instance, shows a notable resemblance to some of those guilds.

Feminine cults, carried out entirely by women were allowed, but they were despoiled of their former social, political and economical influence. Worship of Demeter, the corn Goddess, continued all through Greece. At harvest time, for instance, as part of the *Haloa* festival, the first fruits were conveyed from Athens to Eleusis. There a priestess offered a sacrifice, men were forbidden to participate.

Oriental Goddesses cults (Attis, Cybeles, Isis, etc.) invaded Greece and Rome after Alexander's conquests. As the Indo-European rule was then firmly established, there was no major conflict, apart from traditionalists who complained. Women in Greece and Rome became adepts to these religions.

They all prepared the way for Christianity. When the new religion came, predicating a King who had been sacrificed for the general welfare and then resurrected, with an offering of bread and wine, it carried an irresistible attraction. The emphasis on a strict moral code appealed to those already influenced by the fraternities and the philosophers. Christianity gave the final coup with the increasing veneration of the Virgin Mary, allowing again a feminine influence in the cult. One of the titles given to the Virgin in a Christian temple in Cyprus (the inscription can be seen today) is illustrating: Panaghia Aphroditessa—all saintly Aphrodite. The continuity of an old tradition of veneration of a mother figure is obvious.

The impact on the Basques, for instance, of a cult where veneration of a virgin of that name was important, can be easily understood. They worshipped a goddess of the mountains—the Lady. Her name was *Mari*, also *Mari of the Caves*. Her legend still stands. Even today some old mountaineers speak of a woman of extraordinary beauty who travels through the air surrounded by fire.

Fig. 33. Sketch of a white-stone statue representing a goddess from Mari

In her lore, Mari can transform herself into horses, bulls, rams and boars (the most common animals in Ice-Age-Cave artistry). All of it probably pointing to the aspect in which Mari was worshipped, or the kind of masks used by her priestesses during rituals. In some regions she is said to be able to turn into a wolf.

A notable stalagmite in Bidarray, known as *Arpeko Saindua* (the saint woman of the cave), resembling a human back, was venerated in the past as the goddess petrified.

Mari was also worshipped in Cyprus. On her account the Egyptians called Cyprus *Ay-Mari*, Mari's island or the island where the worshippers of Mari lived. She must have been the ruling goddess of Mari, a city on the Euphrates, whose enormous palace has been found significantly similar to the one at Knossos, both in the architectural design and in the subject and technique of the frescoes. A sculpture from Mari, celebrated as an artistic marvel, treasured in the National Museum of Aleppo, shows the Goddess holding a vase from which water flows down her skirt (Fig. 33)—adequate for a fertility goddess.

She was also venerated at Amari in Minoan Crete. Was she identical to *Mara*, the agricultural fertility goddess adored in the Baltic? Her altars are common in Lattvia and Lithuania *today*. Is it the same goddess? It has been pointed out that Mari originally meant prolific mother: *Ma* (shortening of Sumerian *Ama*, mother) *ri* (to bear a child). Mari could have been just one of the many titles of the Goddess. The expression Fruitful Mother, or its equivalent, is found in many inscriptions and writings, as it could be expected in fertility cults. It is not very surprising to learn that Basques became extremely devoted to the Virgin.

While in the advanced regions the influence came through Mysteries and fraternities, in the most remote parts of Europe, peasants, all dependent on rain and weather, remained as loyal to the old rites of the Goddess as was possible. The ancient rites gave rise to many persecutions, especially when unstable situations made the political or ecclesiastic authorities feel insecure. In times of turmoil, the witch-hunt always became fiercer.

The trials have left quite a record, even if biased, of the old cult. The religion implied a belief in a god incarnated in a human being or animal. The god appeared to his worshippers disguised—as a stag, a bull, a dog, a cat, a bird or other animals.

It is fascinating to notice that some modern scholars studying this part have tended to associate it with the Paleolithic paintings in the caves. They also saw an ancient priestly-king in the stagmen and the birdmen (Fig. 18 a, b) which appeared in some of those prehistoric art galleries. What Robert Graves deduced from Greek myths, traditions and legends coincides with the thought of those who studied both the folk customs and the records of the witch trials.

Those studies started (at least in the open) nearly two centuries ago—when the institutional leaders felt that the old cults had ceased to be a menace. The fertility rites were the focal point for the recorders of the trials.

For the celebrants they were the means to secure the prosperity of their crops and herds. The liturgical ritual, which brought the harshest prosecutions, involved intercourse of the god (the devil, for prosecutors) with some of his worshippers. The main members of the cult, analogous to priesthood, were usually organized in number of 13. Usually a male, disguised as the incarnated animal, and twelve women (again 1+12, the sacred number of the Goddess).

Assemblies usually took place four times a year: Candlemas in February, May-Eve or Roodmas, Lammas in August and the still popular Halloween in November.

People used to come from afar for those celebrations, a gathering of hundreds, a fair with dancing, singing and feasting—and no little sex.

In some of the most backward regions in Europe, an impressive ritual took place: the sacrifice of the god. It happened every seven or nine years, indicating that extension of the life of the sacred king had already been negotiated.

The noted 11th century A.D. historian Adam of Bremen is best known for leaving the first record of the existence of the Viking discovery of America (Vinland). He also left a precious description of the renowned festivals at the gold-gleaming temple of Uppsala, as told by eyewitnesses. *They were celebrated every nine years.*

Victims "*of every living thing that is male*" were hanged from trees "in the sacred grove that adjoins the temple." "This grove is so sacred in the eyes of the heathen that each and every tree in it is believed divine." A man was plunged alive into a sacred well. Nine men were ritually killed—*nine men dying every nine years*—Goddess' numbers at play again. A cathedral was erected in the place of the pagan temple a century later. A fire destroyed that building, and a new church was built—Kamla Uppsala Kirka. Most probably, the many ancient stories about children being sacrificed by witches point to the ritual victim offered yearly in substitution of the king.

Many of those ancient traditions found their way into modern times. Some saints and processions carry an unequivocal air from the old Goddess' festivals—St. John's Eve, for instance, on June 23. It still is a very popular feast in many places in Europe. From Spain and France, to Italy and Germany, the great fires of the traditional midsummer festival maintain their old attraction in many villages, towns and cities. In the Baltic its old meaning, the Ligo festival of Saule, the Sun Goddess, is still fresh among Latvians and Lithuanians, among whom many still celebrate the summer solstice with its ancient symbolism. It is quite popular among many Slavs too.

Carnival, with its erotic license and disguises, is a survival of those feasts. It follows a clear tradition of the ancient, fertility-cult communal celebrations.

Candlemas also became a Christian feast, commemorating, most adequately, the purification of the Virgin and the presentation of the Child in the temple.

Easter is a name that retains an ancient meaning. It reveals the transformation that took place. Easter was the name of the ancient spring festival dedicated to honor goddess Eastres. Who was Eastres? Some fifteen centuries ago, the Venerable Bede cleared this point in his memorable writings on the Church in England. He equaled Eastres to Astarte. The ancient Ishtar—associated to planet Venus— is still receiving homage in that name.

Christmas keeps all the marks of an ancient festivity: it marks the rebirth of the sacrificed Sun God, the solstice—a pagan festival that, through that conversion, kept being the most popular celebration.

Jesus' birth was not celebrated on that date at the beginning. Actually, there is no certainty not only about the exact day but also about the year of His birth. Most scholars agree that Jesus was born between 4 B.C. and 8 B.C., based on the famous Roman census that made Joseph take his family to Jerusalem—but no one dares to put an exact date.

The Egyptian Christians began to celebrate the Messiah's Birth on January 6th. The Eastern Church soon adopted it. On that day the ancient festival of Dionysus took place throughout Anatolia and the Greek Islands—a god who had also been torn apart and resurrected, son of a god and a mortal. An ancient feast, coming from the times of the Mother, when the celebrants ritually killed and ate the king, and then invested his successor, which was liturgically interpreted as a resurrection. The chosen date had an immediate attraction for the people.

The Western Church never recognized January 6th and adopted, nearly at the end of the third century, December 25th as the official birth date of Jesus. It coincided with the popular, pagan, winter-solstice festival. The evergreen pine and the mistletoe kept being religious symbols, incorporated not by theologians but by overwhelming tradition.

January 6th kept being a celebration in the West anyhow, becoming the feast of Epiphany. Not by chance, it celebrates both the recognition of the Messiah by the three Magi and the miracle of the transformation of water into wine—on the date of the celebration of an ancient wine-god—a clever way to mean Dionysus dethronement.

Some scholars considered possible that part of the old beliefs helped to originate the lycanthropy legend—the folk tale of those able to assume the form of a wolf and adopt its habits. It is too close to the ancient tales of the primitive totemic fraternities indulging in some sacrifice at their moon celebrations. The wolf was one of the most common totems.

Our word lyceum, for instance, came from the place where Aristotle taught (archaeologists found the remains of its ancient buildings in 1997). It had been prior dedicated to Apollo *Lykaion*—Apollo of the Wolves. *Killer of wolves* was one of Apollo favorite titles. It probably meant that his Indo-European priests had successfully eradicated some Goddess' wolf fraternities. In ancient times, probably it was not healthy to be strolling near the Lykaion at full moon, if the men from the wolf fraternity had decided to have a meeting.

Folklore is full of all those tales of men assuming the shape and identity of some wild animal; the animals involved coincide with the most common totems of the fraternities.

The ferocity associated with those rituals is not always exaggerated. Sometimes members tried to emulate the totem, accomplishing the execution of the victim with their teeth (see page 117). The legend of the *loup-garou*— werewolf (Basque *guisotso*)—has been especially strong both among the French and the Spanish Basques. A telling point: not a few Basque aristocratic coats of arms carried the picture of a man-eating wolf— a souvenir inherited from some ancestor proud of belonging to a powerful fraternity. D'Artagnan spent his childhood in Loupiac—the city of the wolves.

Vast regions in Europe carried that name. It indicated that in them a cult existed where the Goddess symbol was a female wolf.

The traditional myth of Romulus and his twin brother Remus, founders of Rome, reared and suckled by a wolf, tells us immediately in which cult and fraternity they were educated, and, most probably, which might have been the initial state-cult followed by Romans.

Just like Theseus did in Athens, Romulus banished the priestesses but did not dare to suppress their most important celebration—the Lupercalia—the feast of the Wolves. It was an obvious fertility cult celebration—its ritual pointed to an earlier human sacrifice. Its celebrants were the consuls and a band of dancing youths from the patrician families—the *Luperci*. It is easy to note their similitude with the performer and the Chorus of the Great Dionysia. The Lupercalia kept being the most important and popular Roman celebration until the Catholic Church abolished it. Twenty-seven centuries and a half later, in spite of Her priestesses' banishment, the female wolf is still the emblem of the city.

A spectacular side of the witch trials was the description of flights and many other unbelievable experiences of those who took part in their meetings. The modern view is that the use of hallucinogens was widespread. The experiences described by those who have ingested some hallucinogenic brew coincide too well with the descriptions common in the trials.

Hallucinogens were widely used in ancient times. Euripides wrote that the priestesses of Apollo used certain kinds of wild, toxic honeys in their prophetic trances. Modern physicians have confirmed their hallucinogenic power—they contain some grayanotoxins. Priestesses seem to have used every possible source of hallucinogenic substances.

Recent geological studies have confirmed that in ancient times there was a source of ethylene—a gas that is currently used as an anesthetic—below the temple of Apollo at Delphi. It gives believability to some ancient writings that indicated that an emanation from earth caused the prophecies.

According to Roman writers, the Pythia fell into a hypnotic state after burning or chewing a poisonous variety of laurel. Some plants the ancient Greeks called *Daphne* (laurel) do contain hallucinogenic toxics. Witches in Portugal still use the *Panaeolus papilionaceus*, a small fungus, whose effects are similar to those of mescaline.

It has been argued that Pelasgians were fond of using *Amanita muscaria*. Probably no other mushroom has been drawn and painted as often as the toxic *A. muscaria*. It is the famous red cap fungus with white spots that appears in the illustrations of so many children books, often with an elf or fairy sitting atop.

The common belief that witches used toads and snakes for their concoctions, as described in many trials, could have a very solid ground. Certain frogs and toads produce hallucinogens in their skins, like the bufotenines, a fact that was well exploited by toad-licking hippies in the sixties. Toads are still used with those purposes. The toad was the symbol of Dionysus, the god of hallucinogenic trances. It is less known that the venom of certain snakes also induces hallucinogenic phenomena. That has been offered as an explanation of the many snake cults professed by the ancient Europeans.

Serpent cults were not restricted to Europe. Some people in the Pingri Village in Uttar-Pradesh, India, are still observing that ancient custom. There, thousands of years after those cults have died in other regions of the world, women still offer their arms to cobra snakes (Fig. 34 a, b, c). When the cobra bites they get an instant trip—full of voices and visions. As with the dangerous mushrooms and all the hallucinogenic drugs, sometimes they get a one-way-ticket only. Return is not always guaranteed. If the snake has accumulated too much poison, or the woman who has been stung is not immune or resistant enough, death comes. A few women usually die this way. What is suggestive is that only *women* practise this very ancient art. Old women initiate young women into it. *No men of those tribes try it.* Connection with the many sculptures and paintings of goddesses or priestesses holding snakes is not difficult to imagine.

Serpents have been a religious symbol from very ancient times. They played an all-important role among the Euzkos. Coiled snakes were a common religious symbol for the Picts. Some of the most beautiful Minoan statuettes are gorgeous women holding snakes in their arms. It would not be surprising that they were, at least in their origins, snake cults. Meaning that the venomous fangs of the reptiles induced not a few of the hallucinogenic states.

Fig. 34a. A Pingri woman offering her arm. Another woman assists. Courtesy of Geomundo, 1979

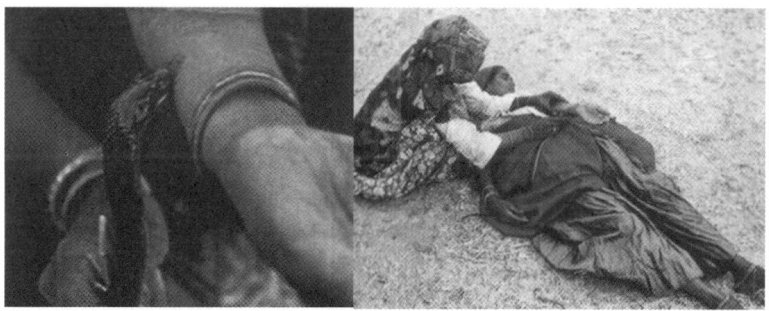

Fig 34b, c. After the bite the woman rests. Her assistant is ready to help her awake if troubling physiological symptoms appear. Courtesy of Geomundo, 1979

According to ancient writers the prophetess at Delphi was called the *pythoness*—from Pytho, the sacred serpent. In the myth, Apollo slained Pytho. The oracular shrine, in Pelasgian times was dedicated to Gaia, the earth-Goddess. So, most probably, that myth is telling us that a snake-cult, where the pythonesses' oracular trances were originally induced by viper's bites, was succeeded by an Indo-European one, where a priestess still had the most important supernatural locus, but the male priesthood, in charge of interpreting the oracle, was now in full command. Not surprisingly, the Greek myths describe numerous encounters of Heroes with supernatural snakes.

One of those episodes is illustrating enough: the already mentioned myth of Herakles slaying the Hydra of Lerna—the monster that had multiple heads—all of them serpents. Herakles went killing the heads—one by one. The heads kept reproducing themselves. So, the Hero started to burn them. As there are many reasons to think that the priestesses were called serpents, the scope of Palemon's famous Second Labor emerges easily. He was commissioned to annihilate a snake cult. Dead priestesses were soon replaced by daring new successors—spoiling Palemon's job. He then resourced to burning them—anticipating the witch burning of future centuries. Herakles was acting well within the Aryan tradition. He was following his family tradition too, and acting a very personal revenge. According to his myth, two serpents had tried to kill him at his cradle—two priestesses had evidently claimed the royal baby male. They failed, meeting their death. Maybe it was not Palemon who eradicated the fertility cult; maybe it took a few generations. By Dorian times they were all gone. All the stories are congruent. Anyway, almost a millennium later, Pausanias described the many monuments to goddesses that abounded near Lerna.

Were those sexy Minoan statuettes—women holding snakes in their hands—depictions of pythonesses?

Snake cults did not become extinct at all with the fall of the Minoan civilization. They were still going strong in Western Europe in relatively modern times—practically in *our* times.

An Arab, Ahmad Ibn Fadlan, wrote one of the most precious narratives about the Vikings—in many aspects the *only one* about them. From him we know that many uses of the old Europeans were still in vigor in Scandinavia in Viking times. He was, for instance, forced to take part in a sudden expedition that took him from Russia to Scandinavia. His involuntary trip was the result of an old *wise woman*'s advice. On her word, a dozen Viking warriors left for Norway, plus forcefully carried Ibn Fadlan. The old woman had said that, to succeed, the Viking war party had to consist of *twelve of a kind plus a different one*—the Goddess again.

A common Viking habit shocked Ibn Fadlan's moral sense: public coition. Something that was also traditional among Picts, Etruscans and Pelasgians.

The Arab traveler also let us know, somehow, that Indo-European influence was already been exerted with full strength at the beginning of the 12th century A.D. in Scandinavia: at a chieftain's funeral a *woman* was sacrificed. The same wise woman, who had recommended the expedition, ritually killed her. The Vikings called the wise woman the *Angel of Death*.

The other mixed cultural influences of that funeral are also significant: the chieftain's body was still being sent in a boat (Euzkan tradition) but then it was set on fire (Aryan tradition.)

One of the most interesting passages in Ibn Fadlans's writings concerns very primitive people, who really had extraordinary features and customs. These primitives had been antagonizing a Scandinavian village. So, they were the real object of the expedition, they were the Viking's adversaries. The expedition was successful. The Vikings killed the *woman* who was considered the heart of that astonishing, primitive people—an old woman, whose role, leader or priestess, was unspecified. Instants before her death, she had been receiving homage from three males of her tribe that were singing, prostrated with their faces on the earth and their hands raised.

What makes Ibn Fadlan's description priceless, in a continent where matrilineality had had such a notable influence, is not only the recognition of the central part that old woman played among her people, but also that she lived in a cavern *full of snakes and human skulls.*

It was the Goddess and the snakes all over again.

Were those crania the usual Heroes' skulls? Sacrificial victims? Unlucky prisoners? The Arab's writings allow us a breathtaking glimpse at what could have been the pythoness' *métier* at Delphi and other sacred-places a few thousand years back. *All that was still taking place in Europe, according to that famed Arab witness, only a few centuries back.* It happened only a century before William the Conqueror left Normandy and set foot in England. Classic Greeks had disappeared long ago, Troy had become a nursery tale, Rome had collapsed many centuries ago, the Church was reaching its first millennium, and still the Goddess was being worshipped in Western Europe.

Archaeologists could produce an invaluable contribution by taking a close look at certain Scandinavian caverns. The peculiar constitution of that primitive people described by Ibn Fadlan could bring out some interesting finds.

Hallucinogens may also have been involved as the reason of many witch-hunts. It has been argued that ergotism might have caused terrible prosecutions in the past. Ergotism is a poisoning originated by the ingestion of contaminated grain. Together with economic and religious reasons, it could have inspired many of the recorded witch-hunting fevers.

At those convulsed times, many people were never short of reasons to torture or eliminate some neighbors or competitors. Not so long ago as we might like to think, even chickens, dogs and cats were submitted to trials. Those were sadistic times.

Ergotism originates mostly through the ingestion of contaminated rye or its bread.

A fungus, *Claviceps* (clubheaded) *purpurea* (purple), that infects many plants, producing a typical black mass of branching filaments, is responsible for the intoxication. The plant disease is called ergot. From the fungus many alkaloids have been extracted—ergotamine among them. When baked it produces hallucinogens. One of those hallucinogenic products has won quite a reputation. It is commonly known as LSD.

Due to the consumption of contaminated rye bread, entire villages seem to have suffered the well-known effects of hallucinogenic trips. Tales of peasant madness, collective hysteria, people running naked through the streets, wild sex in the open, everything seems to have happened as recorded by many chroniclers.

For those who had experienced hallucinogens, during the old-religion rituals, the culprits must have been obvious: witches. They supposedly assumed that witches were purposefully poisoning everybody. Even today, Basque language carries the word *sorgokari* that means stupefacient—linked to *sorgin*, witch. Not surprisingly it is also linked to *sorkari*, to create or generate. All those words are linked to sacred sex rituals, after which a *sorgingosari*, light meal after midnight, was taken. Not surprisingly either that the *sorgokari* allowed to see *sorkeria*, strange creatures, while being *sor* (stupefied, deaf, stun) under its effects. The people knew that witches could produce such drugs.

It has been suggested that ergot might have been used in the Mysteries, where consumption of bread, cereals and wine was common. Those suggestions may have been strengthened by modern lab-analysis of some bog mummies.

For instance, the Grabaulle Man, a body found in 1952 in Denmark, remarkably well preserved by the acidic bog, whose death took place about 2,100 years ago.

How did he die? His throat was cut from ear to ear. His skull was cracked and his chin fractured. Most probably, he would have died without any need of all that: the analysis of his intestines showed his last meal had been grain, totally contaminated with ergot, as the myriads of toxic, fungal spores unequivocally indicated. He must have suffered some convulsions first, and then passed through some hallucinatory phase.

Had he time enough to communicate his visions to the people around him? Could he tell them about some strange voices he was hearing? Or had his killers just to content themselves with observing his agonizing contortions? That was one of the favorite ways to foresee the future of the tribe, according to the widespread belief of those times. His hands, feet and mouth must have felt as if they were on fire. Then, numbness must have followed. Was he lucky enough to lose consciousness before being slain?

The scientists who studied his body and other mummies do not speak about executions. Sacrifice—it is their almost unanimous verdict.

Is it a coincidence that the word *rye*, the name of the ergot-fungus favorite cereal, also meant *king*? Was he a Hero or a substitute victim?

As that hallucinogen is also considered a strong aphrodisiac, was he induced to ritually mate with some priestesses prior to his killing? Or was he offered for some other reason?

Unfortunately, at those times, there was a hideous excess of religious motives for killing people—courts even condemned chickens, dogs, cats and other animals for sorcery. A lot of non-religious causes could also have triggered many deaths. Women and children have also been found in those bogs. In any case, the connection between ergot and witches is not that hard to see.

By the way, *sorcery* is said to come from French *sorcier,* which apparently came from Latin *sors* (lots, fortune). Did it really come from Latin? It is too close to the old Basque word.

Ergotism produced terrible, deadly epidemics in Europe well into our times. The first recorded major outbreak took place in the Rhine Valley in 857, costing thousands of lives. The thousands quoted are no exaggeration. It has been estimated that the terrifying one in 943, in Limoges, France, depopulated the region. They were all over Europe. France was terribly hit in 1039, 1595, and 1674. Germany suffered in 1581, 1587, 1592. They were endemic in Spain, where some notable epidemics took place in 1581 and 1590. It saved the Ottoman Empire from an expedition of Peter the Great in 1722. His horses started dying after eating infected rye. His troops became sick after consuming the bread.

Those were some of the most serious, widespread incidents. Minor cases, involving villages, or just families, were common everywhere, all the time. They must have caused not a few witch trials. Dates of epidemics and trial madness tend to coincide. In modern times, when the real culprits were known at last, rye bread was forbidden. Laws were not always obeyed. Russian peasants, for instance, were forced by hunger to consume it in

1926 and a terrible epidemic followed. Similar causes produced the last outbreak in France, in 1951. Economic crisis made peasants opt for illegal, cheaper rye bread. Three hundred became affected near Avignon. Thirty-one went mad. Four died.

In spite of all witch-hunts the Goddess cults went on until very few centuries back. Gabriel Tetzel of Nuremberg complained in the 15th century about the strong cult of the dead professed by Basque women. He deplored the "stone sepulchers which attract their interest," which were little in accord with the Roman Catholic Church practice. Especially because those Basque women still preferred those stone tombs to churches, which they avoided. In the Basque region the witch trials reached the 17th century. All the lands with a strong witch tradition also tend to show some notable Euzko heritage.

15

Our Own Stone Roots

Many Basque words for modern utensils still carry those roots meaning stone, for instance from *aitz* comes *azpil* (=round stone=dish). The Almogavars were famous for their skill in the use of the *azkona* (a throwing knife, devastating in their hands).

Saying that Basque language carry terms directly from the Stone Age may be misleading. *Because all languages carry terms from the Stone Age.* Everybody is a descendant of Stone-Age people—no matter the person, nation or culture.

Some existing languages, very widely spoken, were originated more or less recently. Spanish, French, Portuguese, Rumanian, for instance, were generated from Latin, some two millennia ago, when metal artifacts were already in use in the European regions where those tongues are spoken. In spite of their modernity, most present words in those languages carry some ancient Latin root, or another one that comes from some other old tongue. Languages are always evolving, being mixed up and reshaped, but some roots are very old. They have a peculiar staying power.

Have we some recognizable stone root in our present day language? The answer is yes. There are not a few examples, but a lot of them, revealing our not so remote stone past.

Would Commander James Bond use an *azkona*? Of course not! We all know that Mr. Bond prefers a Beretta pistol. Besides, Mr. Bond is a Scot. Scots never, ever use *azkonas*. They use *skeans*. That is the name for a Gaelic dagger used in Ireland and Scotland. What would a Scot shepherd do with such instrument? Well, he could use it to *skean* a sheep. Or shall we say *skin* a sheep? Was the *sk* sound of skean inherited from Irish and Scots ancestors, the Euzkos? The resemblance between *skean* and *azkona* would not go unnoticed for any linguist.

The fact is that the *sk* sound has been also independently identified in many roots in Indo-European languages that are far apart from the Basques. It carries a deep, old meaning. The Indo-European root *(s)ker* appears in a very distinctive group of words. Language specialists have long ago recognized that root in some word families. It appears with a remarkable high frequency in words meaning cutting. *Skean* (Irish, Scot), *skin* (English), Both Swedish *skära* and Danish *skære* mean to cut. In many words the *s* was dropped. So came the Latin *caedere* (strike, cut). With equal meaning evolved the French *couper* and the Spanish and Portuguese *cortar*, and the Italian *cortare*. That was also the origin of English *cut*. Comparative philologists tell us that in other group of words the root *(s)ker* became *sek* (Latin *secare*, Polish *siec* and Russian *sec* all mean cut). From that root also came French *scier*, saw, Spanish *segar*, mow. We say *segregate*, to cut off. That is also the use of a *sickle*.

Those are not the only families of words where that root *(s)ker* appears. It is also present in families meaning *shape* (from old English *gesceap*), in the sense of chipping off. With the same meaning: Swedish *skapnad*, Greek *schma*, Polish *ksztalt*, Danish *skikkelse*, Sanskrit *akara*, and, of course, in *sculpture*.

In a similar way, we say *scrape*. What was the origin of that peculiar root *(s)ker*? It is extremely old. It comes, linguists tell us, from thousands of years ago, when the Indo-European tribes had not yet split and dispersed themselves between Asia, Africa and Europe. When they still were one people. Long before they became Germans and Russians, Hindus and Persians, Portuguese and Swedish. The root has to be far older than that. Why? *Because it is also present in Basque words.*

It also appears in other languages, even farther apart than Basque, with slightly different sounds. They have been separated for many dozens of thousand years. At least that is what linguists, geneticists and archaeologists are sustaining. So, it was in use long *before* they became a separated people, with a very different language, through a long process of many thousands of years.

What can be the origin of that peculiar root (*s*)*ker*? Let's think hard. What sort of thing can be used to cut, to strike, to skin, to scrape, to shape, to sculpt? All that happened in prehistoric times, when the use of metals was still unknown. Is there any other solution to that riddle apart from the already evident one? There is only one possible answer—the stone.

That answer is revealing. It tells of an old love and hate history. To be more precise, let's better say an old love and hate prehistory. All of us have some peculiar common habits that defy time. One of them is a critical part of hour human legacy. It is our fondness to invent names. That is to assign a symbolic sound or gesture to a thing or activity, and then to extend it to other things of activities with a similar meaning. A good example can be that sound of the stone: the *sk* sound becoming both the act of skinning and the skin. By analogy (and we are entering the symbolic mind of our beloved common ancestor, the Stone-Age Man) to the surface of an animal, the skin, we *skim* the surface of liquids and *scrape* surfaces of other materials. Is there actually any difference between scrapping and *shaping* a stone? But the love-hate story came later.

Another force shaping languages is the exchange of words between different communities. It serves the purpose of specialization. It brings a clearer perception.

Let's see a modern example. French nationalists are presently protesting frenetically against the increased use of English words in their language. They resent it very much. Wasted efforts, it is a losing battle, given the cultural influence of English speaking groups in many areas. They have gained that influence by their preeminence. On the other hand who would use a different word than the French *bouquet* when talking about wines?

The French resent the use of English words like *market*, whose use denotes the strong U.S.A. influence in their economy (they actually resent *that* influence much more than the English words). They should not complain. After all *market* is a borrowed word in English. It comes from the French *marché*. Which, of course, denotes the dominant power not so long ago. And about resentment, ask the Saxons how they felt when they heard *marché* and many other strange words from the people who accompanied good king William the Conqueror. *Oui*. But thanks to that word *market*, and in spite of what ultranationalists say, French people now have a new perception. They use *market* when they speak about investing in stock and *marché* when they are interested in *baguettes* and *bon vin*. It is the same word, in essence, but different when applied to different activities—the same concept, with a slight variation.

The clearer perception is useful for any human community. Make a mistake in the *market* and bye, bye, *baguettes et le bon vin*.

Through that phenomenon of exchange, French citizens got those *cognate* words, *market* and *marché*.

Cognate means of the same origin. The French and English languages are also cognate. Both are Indo-European tongues. It is interesting to observe the process involved in the use of *market* and *marché* by the French. First, it was the same word, *marché* at both sides of the channel, which through time and isolation, through a small alteration in sound, became another word: *market*.

It requires separation and time, the English channel, and then fusion, through exchange and commerce.

Whenever cognate words appear, they point to those same events taking place: togetherness, separation, togetherness—the love-hate history.

For instance, the voices *fatherly* and *paternal*, another cognate pair, point to a common source, another history of both common heritage and a period of separation. Both words come from the mother word *pater*, akin to the Sanskrit *pitar*. Same words, same meaning, but they traveled different paths. One reached us through old German, *fatar*, and the other one via the Latin *pater*. Those two words mark immediately the influence in our family structure and thought of both the German and Latin cultures.

We have cognate words. We also have cognate cultures. Just the same as Italians, Spaniards, and the French are cognate with the English. Interestingly, many, many thousands of years before those people were still one, eons before all they were sharing the same culture, long *before they appeared as a human group with a separate culture* from other non-Indo-European ones, there were other already old love-hate stories—or prehistories. We also have cognate sounds. Or, from the cultural viewpoint, cognate roots. Actually, stone roots.

What sounds are cognate with that ancient, prehistoric *sk*?

What was the meaning of that sound, the multiple faced *sk*? Only one possibility: the *st*one. And, yes, the *st* sound means just that: stone (Basque *aitz*, Greek *stia'*, pebble, *stear'*, stiff, Sanskrit *stya*, stiffen, Czechoslovakian *stena*, wall, Servocroatian *stijena*, rock, Swedish and Danish *sten*, Rumanian *stinca*, Dutch *steen*). Some languages kept the *sk* root: Polish, *skala*, Bohemian and Russian *skala*, Lithuanian, *skelti*, split, Sanskrit *çila*). Latin conserved the *sk* root in *saxum*, large stone, rock (from it comes the Italian *sasso*) and also in a very revealing word, linking high-tech from the past with today know-how: *acer*, Latin for sharp (from it, Spanish *acero*, steel). *Nihil novum sub soli*. The *st* appears in words meaning stone, solid, *stiff, steady, stable, stand, cast, dust*. Philologists have long ago pointed that origin. Also in words implying *striking*: *stamp, stomp*. Cutting: *stave, stiletto*. From all those stone sounds to *steel* it is just a matter of time.

Specialists in Indo-European tongues have long reached the conclusion that all those terms are linked to *stone*. What we need is to recognize that the word stone is also linked to the stone. It is that sound, *st,* that keeps reminding us of it. Not only the *st,* but also the *sk*. They are cognate sounds. It is a fascinating story. Thanks to it, we know that in an incredibly remote past, our ancestors were one, then they separated, and finally became linked again. We have inherited sounds, through many words, from both groups. There are other cognate sounds denouncing the stone. All of them point to penetrating or cutting instruments, and imply striking or smashing: *speck, spear, spade, spike, spata, spud, spado, spall, splinter, spank, spur, splash, split, spay.* So the love-hate story happened more than once.

When did those separations and fusion or contacts took place?

It would be very romantic to think about Neandertals and Cromagnons splitting and then getting in good terms again. The trouble is, there is no certainty that Neandertals could even speak.

At a recent congress there was a dispute about the position of the hyoids: did it allow them to speak? According to a journalist, scientists were at each other's throats on that subject. Conclusion: maybe they were able to speak, maybe not. Given the many surprising aspects of the Neandertal culture—they had musical instruments, ornaments and a religious cult of the dead—it is highly improbable that they could not speak. It would be surprising that even much older hominids had not been able to do it, as some of their very complex skills imply. The fact is, we are considering a subject that covers such an immense interval of time that many things could have happened.

The lapses in consideration could be nearly a hundred thousand years or maybe some hundreds of thousands. Hundred thousands? *We could be speaking of millions of years.*

When we speak about the Stone Age we tend to think mostly in terms of the time immediately preceding the metal period—the short Neolithic. Stones have been with us longer than that. The Leakeys in Africa found chipped-off stones in deposits that were much older than two million years.

Did it start that way? Was that chipping-off sound what inspired everything? *Tsk, tsk.* Who knows? Nevertheless it is a very tempting possibility. Some stone hits other stone—its sound becomes some onomatopoeic names.

The first use of the stone, archaeologists and anthropologists are telling us, was probably to *scare* animals away. The poor beasts had no choice but to *escape*. From that first tool high-tech arrived: stones used as hammers, the first tool-making tools, were used to produce stone-knives. And, let's not forget, *axes*. (Should we say a*k*ses?). Let's not forget a good *zax* either. From there we got *skins* and *skeletons*. Losing an s, Latins used this word meaning flesh: *caro* (Spanish and Portuguese *carne*. The English cognate is extremely significant: *carrion*). We now hate carrion and prefer roast-beef. Our grand-grand-etc.-grandpas were not so exquisite, we are told, and were good as scavengers.[*]

If we want to inspect really startling coincidences, let's consider this: one of the root sounds that have struck linguists for decades is *skeu*. Why? It links very dissimilar concepts: darkness, concealing, cover, take shelter. Now, is it a coincidence that the root *skeu* is so close to (*s*)*ker*? From *skeu* comes hide, which both means skin and conceal. If that is not a mere coincidence, then we might be looking at some of our most ancient ancestors (perhaps!). In order to link *skins* to *shadows*, we must consider people living in an arid, hot environment, where there were no trees to proportion *cover* (Yes, it comes from the same root!) where *skins* were the only *shelter* to protect from an unforgiving sun. Where *hides* offered the only chance to *hide* or *cover* something. *Skin, hide, cover, shelter, shadows*. All cognate. Are *skin* and *hide* cognate words? Everything points that way. The probable source?

---

[*] scavenger is a new word, or rather a new usage of an old word. Apparently it comes from Middle English *scauager*, from Anglo-Norman *scawager*, toll collector. Maybe some ancestor used it in our modern sense, but we cannot clasify it with *carrion, caro* or *carne*

Some sound similar to *sk* must have been the ancestor word. Most important of all: those sounds have stayed with us. For that to happen, for those terms to survive through eons, there must have been a real need of all that for a long, long time—without a chance of getting *cover*, *shelter* and *shadow* in any other way.

Today anthropologists are pointing to the birth of humanity, a period when a region East of the Riff Valley in Africa became drier. Some apes adapted to it, losing some hair in their skin, perfecting their walking skills and posture to get through the savanna, getting plenty of sweat glands to be able to stand the heat (only ones among all apes and monkeys who perspire, as anyone who jumps into a subway wagon at the rush hour in summer can attest). Some scientists point to a scavenging past, prior to becoming hunters. They speculate that *both* scavenging and hunting must have required the stone. Languages are apparently reflecting all that past. Maybe those sounds were originated not that long ago—maybe not millions, but necessarily implying an extraordinarily long permanence in an arid region at the time language was being born. It happened at a very distant past anyway. Did those sounds originate a few hundred thousand years ago? Are we talking about a *million* years? It is very difficult to know if there will ever be an answer to these and other questions.

While hunting for stone words in different languages a genealogical tree could be constructed. Looking for the differences and similitude in stone words, their geographical distribution, the time of departure or splitting apart of different ethnic groups could bring an answer about the ancestral sound used for stone. It would be always only an educated guess, because the period of the stone culture is so, so long that we will probably have no real way to discern the actual first words.

A genial linguist, the late Joseph Greenberg, created a clear model of the evolution of African languages. He also left a more controversial model for the distribution of American languages before Columbus. Even if his models have been questioned, the American one in particular, geneticists, historians

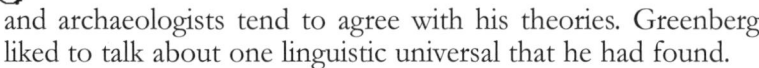

and archaeologists tend to agree with his theories. Greenberg liked to talk about one linguistic universal that he had found.

The sound is rooted in one gesture. The universal symbol—a finger signals "one".

Resonances of the primordial sound can be find in the Greek "daktylos" (finger). In Latin is "digitus". In Nilo-Saharan is "tok, tek and dik" for the number one. It is the Indo-European root *deik* (meaning to show or point, as in in*dic*ate). Greenberg postulated that the original word had been *dik*. It was his most concrete guess about a word in the original human language.

Maybe some symbolic sounds started with an attempt to imitate the sound of stone-chipping. *Tsk, tsk.* Anyone trying that will end with various sounds. No wonder that root *(s)ker* developed later in so many ways. Was it *tsk*? Or could have been *skr*? After all it explains *skinning* and *carrion*, the *kr* that ended in Latin *caro*, could have turned *rk*, giving us *rock*. It seems wild, but the fact is that the spectrum of stone sounds is far wider than those two—much wider, and not so wilder. Sometimes it could be what has been common in languages all around the world: an exchange or evolution between *r* and *l*. A wild guess? Maybe, but a *killing* one. Did that make something *click*? Yeah, there we have another branch of our family tree. What a family! The *kr* turns into *kl* and bingo! A lot of words *clanking, clonking, clashing* and *clacking* of stones, cutting, *clubbing, clipping,* talking to us of objects used to *cleaver,* to *clear* forests, to *claw*. People trying to *climb* or *clamber cliffs*. You can bet they would try to *step* on a *cleat* to avoid falling down on *clinkers* or on a *clod*. Perhaps they prefer to go through *cloughs*. What can *clink* better than a stone? *Clatter, clay, clastic, clava, cleavage, clap, clank, clink*. It is *clobbering*. What in the sea resembles a stone better than a *clam*? And that *kill*? An interesting proposition: let's try to pronounce it without the *i*. The sound will be identified by anyone as the same. Tempting? Was that the primordial sound? *Scaring*. Were *cloaks* and *clothes* made from *hides*? And be *careful*, but not *scared*, all this stone-*chipping* will not *chop* your head off. Yes, we keep meeting long lost members of our extensive stone-family-tree all over the way. Maybe all this *clipping* will take the *chips* from our shoulders. By the way, or by the *shoulder*, are they not telling us that our ancestors used both stones and bones for similar purposes? What an occurrence! Who on earth would use *spines, skulls, scapula, claws* or any other part of any *skeleton* as *cleavers* or *clubs*!

What a beautiful love-story. Our forefathers may be long lost, but their words still *clink hard.*

16

An Astonishing Map

How far did those Euzko ancestors extend themselves? Arana Goiri left a long list of places and peoples that could be connected with the Euzkos. It covered all of Europe, and a good part of adjacent regions. He believed, for instance, that the Vosgos Mountains had gotten their name from them. (Vosgos is phonetically close to Basques).

Some readers may find Arana Goiri's ideas an outrageous proposition. If so, they are in for a big surprise. *Modern scholars have a present image of old Europe that surpasses even the wildest of Arana Goiri's concepts.*

How have they come to such novel conclusions? Because they have used the same tool than Arana Goiri and other Basque intellectuals had a century ago. They used it in exactly the same way. They just considered *ancient European names.*

Basque was the original language of the continent. That was the title from an article in the May issue in 2002 from *Spectrum of the Science*—the German edition of *Scientific American* magazine. Elizabeth Hamel and Theo Vennemann, two German scientists, presented to the readers some of the front lines of linguistic thought.

They believe that—a few thousand years ago—people that spoke languages linked to Basque occupied most of the continent. To understand their extraordinary conclusion readers need only to go to a map. They will notice what was said about Pelasgians and Etruscans in these pages—what ancient authors mentioned all the time—the singularities of certain geographic names that appear in many different countries.

Hamel and Venneman point, for instance, to what had been considered an authentic German name: Ebersberg—a pre-Alpine town on the Ebrach river. The name has a clear meaning in German: mount or mountain of the boar (Eberg = boar, berg = mount, mountain). The shield of the town shows a boar. It is not the only one with that name: the German post-office registers seven municipalities with the name Ebersberg. There are also nine Ebersdorf and sixteen Ebersbach. Hamel and Venneman counted no less than eighty cities whose names included *Eber*—all supposedly coming from boar.

Any traveler can assume that all those names came from the abundance of boars in those places. That supposition starts to fail once boundaries are crossed.

The same root is found in many places all over Europe. From Britain to Scandinavian countries, from Spain to Italy, even in Ukraine names that can be linked to *eber* abounds.

In France, for instance, some of the names that linguists link to *eber* are: *Ebréon, Ibarolle, Evrune, Ivry, Averdon, Avricourt, Avrolle* and *Yvré*. Then the problem appears. Because the word that means boar in French is *sanglier*, not *eber*. The same happens in many other places, with other languages. The same root *eber* keeps appearing, but it is unreasonable to link that word to boars. It also appears in the Iberian Peninsula—a place that no Indo-Europeans reached before the names were given to places. Take the *Ebro* River—called *Iberus* by the Romans. They called Iberi the people living near it. It gave the name to the whole peninsula.

So, where does the root *eber* come from? Linguists have pointed that all those places are rivers or close to rivers. In Basque *ibai* means river, *ibara-ibarra* mean field near a river, valley. The Basques were living by the Ebro at Roman times.

Ibar is exactly de name of a river in Montenegro and Servia. There are two *Ebrach* in southern Germany—also many rivers called *Eberbäche*. *Ibra* is the name of a river in Oberaula, Hessen.

For more than a century, some scientists had noticed that there were common names all over Europe. They were recognized as "fossil" names. Linguists tried in vain to link them to Indo-European tongues. After their failure it was logical to attribute them to some vanished population.

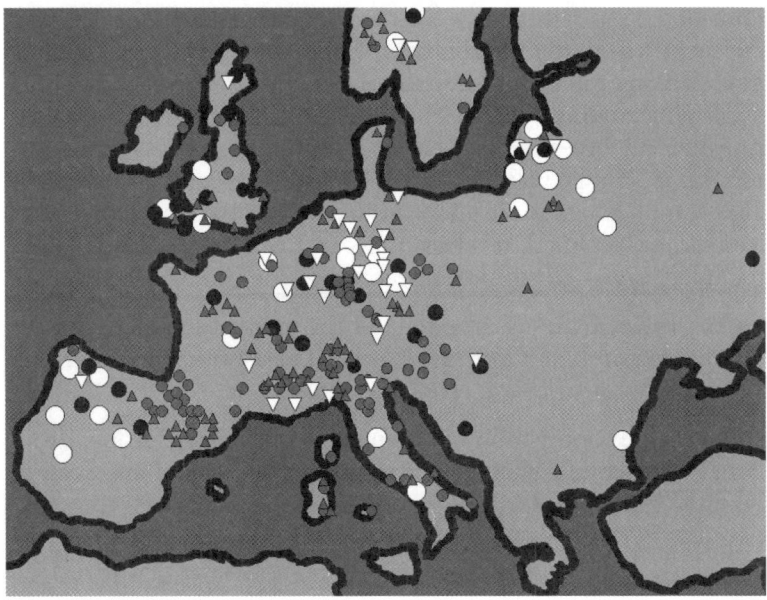

Fig. 35. Water currents in Europe that include Basque linguistic elements in their names. ○ Names with *Al-/Alm-* ▽ Names with *Var-/Ver-* ▲ Names with *Is-* ● Names with *Sal-/Salm-* ◉ Names with *Ur-,* after E. Hamel, T. Vennemann, *Spectrum of the Science,* p 32, May 2002

Suddenly scientists are observing what Arana-Goiri and other Euzko thinkers had noticed. This time the linguists are armed with more precise tools and a vast pool of data and historical knowledge. They use statistical analysis and computers to obtain a clearer view. They think that the people who first came to a place tended to name it for its characteristics. So a river was called that—a river.

Hamel and Vennemann points that many European rivers have short names. There is a striking coincidence between those names and words connected with water in the Euskera—*ur/aur, var/ver, sal/salm, al/alm,* and *is/eis.* (*Ur* = water in Euzkera. *Ura* = water, water current, *is* has a similar meaning).

Hamel and Vennemann quote some of the rivers with *ur*: Urula (Norway); Irwell (Great Britain); Ourthe (Belgium); Auerbach, Urbach, Urach, Aurach (Germany); Irrsee (Austria); Aroffe (former Urofia), Huriel (France); Urura, Urora (Spain); Urwiss (Poland); Ura (Russia). With *is*: Iselfjorden (Norway); Isa (Italy); Isainka (Russia); Iesla (Lithuania); Jizera (Czech); Ijssel (Holland); Ismaning (former Isamaninga), Isen (former Isana); Eisolzried (former Isoltesried) (Germany); Isen, Isel (Switzerland)

They give river names in Germany: with *var/ver*: Warne, Werre, Warmenau, Warme Aue; and also with *sal*: Saale, Sale, Salz (former Salusia), Selke (former Salica); or with *al*: Aller, Alm, two Alme (formers Almana and Almara), Ahla, Elke (former Alantia), Elz. They also mention rivers in the Iberian Peninsula: Alba, Alenza, Almar, Almanza, Almonte, and Almantes.

A map (Fig. 35), covering some of the river names—which include the quoted linguistic elements—gives a surprising vision of the extent of the Basque population in prehistoric Europe. It covers practically all the continent.

Were they really Euzkera names? The cathedra of Theoretical Germanistic and Linguistic Studies under Venneman analyzed the river names in Germany. More than half of them start with a vowel. The *a* is the most common starting vowel (the name frequently often includes additional *a*'s). Names starting with *i* or *u* are also common. That is not the frequency expected in ancient Indo-European names, where names starting with a vowel were scarce, and the most common vowels were *e* and *o*. The analysis pointed to a Basque origin of the words.

River names are not the only geographical elements that linguists have found which have a Basque inheritance. Many places all over Europe, for instance, carry the Euzkera word *aran* (valley): Arundel (Great Britain); Arendal (both Norway and Sweden); there are dozens of Arnach, Arnsberg, Arnstern, Arensburg, and Ahrensburg in Germany, also including the

Ohrenbach (former Aranbach) and the Morhenstein (former Marstein = in the Arnstein.)

Vennemann does not believe that München means "a place where monks live." He thinks it also came from Basque. *Munica* was the original word, in his opinion. It means riverside platform—coming from Euzkera *bun* (slope, mound, hillock). It points to the original place of the city—the Petersbergl hill, close to the *Isar*. So, it seems that Euzkos were the original founders of the notable, ancient capital of Baviera.

Linguistic analyses are enlarging the list of Basque original words. They are discovering that Euzkera roots are not only hidden in geographical names but also in many words of current language. Linguists have argued for years that it is the origin of the word *land*, for instance.

More surprises are coming. Linguists have discovered in Western Europe many examples of influx of Camito-Semitic tongues. It probably means that peoples speaking this tongues migrated northbound along the western coast.

While all these scientific developments took place in the fields of linguistics and prehistory, other developments are beginning to back those modern views. Not surprisingly, the new understanding came from the study of a far, far more ancient language. One that we all are still used to talk, even if we never notice it.

The analysis of what is left in us of that old, old language has pointed to an amazing notion: for some scientists there is no problem in considering the Etruscans or the Pelasgians as Euzkos. For them, *most of the modern Europeans are still Euzkos.*

17

The Oldest Language

Until just a few years ago there was an accepted version of the occupation of Europe by Homo Sapiens Sapiens.

According to it, different waves of hunter-gatherers came first—most probably from Asia. They got in touch with the Neandertals and finally replaced them. The Basque ancestors came among these intruders. Then, after the end of the Glacial Age, some agricultural tribes, the Aryan wave, came from Asia. The farmers slowly replaced most of the hunter-gatherers. Their farming techniques also originated a population explosion.

The study of some language characteristics has changed all that. Which language? It is considered the oldest one. Scientists deciphered it only a few decades ago. Neither archaeologists nor linguists broke its code. Biologists did it. It is the language that cells use to talk to themselves and to each other—the genetic code. Cells use it to pass their characteristics to their descendants.

Curiously enough, in a continent where the alternating modes of the male-female relationship have been historically so important, genetic investigators have centered their search in genes that are passed from woman to woman and from man to man.

Scientists trying to establish a philogenetic tree use as search tool the mitochondrial DNA (mtDNA) inherited only from mothers, and certain segment of the male Y chromosome, that is given only from the father.

In 1967, Allan Wilson and Vincent Sarich shook the human family tree. They claimed, based on immunological comparisons of serum albumins, that humans, chimpanzees, and gorillas had a common ancestor five million years ago. At that time paleoanthropologists had already settled on a common ancestor about fifteen million years ago or more. They strongly resented the invasion of their domain by outsiders and fiercely challenged it. Nevertheless, most anthropologists now accept human emergence taking place some five to eight million years ago.

DNA allows a more direct, closer look into our genes than the proteins. So, when maternal mtDNA became an accepted research tool, scientists started to use it to study human evolution. Allan Wilson (posthumously), Rebeca Cann and Mark Stoneking published their results in a 1987 article in *Nature— Mitochondrial DNA and Human Evolution*. Studying the mtDNA from 134 individuals from different places of the world they concluded we all came from a genetic "Eve". They concluded that "Eve" had most probably lived in Africa some 150,000-200,000 years ago. It means that our ancestors first displaced or replaced our older hominid relatives from Africa and later continued that process in other continents.

Some scientists have challenged the mathematics and the conclusions of that research. In spite of the original questioned methodology, reanalysis of the original data showed that the Out-of-Africa model was weakened, but not rejected. The dating of Eve—based on that study and also other data—is now in the 100,000-230,000 years ago. Not much difference from the original conclusions.

Good for Africa. What happened in Europe?

A team of scientists, mostly from Great Britain and Germany, tried to find the answer to that question. Martin Richards, H. Corte-Real, P. Forster, V. Macauley, H. Wilkinson-Herbots, A. Demaine, S. Papiha, R. Hedges, Hans Jürgen Bandelt and Bryan

Sykes published their results in the *American Journal of Human Genetics* in 1996: *Palaeolithic and neolithic lineages in the European mitochondrial gene pool*. They had found that practically all Europeans could trace their origins to one of only seven mutant mtDNA categories. They could also estimate the antiquity of each mutant mtDNA category sampled in the continent. And then, a most surprising fact emerged from all data. Against the belief that most Europeans were the descendants from farmers coming from the Middle East only a few thousand years ago—the so called Indo-Europeans or Aryans—they established that only one type of mtDNA had come into Europe during the last ten thousand years. It is present in only 15-20% of the European population, the variations depending on the zone. It all meant that most Europeans, 80-85% of them, were descendants of *people who had been there before the Indo-Europeans arrived*. They all descended from the other six types of mtDNA. It was a shock for all those who had been studying the genetics of human population.

That study brought a considerable amount of arguments and tensions in congresses—at least for a time. The final coup came with another study. It concerned the male genes—the Y chromosome.

Scientists from Italy, USA, and Eastern Europe carried out that research with the Y chromosome and published it in *Science (november10, 2000)*. *The genetic legacy of Paleolithic Homo Sapiens in extant Europeans: a Y chromosome perspective* by Semino O, Passarino G, Oefner PJ, Lin AA, Arbuzova S, Beckman LE, De Benedictis G, Francalacci P, Kouvatsi A, Limborska S, Marcikiae M, Mika A, Mika B, Primorac D, Santachiara-Benerecetti AS, Cavalli-Sforza LL, Underhill PA. They studied the Y chromosomes from 1007 men from 25 regions in Europe and the Middle East. They concluded that practically all men fell into ten chromosome categories. The differences among them were mutations. After calculating the probable antiquity of each mutation, they established that approximately 80% of all men had a Paleolithic ascendancy and only some 20% of the chromosomes were as young as necessary to indicate some Neolithic newcomers.

Both the male and female genetic materials indicated the same: *most Europeans descend from Paleolithic ancestors*. Hunter-gatherers who were there long before the Indo-Europeans arrived with their new life styles. It is very interesting to see that using two different techniques the investigators reached the same conclusions. That helped a lot to strengthen the new proposition. Even more, different teams of researchers usually use different genetic markers whose characteristics are not usually easily revealed to competing scientists. So, even studying the same chromosomes, different genetic trees are built. In spite of all those technical differences, the same overall conclusion emerged: the Indo-European genes proportion rarely passes the 15-20% in most regions.

The Oxford team who had used mtDNA to build the tree had felt a little unease about those 15-20% of genes attributed to newcomers. Supposedly they came with farmers from the East. But, did they really? According to that supposition, the percentage of appearance of that Neolithic mutation should be considerably greater in eastern regions. They had a number of samples from people from Saudi Arabia. They tested their mtDNA. The results closed the argument. That mutation, which only shows in 15-20% of European mtDNA, appeared in about 50% percent of the Saudis tested.

While about just one in six Europeans showed that Indo-European marker, one of every two Saudis had it. *There had been an invasion from people from the East in Neolithic times.* Genetics and archaeology were in good agreement there. Something that those scientists did not point, but central to this book, is that *the invasion coincided with the gradual decrease in women's rights in European cultures. That decrease also took place from East to West.*

What about the Basques? A team from the University College in London, for instance, wanted to study the genes of Celtic populations. They assumed men living in Castlerea, in central Ireland, and Anglesey, North Wales, could represent the original inhabitants of Britain—no foreign people invaded those regions. They established that *Y chromosomes of Celtic populations were practically identical with those of the Basques*—"statistically indistinguishable" was the verdict. The Celtic-speaking men, since genetically very close to the Basques, must also be drawn from the original Paleolithic inhabitants of Europe, and probably represent the first modern human inhabitants of Britain who settled the islands some 10,000 years ago. The genetic study confirmed the strong cultural link between them. Asterix was a Celt and a Basque at the same time. Both people were genetically identical.

The reason of that connection between Basques and Celts was evident for those studying their genes. They thought it was a consequence of the climatic conditions in Europe at the time of Homo Sapiens Sapiens arrival.

How did all these Homo Sapiens Sapiens enter into Neandertal Europe?

The variability of the glatial climate had produced hard, extremely cold periods. It caused large migrations of fauna, which moved away from the ice-covered north and central Europe to its southern areas. Similarly, the herds of animals that had inhabited the warm areas of south Europe moved farther south, towards the areas of North Africa and Asia. Then, when conditions improved, fauna and flora replenished themselves, and men followed them.

In Nature, such retreat-advance conditions usually favor the apparition of opportunistic invading species.

It was probably during one of the last interstadial warming episodes of the Würm Glaciation that one of those opportunistic species—modern Homo Sapiens Sapiens—entered Europe.

Both the archaeological finds and the modern DNA analysis (results obtained both through the maternal mtDNA and the paternal Y chromosome techniques) agree on the time of their entry—35,000 to 40,000 years ago. There was a warm episode about 40,000 years ago. It lasted a few centuries. Then another warm interval started about 38,500 years ago, lasting nearly three millennia. One that lasted some 1,500 years started some 35,000 years ago. They could have followed all the animals that entered to graze in the new available pastures.

The DNA studies show that first Homo Sapiens Sapiens entered from the East and spread through Central and Western Europe. It was the Aurignacian culture. They used bone tools and blade flint technology, with scrapers and burins. Their descendents represent about 50% of today European genes. Of course, they predominate among the Basques. They were the tall Cromagnons—taller but less muscular than the Neandertals.

If we owe Neandertals for the great cultural symbolic explosion, these newcomers added a new cultural dimension. They kept tabs on the seasonal changes and the lunations. They were aware of time in a grand scale. The first symbolic *writing* was theirs.

They exhibited typical dolichocephalic, pentagon-shaped skulls, as many of today Basques. In France, their rests were associated with the Cromagnon finds. Blowing pigments through a tube, they left the negative print of their hands in the walls of caves, one of the first artistic manifestations in every continent. Female genitalia are also shown in those cave walls, in sketched figures or in some tridimensional rough sculptures.

Their carvings in bones, antlers and ivory were so numerous that the Aurignacian is known as the *Ivory Period*. *The first personal ornaments were found in layers associated with them.*

Maybe aided by the implacable climate, maybe for other reasons, but the Cromagnons completely replaced (or displaced) the Neandertals after the coldest episode of the last glacial period. In many archaeological sites, objects typical of the Aurignacian culture of the Cromagnon suddenly replaced those of the Mousterian culture of Neandertal man.

What happened to the Cromagnons? The Basques exhibit the highest frequency of the M173 (haplogroup R1b) associated with them. The frequency of R1b decreases from west to east, being virtually absent near the Ukraine. On the other hand, the other marker associated with the Cromagnons, Haplogroup R1a is more frequent in the East and it is virtually absent in Western Europe. Its frequency increases eastward and reaches a maximum in Poland, Hungary, and Ukraine. R1a is indicative of "Viking blood" when seen in the British Isles.

Where is it possible to find a Cromagnon today? Can the reader touch a Cromagnon? Of course!! Nothing can be easier than that. Almost any reader of European ancestry needs only to extend one hand… and then touch the other hand. No need to worry about left or right hand. It is a more than safe bet that nearly half the chromosomes from the cells of both hands might be of Cromagnon origin.

How can anyone be so sure of that?

It is pure statistics. Those genetic markers tied to the Cromagnons are from the segment of the Y chromosome *that does not recombine*. That makes that segment precious to follow our genetic history and evolution. As it is passed from male to male intact (except for some spontaneous mutations that allow geneticists to date them) the Y chromosome allows the construction of an ancestry tree. The female mtDNA markers do not recombine either—allowing a maternal tree. But *all other genes do recombine at each generation*. That allows an incredible shuffle and reshuffle of genes. *They spread around and mix all over.* As humans have in the order of 30,000 genes simple statistics apply. About half the genes of most Europeans must be Cromagnon ones. But wait, that assumption would be valid *only if it is accepted that Cromagnons mixed with other people...*

Did they?

That brings us back to the rest of the story. According to genetic analysis a second wave of gene markers arrived with some tribes from the Middle East 20,000 to 25,000 years ago. They are associated with the Gravettian culture. The new tribes could have entered, for instance, favored by a warm phase during that glaciation. It started about 24,000 years ago and lasted a millennium. Maybe a few tribes got into the continent in two prior shorter interstadial warming intervals that took place 28,000 and 29,000 years ago. These genetic markers are most frequent in central Eastern Europe and also occur in Basques and Sardinians. These genes are believed to have been common within Viking populations.

The Gravettians gave us most of those splendid Venus figurines. The Venus in the cover of this book belongs to them. Among other refinements, they already knew about ceramics—the baked clay Venus from Dolní Vestonice (25,000 years ago).

Geneticists tell that members of the Aurignacian and Gravettian cultures *did mix*—as told by the analysis of today European genes. *Almost all Europeans have genes from both groups.* These genes also tell an additional terrible story.

It is a magnificent example of stories being written in the DNA—before any other symbolic record could be kept. That frightening DNA tale is also a good example of the implacability of the glacial conditions. The study that linked Celtic and Basque genes showed a surprising *uniformity* of Y chromosomes—a genetic bottleneck.

Some stressing, catastrophic episode had reduced the population to a few families—decreasing the genetic diversity.

Scientists believe that all those modern European genes come at best from *no more than a thousand prehistoric individuals*—the scarce survivors of the rigors of the Ice Age. Maybe that is an *optimistic* evaluation. The researchers knew that *as few as fifty individuals* could have brought the same statistical results in the genes of their descendants.

Does that make clear what the Ice Age meant? It left at most only a few hundred survivors struggling with the unforgiving climate in Europe—in Spain and in an area of the northern Balkans. The tragedy happened during the Last Glacial Maximum (LGM, the peak of the Ice Age, from 20,000 to 13,000 years ago)

The new DNA evidence suggests that those few hundred survivors of Stone Age hunter-gatherers were the ancestors of many modern day northern Europeans.

One theory is that the population expanded from those two small enclaves to the rest of Europe once the present warm stage began. It is the cause of the surprising uniformity of the genes of the European population. Most of them descend from those scarce survivors.

It explains why all Europe is covered with prehistoric names with the same linguistic roots—akin to the Basque—Euzko names everywhere. It also explains the religious homogeneity that had astounded Robert Graves and others.

A few female-structured Paleolithic families survived and spread all around. The public sacred coupling ceremony at the center of so many ancient societies could point to their Ice Age rituals. Maybe twice a year the people of the villages stopped their hard daily toil to celebrate their most cherished and respected feast. Then came the precious moment, as they joyfully watched the just chosen King copulating with their Queen-Priestess. At certain times it must have been a Romeo and Juliet age couple, in a naked celebration of the most important subject for any people at the border of extinction: the continuity of life..

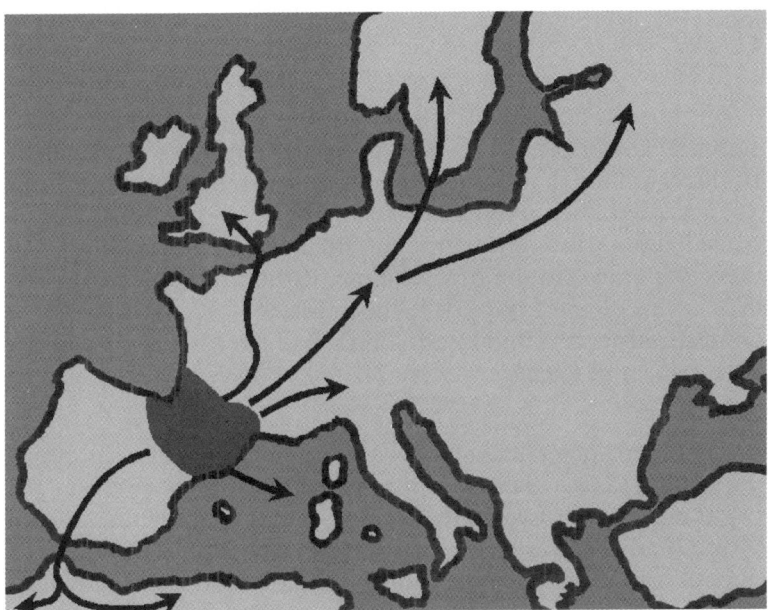

Fig. 36. According to geneticists, people from Spain and France living near the Pyrenees repopulated the west and north of Europe, after the Last Glacial Maximum, after E. Hammel, P. Forster, *Investigación y Ciencias,* p 68, Jan, 2003

Then the third wave came from the East—Indo-Europeans or Aryans. The genetic history agrees with the dates of the archaeologists. They started coming some 8,000 to 10,000 years ago. The critical struggle of their entrance and the cultural shocks were described in former chapters.

How could so few Indo-Europeans impose their language and customs over almost all Euzkan Europe? Their genes scarcely reached some 15-20%. A much modern invasion history in South and Central America is a good example. A small number of Spanish and Portuguese invaders imposed their language and culture over huge numbers of native people.

Another example? A relatively small number of Arabs imposed their language and religion over the numerous Copt-speaking people in Egypt in the 8th century A.D. The difference at that time between speaking Copt or Arab was just a little more tax. In just one generation Copt was a dead language—with the only exception of the minority Christian Copt Church—only their priests speak the ancient language of the Pharaohs today.

All those genetic analysis have confirmed the former supposition in this book that Etruscans and Pelasgians were Euzkos. If, disregarding all the notable cultural links, that supposition is not accepted, then the hypothesis of the *vanished tribes* should be considered—tribes that brought their genes and culture and then evaporated in the mist of time, without leaving any genetic or archaeological trace. It is much easier to accept what some linguists, historians and mythologists had already proposed, that Pelasgians and Etruscans were related peoples—related also to the Basques.

The small percentage of Neolithic genes in the European population also makes clear that racial theories in vogue at the beginning of the twentieth century—used as a justification of World War II—were senseless. It explains the present refusal of scientists to recur to racial models. They found them unreal. It also shows the formidable impact of culture in human society—its influence transcending any genetic frontier.

In the introduction of this book there was a curious affirmation. Just like in the *Asterix* stories, some people had thought that Basques had traveled to America. Is that possible?

There was no proven connection between Europeans and America before Columbus. Right?

Wrong.

It seems that a lot of people from Asia, Africa and Europe had discovered America, before Columbus, before the Vikings and before writing was invented. Interestingly, Asterix is portrayed as an ancestor of the French people, and yes, the Paleolithic Columbus seems to have sailed from some point in the French coast.

The story starts in 1933. Diggers unearthed a flint spearhead at Clovis, New Mexico. It was beside a mammoth skeleton. The spearhead was distinctive because it had two faces, where flakes had been knapped away from a core flint. They dated it as from 11,500 years ago. Soon similar spearheads were found in 48 of the USA states. It became an archaeological icon. It was considered the oldest evidence of human occupation of the continent.

The Clovis point later brought a bitter debate. A few archaeologists claimed finds much older than them. Their colleagues firmly denied those finds. The scientific community ostracized the finders. Another complication became evident some decades later. Assuming that man had entered the Americas using the Asian-American connection of the Behring strait, where were similar spearheads in Alaska and Asia? None was found.

Two prominent archaeologists, Dennis Stanford and Bruce Bradley looked around for examples of the stone workers style—the unmistakable off flakes produced by their peculiar spear point making. They found them—*not in Asia, but in France.* A rummage through the unattractive flint off-cuts in the storerooms of a French museum convinced Bradley of the similarities of the technique. A remarkable society had discarded those typical flint byproducts. It was the most innovative and adaptive of the time: the Solutrean people.

Stanford thinks that people connected with them left the south west of France and traveled to America. They had implements and technology very similar to that of today Inuit Eskimo. The Inuit manage to travel long open sea routes in their small traditional open boats. They still prefer them to modern boats. They made their boats with wood, sealskin and whale oil. These seemingly fragile vessels are extraordinarily resilient and easily maintained, and they can tolerate seas and weather conditions much better than modern boats.

The Eskimo also consider their typical, impermeable, skin suits better than any other garment to survive the Arctic extreme conditions. Clothing makers from Barrow, Alaska, could find no difference between their classical bone needles with those of Solutreans.

So. Solutreans could have crossed the Atlantic—crossing from iceberg to iceberg—in a typical Inuit sea travel.

The final proof of ancient European visitors came from another field.

Using mtDNA, Douglas Wallace mapped the geographical ancestry of all the Native American peoples back to Siberia and northeast Asia. His dates? The maternal mtDNA studies pushed the arrival dates way, way back. The first genes had entered some 30,000 years ago, at least (some researchers claim far older entries). Did all of those genes come from Asia? No.

The genes from some tribes showed an unexpected component: some markers of irrefutable European origin. A mtDNA lineage predominantly found in Europe got to the Great Lakes 14,000 to 15,000 years ago.

Using another technique, human lymphocyte antigens, researchers have found blood types connecting not only Europe but also Africa to America during prehistoric times. And many of the Amerindian genes are connected not with Siberian ones but with genes from southern Asia and from the South Pacific Islands.

What is clear is that some of Asterix's ancestors had traveled to America.

It fulfills the last claim from the Introduction.

It is about time for the last two Chapters

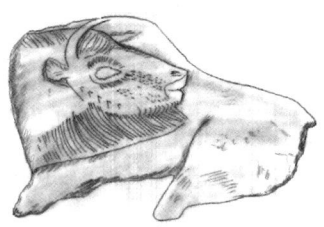

18

What Homer did not Tell

A short review of prehistoric Europe has been given throughout these pages, with a glimpse of the traumatic transition from matrilineal to patrilineal structures.

Some of our oldest linguistic links to the stone, older even than the Euzkos, were analyzed.

A few of our psychic, cultural links to the matrilineal Euzkos have been examined.

One of the problems of generalizations is that in order to get a global view many differences tend to disappear or to be minimized. Even if some genetic, cultural and linguistic links seemed to be well spread among our prehistoric ancestors, the gaps among them are not a few. Even among peoples or tribes living in relatively reduced areas, the Pelasgians for instance, groups could show many differences. Even if only groups living in continental Greece are submitted to study, a surprising variety arises. Even if smaller regions are observed, the heterogeneity is evident.

Take the island of Crete. No less than four different cultural or ethnic groups seem to have been simultaneously present during the period from 4,000 to 3,000 thousand years ago. Herodotus points to at least five different languages spoken there at his time. Apart from the evidence of cremation habits, typical in Aryans, the influence of other groups with widely differing funeral traditions can be detected. Skulls and skeletons also tell their own story of differences. Dissimilarities also appear in pottery, ornaments and architecture. What happened in Crete was common to all Europe.

The difficulties for land communication seemingly allowed a greater degree of heterogeneity than anything we can imagine. In spite of any heterogeneity they all seemed to have at least something in common. In the words of Robert Graves (in his introduction to "The Greek Myths") "the whole of Neolithic Europe, to judge from surviving artifacts and myths, had a remarkably homogeneous system of religious ideas, based on the worship of the many-titled Mother-goddess, who was also known in Syria and Libya".

The worship of the Goddess underscores their more important features—their matrilineality and the high status of their women. The differences between all those cultures and populations were deep in some cases. *In spite of all their many differences, the sharp contrast they offer against the patrilineal Indo-European customs is so marked, that they emerge, no matter their disparities, as a surprisingly homogeneous group.*

How old was that religious influence? Coming from the remote past, until the Aurignacian culture, commonly associated with Cromagnons, nothing can be said. Only a rock sculpted like a vulva is not much of a sign. With the next culture of the upper Paleolithic, the Gravettian, the first Venuses became common—steatopygous and with peculiar hairdos. That dates it back to some thirty thousand years. The oldest baked-clay figurine known is a beautiful, dark piece 25,000 years old, a Venus from Dolní Vestonice in the Czech Republic. The sexy statuettes remained through all the Solutrean culture and then the Magdalenian one, whose more recent remains date back more than 11,000 years. From there the Goddess made Her presence felt all through the modern, almost contemporaneous cultures. Its vestiges lasted in modern Europe until scarcely three centuries ago.

How far did it reach? Surprisingly far. Archaeological confirmation comes from all Europe—and then more. Finds extend through Siberia, Northern China, Asia Minor. In Africa some cults survive which are closely linked to those that were common along the coast of the Mediterranean Sea more than two millennia ago.

In India, goddesses are still worshipped today.

There are matrilineal tribes, or retaining some matrilineal traits, in all continents. But the times of the Goddess empire over all subjects are gone everywhere.

A tale of Her decline can be obtained analyzing the emerging cults through the ages.

When the first patrilineal tribes arrived in the Mediterranean area they could not overcome the already dominant Goddess tribes, so a first compromise is evident: the gods were adopted as sons—incorporated to the spiritual royalty but in a lesser, dependent position. The figure of the Goddess and Her Son became common everywhere. In Egypt Isis and her son Horus appeared. Sometimes the Sacred Son could point to that other ritual innovation—the son as substitute victim—especially when he appears crowned.

Then, as the incoming patrilineal groups gained more power, the sons became husbands. The metamorphosis was evident in the role of the sacred king—at the beginning merely a companion, not the important figure. His sacredness derived only from his marriage to the Goddess. It was borrowed power. In Sumer they were Innanna and Dummuzi, later Ishtar and Tanmuz. In Egypt they were Isis and Adonis. The male counterpart kept growing in his survival period and influence, until the Aton phase was reached—Aton-Rah, the Sun god, the one and only God. The new Egyptian rulers left no place for a female in the heavenly top anymore, just as Zeus became the victor in Greece, Jupiter in Rome and Odin in Scandinavia. The pace and the type of displacement varied with the places and the peoples.

The displacement was complete but left many telling signs. Take Dodona for instance, an ancient city of northwest Greece. It was the site of the most prestigious sanctuary devoted to

Zeus in classical times. Actually, the shrine was much older and of Pelasgian origin. Scholars who first studied the cult were astonished by the recorded priests' behavior: they all went naked and barefoot, making a point of sleeping on the bare earth. Even those experts whose majors were not the Greek religion understood well the meaning of that apparently eccentric conduct: remnants of an ancient cult of some Earth Goddess. Her priests always slept naked on the earth in order not to lose contact with Her at any moment.

The apparent contradiction was clear: even when Zeus already dominated the scene, even in the most respected of his sanctuaries, no one dared to break the old customs and to affront the Goddess. Traditions and beliefs, especially the religious ones, are hard to suppress.

Many ancient names are also revealing. In France the Marne got its name from Matronae (meaning the Triple Goddess) and every time a Parisian mentions the Seine is paying an unknowing homage to goddess Sequanna. In Britain the Severn owes its name to goddess Sabrina and the Clyde to goddess Clóta.

The change was not simultaneous. Great centers of worship of the Goddess in the western areas persisted much longer. Besides, the masses were much more conservative in their worship than the new Indo-European masters arriving from the East.

It is not surprising then that in Chartres, the great heart of Druid cult and yearly pilgrimage, the Goddess and her Sacred Son were revered until the first centuries of the modern era. Revealing, at the same time, that the Indo-European religious influence was still counterbalanced in the region.

The wooden image of the Black Virgin and her Son, center of veneration in the Chartres Cathedral, is apparently the remake of a pre-Christian one. It still is a renowned center of pilgrimage. The image was supposedly adopted by the Church to channel an already old and potent religious feeling in the region.

The recent joyful celebration of the eight-hundredth anniversary of the monumental Cathedral, with the happy and hearty participation of neighbors, and the continuous affluence of tourists and believers from all regions, is testimony that the choice was quite sensible. Not surprisingly, as in ancient times, the Lady and the Child kept being the religious center for today's visitors.

The Chartres tradition is not unique. The Black Virgins, as they are called, are more than one. They exist at Le Puy in France or at Einsiedeln, in Switzerland. In those places, and many others, they keep evoking strong feelings. Their cults are still alive and powerful, impervious to time.

Take the Virgin of Czestochowa, the most sacred of Polish icons. The veneration for an image in a cloth is many centuries old. Native and foreign pilgrims crowd the towering Paulite monastery of Jasna Góra every year. One of the peculiarities of nationalism in Poland, that always calls the outsider's attention and always ends unexplained, is the traditional Polish tendency to defensively cluster around the veneration of the Virgin, when it comes to protect their territory or rights. That happened recently, even during the period of Communist Party supremacy. Both the Kremlim and Washington were awed by the strong religious feelings externalized by the Polish. It all looks like an old center of ancient amphictyonic alliances that keeps alive its many traditional, psychical ties even in the present. The communists were just experiencing what invading Turk horsemen had lived centuries before, and probably just what the Hun hordes had earlier learned at their cost in pre-Christian times, when nationalisms were not yet linked to a crown but to a shrine.

It is always the Lady and the Child. Their golden statue is still the central point in Munich. They appear everywhere in Europe, big cities or small towns, marking to whom loyalty and devotion were expected as a citizen's duty, as ancestral legacy.

When it comes to religious traditions practically nobody can beat the Basques and their neighbors. The region of northwestern Spain has been a center of pilgrimage for eons. The chapel and the hospice for travelers and pilgrims built by D'Artagnan's ancestor in 1605 were destined to those who followed the renowned Chemin de St. Jacques or Way of St. James, to Santiago de Compostela in northwest Spain. D'Artagnan, as a child in southern France, must have seen many of the thousands of pilgrims who traversed the Pyrenees each year.

Compostela was then a Christian religious center that ceded only before Rome and Jerusalem, creating an international emotional link among visitors that was crucial to European consciousness. It still is a pilgrimage center, receiving each year hundreds of thousand of visitors that now use the new tourist facilities for traveling. It is not surprising that it has been also strongly linked to nationalism; the whole region was the motor center for the Reconquest of Spain from the Moors and it was important for the growth of Spanish national feeling. "Santiago!" (Saint James!) became the traditional war cry of Spanish fighters everywhere; people from all regions fell safely united under such a banner.

The Way of St. James, anyway, is far older than that. The then Christian pilgrims were crossing a region that is famous for its caves, full of prehistoric murals. It seems to have been a fountain of both religious inspiration and experiences for so, so long a time that our present concepts of history or tradition lose completely its meaning in comparison to it.

What about the Basques? How did they manage to keep their lands for such an incredibly long period? Such a continuous occupancy of a land by the same people in a region that is the almost unavoidable door between two continents, natural crossing of both the Atlantic and Mediterranean marine paths, where there has been a perennial migration through the land or sea, is unheard of except in the Basques' case.

How was it possible? How did they preserve their language and their customs?

In part, the explanation may reside in an old, religious link.

All observers have noticed a singular religiosity in the Basques—typical in all Euzkan people. It must be attributed to some unusually deep, religious experience coming from the past—attaching extraordinary people to an extraordinary land. Religion is, in part, a social agreement—keeping together—adjusting.

Other partial explanation comes from their way of life. When Lycurgus, the Spartan lawgiver, intended to free his countrymen from invasions, he gave them a strong legislation to keep them free from riches, always tempting to outsiders, and to train them into a nation of formidable soldiers. What the Spartans deliberately did, the Basques seem to have attained in a most natural way. Their simple, pastoral way of life, and their fierce individuality were key to it.

The same trait that made their cohesion difficult, a trait notably shared in different degrees by all the peoples with Euzko ancestry, helped them to survive through the ages.

The lack of a strong, central leadership impeded them from becoming an influential political power but at the same time preserved their independence.

The success of great conquerors is normally easy, once they defeat the central power that is trying to contain them. Then all the population, already used to obeying a strong government, falls in line with the new authorities. Not with the Basques—they could always be counted to unit behind a leader *only* when foreign troops menaced them hard enough—and then not for a long time.

Their story is very similar, and not at all by a mere coincidence, with what happened to Scots, Irish and Welsh, three Celtic groups sharing practically the same Paleolithic DNA with the Basques. There the invading English troops could easily defeat any isolated count's soldiers, thanks to the defenders' almost anarchic lifestyle. As the invaders immediately learned, that did not mean the control of the whole region. They also had to successively beat his brother, his son or his nephew. Even when entire populations were decimated the war never seemed to end, only battles were postponed until a new generation, never less ferocious than the last and always more experienced, was ready to pursue on the combat.

Sometimes, in extremely rare occasions, Scots, Irish and Welsh surprised the invaders, and above all themselves, by achieving some kind of unstable national unity that gave them unusual fighting power. That was the whole Basque history. As long as neighbors did not bother them, or temporarily successful invaders did not interfere with their immemorial traditions, they kept almost quiet, but any intrusion or any menace to their old, old way of life was enough to arouse them. Then they fought with all their abilities and with the ferocity that had made them famous, beating or resisting more numerous and technologically advanced armies.

Indo-European societies—where children grew under an overwhelming paternal authority—tended to emphasize power structures. Obedience to a strong central leader was usually common in them. Euzkan societies tended to abhor such organizations. Their members had grown in an atmosphere where paternal authority was restricted. They relied extensively on customary law.

That characteristic of Indo-Europeans made easy the continual growth of central powers. The Euzkan inclination tended to produce a multiplicity of powers. One kind of society inculcated discipline and total obedience to the leader. The other one showed an extraordinary appreciation for *personal freedom*. While there is no pure example of any of those two kinds of organizations—most tend to be hybrids—historically the model applies in most cases.

When the Gauls confronted the Romans, they were almost always unable to coalesce against the formidable legions. They could not tolerate any strong leadership.

A singular symbol illustrates a surprising continuity—certain signs linked to personal freedom through history. Combatants on the Trojan side were often represented in Greek iconography by assigning them a peculiar headpiece. A soft felt or wool conical headdress fitting closely around the head and characterized by a pointed crown that curls forward. Paris is seen in many vases using that characteristic hat. Amazons covered their heads with it. It was called a Phrygian cap.

Phrygians were apparently related to the Thracians. Both peoples sided with the Trojans and never attained much importance on account of their permanent political fragmentation. They were also famous by their love for music and poetry, and of course, for their extreme devotion for the Goddess. Their neighbors attested to their warring skills. Yes, yes, it sounds like a familiar story. Celts, Etruscans, Pelasgians and all Euzkan societies would have agreed on that. Spartacus was a Thracian. He conducted the most famous revolt of slaves.

Which are the historical coincidences?

Funny, in Rome the Phrygian cap was worn by emancipated slaves as a symbol of their freedom. It was unconnected with the Spartacus rebellion, but...

Later the Phrygian cap suddenly became The Phrygian Cap.

It happened some three millenniums after the Trojan War. Members of the American Revolution used to plant a Liberty Pole in a public square to call the people to an assembly. It was just a pole...with a Phrygian cap on its top.

Almost simultaneously, French Revolutionaries adopted it as "the red cap of liberty." It continues to be associated with their national allegorical figure of Liberté.

Perhaps the fact that Freemasons stimulated those processes at both sides of the Atlantic could help to explain the symbolic continuity. Freemasons associate themselves to old fraternities from the past. Curiously, they postulate the birth of their Order near the time of the Trojan War.

George Washington, Benjamin Franklin and many of the American Revolutionaries were Freemasons. They contributed to establish a most revolutionary innovation: a cyclic government system. They managed to curtail the power of the main executive leader, the president. Among other social revolutionary innovations, the obligated renewal of the top executive was key to all that. It all carries similarities to the Mother Goddess cyclic matrilineal systems—the demotion of the sacrificial king. They all looked as planned to obtain a similar result—the restriction of the king's power.

The Basques, above all peoples, could easily sympathize with both Thracians and Phrygians. Basques were a quarreling lot, never considered a too tempting booty and always recognized as too dangerous and determined adversaries—never worth the nasty trouble. Caesar and Charlemagne could tell it. Vandals and Moors, Visigoths and Gotts, the Nazi airplanes and Neandertals... Wait a minute!

What was it? *Neandertals??* Yes, Neandertals. Exactly that. Neandertals.

Archaeologists concluded, from evidence collected in the cave of Zafarraya, near Gibraltar, that Neandertals were around in Spain not more than 29,000 years ago.

Let's notice that the real time could be surprisingly shorter. That estimation means only the last approximate date at which some remains were left and preserved. They could have been around much more recently. Even with that larger lapse in mind, according to some paleontologists' view, Basques' ancestors have been contemporaries with Neandertals.

Their opinions are not going to be refuted easily. After all, cranial measurements and bone particularities are considered hard evidence in that field. *The same people that survived the assaults of the Kondor bombers of the Hitlerite aviation may also have successfully battled with Neandertals.*

Come to think of it, that old and cherished Basque legend, the *Basojaun*, the Lord of the Woods, primitive, hairy and extraordinarily strong first inhabitant of the woods, *who was there before the Basques*, and from whom they learned everything, is enough to give any anthropologist gooseflesh. *No one except Neandertals seems to have been there before the Basques.* Actually, many of their traditions and legends create gooseflesh in scholars. It comes naturally, being ancient people from an old age.

Still, nothing can upset specialists more than that old Euzko tradition: their women.

Archaeological finds do nothing but confirm the extraordinarily high status that women enjoyed in ancient Europe. Excavations bring confirmations everywhere. Sometimes in places where there is absolutely no need for it—as Crete. No need, given the extraordinary amount of frescoes, jewels and statues that emphasize the high role played by court women. It is they who always appear in the center of processions and offerings in the Minoan scenes. Nevertheless, archaeologists manifested their surprise in 1965 when they found in Arkhanes a tomb whose chamber containing the skeleton of a woman with no less than 140 pieces of gold jewelry.

In 1975 a second woman, also with rich jewelry, was found in Crete. In both cases the types of jewels pointed to a religious status. Queens or priestesses? That cannot be told. It could be both. What archaeologists know, without any doubt, is that these were *women in office*. Ornaments pointed to a belief in the death and resurrection of the god. They had their place in rituals—high status women. The tombs were just confirming what everyone already knew from frescoes, seals, jewels, urns and pottery.

Few visitors, if any, to the famed Viking Ship Museum in Oslo can help a feeling of awe when they enter the Viking Ship Hall. For the tourists the Museum is an unavoidable point. It contains an unbelievable rich collection of items retrieved from three burial ships. The top stars are two of the ships, the Oseberg, a royal barge, and the Gokstadt, a longboat.

Contemplating the rich sculpted decoration and delicate lines of the seventy-feet-long Oseberg ship, its tall, serpentine prow and perfect proportions, the spectator cannot help but agree with experts that qualify it more as an unequaled piece of art than as a navigational tool. Even more remarkable, the ship, which had seen sea duty for no less than half a century, according to experts, became after that the sepulcher of two ladies. One was old and arthritic, the other young and apparently healthy.

There have been speculations about the young woman been sacrificed to accompany the older one. There are absolutely no speculations about the status of whoever was in such a precious coffin—extraordinarily high. The jewels that accompany them are an unnecessary comment on their situation. No much need actually of the ship either to confirm something already known: the high status enjoyed by Scandinavian women in the past. They were able to divorce hubbies at will and then retain property—not exactly an Indo-European custom. Far from it, it went against all their conceptions, prejudices and customs.

What saved Scandinavian women's status was the delay, probably for geographic reasons, of the Indo-European wave in reaching the region. The fact that there still were matrilineal royal houses around, as recently as mid-ninth century, might have helped a lot to the lady in question to be buried in such a regal enclosure.

For the Scandinavian population the high status of women still was usual. So Scandinavian females retained more rights than in other parts of Europe, where the matrilineal-to-patrilineal change had happened more than two thousand years before. *In some of the Scandinavian countries women have today a higher school-enrollment and higher education than men.* They enjoy health, education, rights and status that can only be dreamed of by women abroad. If that is happening now, after a millennium of dramatic change, one can only wonder at the status that European women must have enjoyed respect of men *before* the Indo-Europeans arrived.

What makes all these burials surprising? We must excuse a few traditional archaeologists for having an Indo-European frame of mind. With such a view, a rich burial for a woman could only take place *beside* a man's. Also, fortifying their prejudices, in many places of the world, kings have been buried with their entire court, including wives and concubines, not mentioning a lot of pets or favorite animals. Sometimes all these people and pets were sacrificed immediately after the king's death. *Any richly adorned woman only pointed to the high status of the king.* It was just one more item among his many belongings—another pleasure object, just like some of his garments or any of his favorite meals.

So, these lonely, high-status women in their spectacular tombs are quite unusual. They break the traditional scheme. They point to a different arrangement of intersexes relationships in ancient Europe.

The burials also serve to delineate where and when the old culture still had a certain weight.

At 550 B.C., for instance, a 30-year-old woman was buried in a funerary wagon on Mount Lassoix, near Vix, close to the Seine River. It was full of astonishingly rich adornments and artifacts. Many consider that the Vase of Vix was the most valuable piece recovered—the biggest bronze crater ever found, able to hold 1,100 liters (290 gallons) of wine. Those who are lucky enough to contemplate it at the municipal museum of Châtillon, will marvel at the frieze of warriors and chariots that symmetrically decorates it. That 460-pound, Greek wine vessel is not the only peculiarity: of three kinglike tombs found in Vix, two are of women.

That is not surprising. Not even limited to Europe. In Assyria, where the Indo-Europeans had struck much earlier, it was discovered under the royal palace of Nimrod in 1989 a chamber containing the remains of three women from about 600 B.C. Hundreds of pieces of jewelry, astonishingly well preserved, were adorning them. It was not the first surprising entombment with royal women found in the region and most probably neither the last.

Those are not even the richest tombs. The Goddess also had followers in other lands. Digging in Afghanistan in 1978, near the outbreak of a terrible civil war, archaeologists were dumbfounded when they exhumed a bewildering treasure from two millennia ago. In a burial complex in a formerly unassuming mound (Tillya Tepe, adequately meaning Golden Hill) they found eight tombs. Six of them contained the rests of extraordinarily jeweled women.

No other find, with the single exception of Tutankhamen's tomb, can be compared with the riches discovered: only the gold artifacts numbered 20,000.

Where else could be found a collapsible gold crown of surprising portable design that could be easily disassembled? They were fittingly called "nomadic high-tech" by journalists. Golden statuettes of the Goddess abounded, of course—beautiful Aphrodite with surprising wings, goddess Anahita surrounded by animals. An erotic couple was riding that Goddess' symbol, the Chimera. Seated Athena was also present, exhibiting both her weapons and wisdom. Queens or priestesses, even in a region where women's status has been traditionally high, due to nomadic customs, the finds have understandingly produced a scientific earthquake.

That is not the only earthquake that women's tombs are producing in the world. They are not absolutely limited to the scientific circles either. Something like an atomic bomb has hit China—an ideological nuke missiling from the past, exploding in the most unexpected of all sceneries.

Let's remember that in China emperors were normally buried with all those tedious females who had desperately pursued him—if not all the women during his life, at least his last favorites. Something is certain, their mourning could be nothing but sincere. They were all immediately granted the golden opportunity to accompany him to the other world. Adequately encouraged by armed court-members who wanted to follow traditions. Even if Mao's revolution did certainly improve women's status a little, not even hard believers would point to today's China as a women's Paradise. It is tradition. So, who is one of today's troublemakers that is worrying Chinese authorities in the enormous Xinjiang Uygur Autonomous Region? Answer: a five-feet, brown-blond woman.

Is she one of the many protesters by the use of the region as a nuke test-zone? No, actually she is rather quiet and has not participated in any recent demonstration.

So, why all that fuss about her? The problem is, she is 3,800 years old.

Found in Lulan in 1980, the delicate features of the well-preserved mummy charmed her discoverers. No doubt she was a striking belle in spite of her centuries. The diggers instantly called her "the Lulan beauty."

For the traditional Uygur minority, which is always striving for political independence, the mummy instead became the Mum. She has stirred their hearts and now they call her "the mother of our nation." An artist has recreated her features. The obvious Caucasoid face has done nothing to dispel the consternation of the Party. She is inspiring some songs. Her cassettes sell well. Wow! Not bad for a fair lady that old. Even gorgeous Helen of Troy could get jealous with all that success. After all, the Lulan beauty preceded her by some 500 years, even if being contemporaneous with other girls of the Minoan Civilization.

Today archaeologists do not find anything strange in women's tombs in that far away area. They are common all throughout Siberia. They are discarding old misconceptions. A woman and a man in a tomb do not mean anymore that she had been sacrificed to him. Sometimes it does not even signify that she had been in a lesser social status. In some cases that is obvious. Digging a *kur-*

gan, a burial mound, in Siberia in 1993, in Ukok, to the north of the Russia-China frontier, a man and a woman were discovered.

For the scientists it was obvious that the tall, high-ranking lady unearthed had been buried separately, in a well-built funerary log-chamber, along with two horses in splendid regalia. No wonder that her felt saddles were adorned with chimeric winged lions—the Goddess again.

People of a different culture had then added a man's body and horses on top of that elaborated kurgan of more than 2,000 years. But even had the burials been apparently simultaneous, as one the same archaeologist had found in that region only two years before, the modern conclusions are not respecting some old viewpoints. That time the finder did not believe that the girl found with the man had been sacrificed to him and found it hard to presume that she even was in a dependent position. He did not even consider them warrior and concubine. Each corpse had its own set of sacrificed horses around and (fasten your seat belts!,) much more important, each one had *their own weaponry*.

Weapons with a woman's body? Yeah, battle-ax, knives, bow. The startled archaeologist found himself quoting a priorly disdained source. Nobody had paid much attention to Herodotus when he mentioned women warriors carrying javelins and bows. As Homer, he was counted just as an entertaining make-believe, narrating mostly fairy tales but nothing more, with not enough sense to distinguish between fable and truth.

Now archaeologists are hurriedly dusting their volumes of poor, old Herodotus' History and ceasing to sneer at his presumed inventions. The buried horses also bring remembrances. They make us recall that funny word, Amazon.

In some languages, Spanish and Portuguese for instance, it still retains some of one of its older meanings: woman rider.

Herodotus described these warlike women living among the Scythians. According to myth, similar women fought Theseus, Jason, Herakles and their colleagues.

Most persons (including, it must be confessed, the embarrassed author of this book) considered that one of Herodotus' narratives could not be true: a tribe where riding women were in charge of fighting and other traditional man's pastimes. Who could believe Herodotus (shame to the author!) when he also mentioned that in those tribes men played the traditional woman's role of family raiser?

It seems that burials have the offensive habit of not keeping in pace with prejudice. Dozens of burial mounds have been recently excavated in the steppes of Ukraine and Russia. Women and men have been found there. Uncanny thing, women rest with their weapons. Men? With mirrors and skeletons of children.

Archaeologists do not believe that the javelins, bows and arrows in the tombs of those ladies of the plains where mere adornments, or just tokens of devotion from their families. It all looks like these where really *battling* women. Their bones show the kind of injuries that were typical in combat. One, for instance, had still an arrow tip deep inside her body—tough ladies indeed.

The old tales and traditions of women accompanying warriors to battle, or of warrior-women battling on their own, are not been laughed at any more. These stories are well spread all over Europe. Curiously enough, those traditions of independent, aggressive women tend to appear among peoples who painted themselves with blue pigments, like the Picts, or tended to blue adornments and decorations. Ancient royal houses all along the coast of the Mediterranean Sea tended to show over display of lapis lazuli.

In both Sumerian and Akkaddian cuneiform tablets, for instance, it is found the prescription to depict royal hair with lapiz lazuli. Players involved in ritual games in Thera and in Crete show the same adornment.

Those Amazons... What were at first just whispering comments around the fire in night camps about the fighting women, then shy remarks in scientific journals, have become a subject of open discussion. An example? The January '97 issue of the prestigious magazine *Archaeology*. The title of one of its leading articles? *Warrior women of the Eurasian Steppes*. The subtitle could not be more suggestive: *New evidence suggests that tales of Amazon war-*

riors may be more than mere legend. The author, Jeannine Davis-Kimball, quoted Strabo, Hellanicus and Herodotus, comparing the classical writers' comments and the increasingly corroborating data thrown up by the new excavations since the fifties.

That is quite a change.

That archaeologist would not have even dared to write that title just a few years before. Most scientific journals would have refused to print it. The new tombs are turning old concepts upside down everywhere. Those riding women, whose frightened neighbors called them *oiorpata*, killer of men, are starting to regain their old credit.

It is about time. The silence about them has been too long. A silence that seems suspiciously conceived sometimes. A silence that starts, for instance, in the times the *Iliad* was written. Homer did not tell all about the whole Trojan War. The wonderful epic describes only a relatively short time after nine years of siege. He seems to have put emphasis anyway in describing all the contenders, all the allies from both sides. Well, actually, all the contenders? There was a singular omission.

This enigmatic Homer's omission has been evident through the ages. Notice that Homer was a splendid storyteller—for most scholars that is a wild understatement. He is considered the best one. He never lost a chance to move the reader (or the listener, because it was an oral rendition at first.) Yet he never described the most impactant contender: a *woman*—Penthesileia—the Amazon Queen. Her name means the one who forces men to mourn.

We learn about her and her death by Achilles through other authors. Her noticeable absence has always shocked many scholars. She appears in scene carrying the sacred double ax—the *labrys*. Twelve Amazons accompany her into battle—*twelve plus one again*—everything shows their adhesion to the Goddess.

Frederick Combellack translated the *War at Troy* by Quintus of Smyrna. It starts just where Homer left—at the memorable combat between Penthesileia and Achilles. Combellack felt compelled to add an interesting subtitle—*what Homer did not tell.*

Quintus wrote at a time when women were not contestants for power anymore—many centuries after Homer. He could write freely on subjects that would have meant a banishment or execution at earliest times. His books were considered songs—just a story. Homer's writings were *religious books*. They had many meanings and undertones clear only for the elite.

The combat between Heroes and Amazons was considered the most important religious subject. It was part of the freezes of the Parthenon at Athens and of other temples—at Olympias, for instance, where the most relevant— religious panhellenic ceremony took place—the Games. It was extremely important to show there who had been the victor. But sculptors mostly started to depict them only centuries after the Amazons had been defeated. When the Indo-Europeans rulers felt secure enough.

Bellerophon, Theseus, Hercules, Achilles—*three or four generations of Heroes battled the famed Amazons. Those Heroes were the Founding Fathers.* The Amazons hit back. They sieged Athens in Theseus times for more than four months, until an armistice was reached.

All those combats were depicted in jewelry, freezes, statues, paintings and an in extraordinary variety of painted vases.

Were they a women's army? Or just female leaders of armed men? It is almost certain that they were important priestesses. How can we know that? *Greece was full of Amazon tombs where they received cult and homage.* Pausanias, the genial geographer and traveler describes them in many places.

The Amazons seem to have founded not a few important cities: Ephesus, Smyrna, Paphos, Sinope among them.

The Athenians proudly boasted of their role in that war. Theseus struggle against the Amazons was not just a local Athenian tradition. When the Greek army battled the Persians at Plataea, the Athenians were allowed to form the right wing on account of their famed resistance against the *androktonei* (man killers). Their stories abounded all around continental Greece, the islands and especially in the Ionian region. No wonder that Quintus started his story with Homer's omission.

Robert Graves, for instance, believed that politically correct redactors had imposed that noticeable silence on Homer's verses in Pisistratus times. Whether the genial aeda did it or later censors examined and mutilated his Iliad is no clear. It will continue to kindle discussions among scholars. What it is obvious is that it did not show the feminine participation in the war.

It really was an episode of a religious combat between genders.

At the time of Troy *there was a parallel battle. It had started generations before and continued after it. Women lost that battle.*

And silence was one of the most effective weapons.

19

Return

The return took place in parts of Europe where the Euzko influence was still strong. The most notable change came in what is the clearest indicator of the male-female relation in any species—courtship.

In fishes, birds, reptiles, amphibians and all the mammals, courtship is a complex ritual—to be meticulously observed in its minimal details, always demanding, always fixed. The pair involved cannot escape from the predetermined steps of the old *pas de deux* of their own species.

Biologists do point out that in humans the ritual also is of a fixed nature. Nevertheless, it seems that in our species the overdeveloped brain-cortex allows a surprising freedom interval of less restricted choices among the rules—meaning an awesome number of new possibilities.

The many examples of courtship ritual among different cultures illustrate this singularity of the man-woman courting. Love in the couple is very different now from what it was some centuries ago. The right of women to choose their future partners is quite a novelty for Aryan or Indo-European customs.

The tender premarital display that allows a couple to decide if they are going to turn their relationship into a stable one is a breathtaking innovation. What a good Latin, Dorian or any Aryan or Indo-European ancestor had in mind was quite different—something much akin to many present weddings in India or Arabia. The family still prearranges them. Brides have never much part in it. In the old Aryan tradition a few odd families would take their feelings in consideration if they disliked the candidate that much. The Gothic kings, among the Franks for instance, used to send their daughters as signs of good will or alliance even to their enemies.

Our present conventions owe much to a development that took place in Europe and revolutionized the traditional Indo-European pattern forever. It was named *courtly love*.

Those who studied the evolution of courtly love point unequivocally to southern France., the Euzkan Languedoc, as the place of its birth. Indo-European trickery again, or perhaps just mere blindness or ignorance, there had not been any birth at all. It was conservatism, not innovation; it was new only for Indo-European uses.

Cyrano's tender love for Roxanne and his extreme fascination for the moon—the old Goddess' symbol—were just his regional, traditional upbringing surfacing.

Two points are all important. First, in the supposed *nouvelle vogue*, the male lover was in a dependent position in respect to the lady in question. Second, he always thought of himself in a semi religious context—a sublimated, fertility-cult tradition well kept.

The new attitude buried the old view. Court women ceased to be considered only producers of offspring. They became persons. Men started to enjoy a bonus besides sex—their delightful company.

Most sources agree that a temperamental woman had a decisive influence—Eleanor d'Aquitaine.

One of the most interesting women in history, Eleanor married Louis *le Jeune* in 1137. He became Louis VII of France. less than a month later. Disliking his "monkish" attitude, Eleanor divorced Louis fifteen years later, kept her two daughters and also her duchy of Aquitaine—not bad for a lady in those times.

She evidenced the old Euzkan-female character in all her moves. Maybe she found intolerable the ambiance of the French court. The Franks. were not very polite at those times, and there was not enough space for a spirited lady like her. No woman has sat in a throne in France, a revealing fact. She threw her lot with the English court, marrying again with good eye who later would be Henry II, and producing an awkward situation between England and France that would finally explode in the One Hundred Years War.

During all those daring ventures she was loyally backed by her Gascons. The Euzkos never wavered in their support. Tradition again, she was a Queen in the only land where a Queen could really command. They were all significantly for her until she died. Such undivided loyalty to a woman in the all-male 12th century was a rarity. Curiously enough, Gascons always felt a weakness for the British too, probably encountering a greater cultural affinity with them than with the Frank nobility.

Eleanor was the subject of some of the best poetry of her times. She was a patroness of troubadours and their new love poetry, producing with that a considerable impact in the manners and taste of the English court. The Queen influenced the French court too. Nevertheless the French knights had still to await the Love Revolution for more than three centuries, until their good king Charles VIII invaded Italy in 1495.

The French cavaliers were delighted by the looks and manners of the sophisticated and lively Tuscan ladies—that surpassed all their experiences. As a military and conquest campaign it had not much success but it brought the Renaissance to France, including courtship and table manners and invading the ladies' boudoir. The abbé Brantôme, the famed arbiter of wooing, recognized all that a century later.

Another strong lady, Catherine de Medici gave the French. court the *coup de grace*. She brought a breeze or, more precisely, a gale. She returned the prior French invasion to her ancestors' Tuscany by the more gracious way of marrying Henry II of France. French *parfumerie* started right there.

The recognized date of birth of the ballet libretto is 1581. That year Catherine celebrated her sister's wedding. In the feast, she and the ladies of her court presented the *Ballet Comique de la Reine*. She was introducing her subjects to the court festivals that were typical in Florence. No surprise that the ballet story was the legend of Circe, an echo from a time when women had a more significant status.

Not all was song and dance. Catherine did not content herself with giving some hints through ballet and other arts. The French were unused to strong women in the house. Catherine gave them more than enough to learn, mixing in politics all the time. A typical Euzkan lady of her times, she became the man of the kingdom. Regent during the minority of her son Charles IX, she kept the real power until his death—some fifteen years in all.

All that now seems just old history, but present feminine movements would have been almost unthinkable without that continual Euzkan prompting.

It is also very interesting to point at something that should be evident but is strangely missed: the best of European cultures always came out not when they were starkly matrilineal or patrilineal, but *whenever there was enough of a mix*.

It happened during the Minoan upsurge—then again in the Ionic cities and Athens. It happened again in Tuscany. When the Indo-Europeans were extremely predominant, as in Sparta, their culture was militaristic and embarrassingly dull. Matrilineal tribes seem also to have had their part of it, when alone. Both cases point to domination, not conviviality. The equilibrium brought, in daring splendor, civilization.

If, as a sign of our times, feminine participation in society continues to expand, and equality between the sexes prevails, then it can be foretold that a new world rebirth is at hand. It might extend and surpass the promise of anything that the new toy, technology, is offering at present.

Previous experiences have shown a cultural explosion—a remarkable growth of science, commerce and the arts, a tendency to enjoy life as a pleasure.

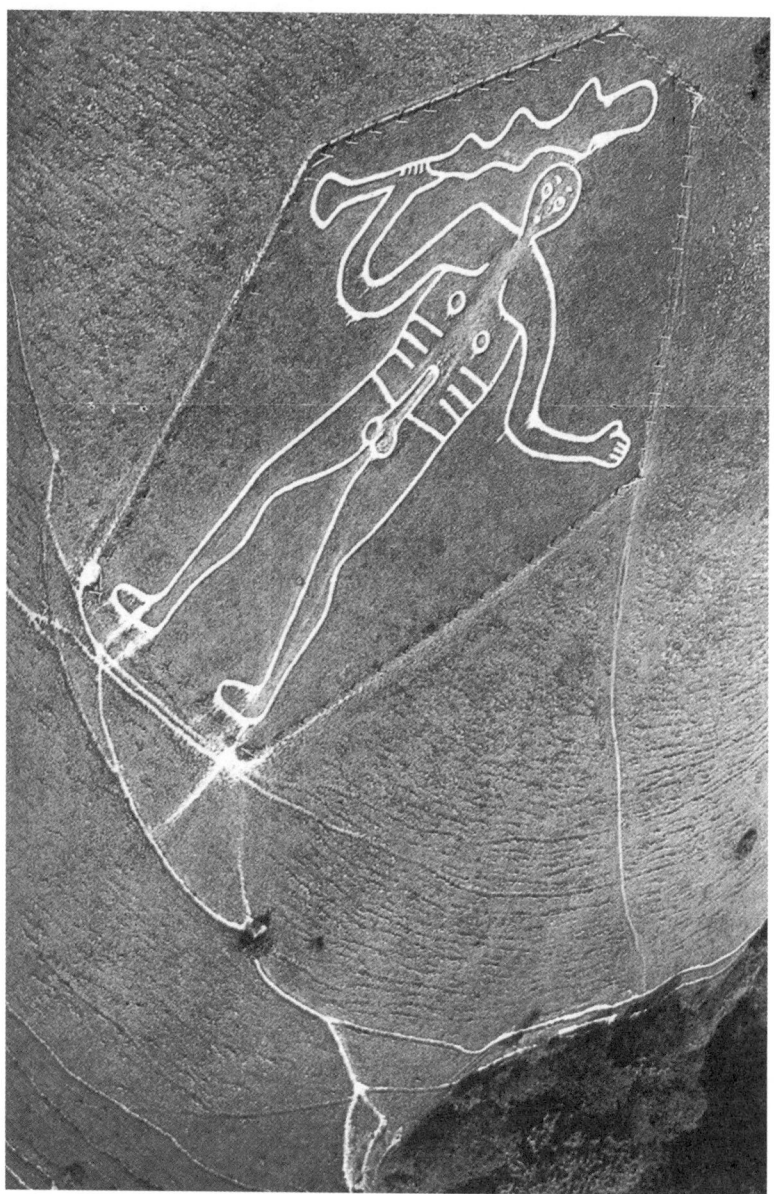

Fig. 37. The Cerne Abbas Giant

On the other hand, should that tendency fail, the dark side of human nature would prevail. Our warmongering societies have a dangerous new toy. They are able to produce a new kind of colossal, hallucinogenic fungus—like the ones that blasted Hiroshima and Nagasaki. Those ghastly visions exceed anything any intoxicated celebrant could fear in ancient times.

The European civilization has been challenging other cultures and civilizations for centuries. Probably one of its best assets has permanently been what people from other regions have found always their most shocking custom, and what could be their best export ever, the relationship between that funny couple, man and woman.

At a moment when entire Europe and its many cultural colonies are permeated by that old Euzkan influence, the old ties seem to become diffuse and forgotten, in spite of some old, apparently crazy, regional habits, which seem hard to die.

In Cerne, Dorset, for instance, not far from London, some surreptitious women still expectantly spend a night on the top of a queer mound, while computer-controlled jets cross the starry sky, and the moon illuminates the cloudy lines left by their engines.

On the top of the mound, surviving the ages, there is excavated the giant contour of a nude man, the famous Cerne Abbas Giant, carrying a club and with a conspicuous erect phallus (Fig. 37).

Investigators, thinking it could be the image of an old Herakles., have studied the electrical conductivity of the terrain, searching for another clue, its mythical lion-skin. They discovered that there was, and is lost now, what can be considered a delineation of a cloak hanging from his left arm. They identified it with his old traditional pelt. Just as one of those big-cat skins is shown in an sculpted image of a deity in one of the walls of the tomb of king Seti I at Thebes—a priestly mantle—telling the sacramental role of the user, the priest of some ancient fertility cult.

The ladies who hopefully visit the mound probably do not know they are spending the night near the ancient symbol of a sacred king, who usually died in the belief that his death would ensure the tribe survival.

Behind the Giant there is a rectangular lot. Locals call it the Trendle or the Frying Pan. Midsummer Maypole celebrations took place there. According to William of Malmesbury, that region was stubbornly addicted to paganism until the 12th century.

Nobody knows if there are sacred-kings' bones buried in the mound or near it. It is difficult that those female visitors know that they are following an old ritual of the Goddess, begging Her old best gift—children. If they do, it is a secret they keep to themselves. They do not tell either if they have slept there with their panties off—as old folks knowingly advise. The ritual name of the sacred king is forgotten. But women, in the Space Age, keep going. Old habits do die hard.

What about that remnant from the past, the Basques, the oldest Europeans? In the age of communication they look minimized.

They are now only a small fragment of both Spain and France, and an even smaller one of that new device, the European Community.

We can all imagine a time, probably some centuries or millennia in the future, when in a meeting of the Assembly of the World Peoples, a proud representative will rise from his chair. Carefully throwing his tunic over his shoulders, he will remain for a while in well rehearsed silence. Then he will smilingly tell the House: "I have the honor to inform the members of the House, that at this moment, all the peoples of the Earth have finally decided to accept the World Government." We can well imagine the applause, the commotion. We can also imagine, when the excited members calm down enough, an embarrassed representative standing up and, after clearing his throat, nervously stating: "I hate to mention this, but there is still these people in the western slope of the Pyrenees that..."

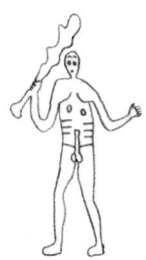

20

Further Readings

A QUICK GLANCE

The following literature does not pretend to be inclusive. It is not modern. It does not contain the latest discoveries. It gives only as few texts as possible for those interested in a quick vision of both the European and Mediterranean past. The opinion of the authors do not necessarily coincide with the views expressed in this book. But they offer a wonderful glance at many of the subjects and peoples treated here.

BASQUE PAGE: unfortunately the literature on Basques read by the author is mostly in Spanish, to be found in REFERENCES. Cybernauts can anyway fill more than adecuately the vacuum with the wonderful *BUBER'S BASQUE PAGE (buber@u.washington.edu).* Courtesy of Blas Pedro Uberuaga. It contains lots of historical and geographical data and very detailed nine pages of folklore and traditions. Indispensable for those planning a trip to the Basque country. For those allergic to the WEB sites, the Encyclopedia Britannica or the reference from the National Geographic can help.

THE SEVEN DAUGHTERS OF EVE Lane,by Brian Sykes (Norton, New York, 2001) Splendidly written. Just his very clear exposition of the DNA research methods and its problems and limitations makes it a jewel. It is a genetic history of Europe by one of the top scientists in the field.

THE GREEKS, by H.D.F. Kitto. (Penguin Books Ltd, 27 Wrights Lane, London W8 5TZ, England, 1951). It is absolutely impossible to read this book and not to be carried away by its author's enthusiasm. Nearly half a century after its first edition it keeps being contagious, written by one of the top specialists on Greek tragedy. It deals with the ethnic conflict and the evolution of Greek thought, art and institutions. It can be usually found in the big libraries.

THE GREEK MYTHS, by Robert Graves (Penguin Books Ltd, 27 Wrights Lane, London W8 5TZ, England, 1955) . The first modern dictionary of Greek mythology. The fastest entry to our ancestors' souls. Being the son of Perceval Graves, the Irish writer, Robert Graves had the unequaled background of a deep knowledge of the Gaelic lore which, given his aquaintance with Latin and Greek authors, gave him an unparalleled viewpoint of European and Mediterranean ancient myths, cults and traditions. The many cross-references and commentaries make this masterpiece invaluable, making it possible for any reader to delve into the classical, original writers and to compare the many versions or twists of every myth and also to ponder on Graves' own interpretations. Graves'commentaries are, some times, even more interesting than the myths themselves. An enlightening approach to our ancestor's minds. Another of Graves controversial books, *The White Goddess: a historical grammar of poetic myth* (Faber and Faber, London,1961) while also enlightening is of a different nature, lacking the academical rigor of *The Greek Myths*. Perhaps for that same reason, it is more amenable and has become a classic among poetry lovers. Another fruit of his incredible erudition, it allows a penetrating glance at not only the Hellenic world but also to practically all European cultures and to many of their Near East, Asian and African contemporaries.

IN SEARCH OF THE TROYAN WAR, by Michael Wood (University of California Press, 1998). An excellent commentary on last developments on the excavations of the place. It contains valuable information about some of the contemporary kingdoms.

ETRUSCOLOGY, by Massimo Pallotino (Penguin Books Ltd, 27 Wrights Lane, London W8 5TZ, England, 1955). Archaeologist Pallotino, considered by many as the top expert on the Etruscans, presents a record of different finds on multiple aspects of Etruscan culture.

A DICTIONARY OF SELECTED SYNONYMS IN THE PRINCIPAL INDO-EUROPEAN LANGUAGES, by Carl Darling Buck (The University of Chicago Press, 1955). The subtitle is an understatement: *A contribution to the history of ideas*. A jewel written by a master in comparative philology with the aid of colleagues and assistants. For anyone intending to trace the origins of some words. Unfortunately, it will be found only in a few libraries.

WHEN GOD WAS A WOMAN, by Merlin Stone (Harvest/Harcourt, Brace, Jovanovitch, Publishers, New York). It is a dramatic narrative of the dethronement of the Goddess and of Her female worshipers in the Middle East.

ENCYCLOPEDIA BRITANNICA. Many readers may have it. It is probably the fastest medium for an overall view. It is common in public libraries. It excels in classical subjects. For those lucky mortals who have the CD-version the criss-crossing through references will be speedier and many more will surge spontaneously. The initial subjects suggested are:

Basques	Dodona	Iona	Rome
Crete	Etruscans	Lemnos	Zeus
Delos	Greece	Linguistics	
Delphi	Homer	Pelasgians	

For those lacking the CD-version the Index will provide additional interesting points.

A PICTORIAL TRAVEL

Images are stories in themselves. The following books and magazines give the reader an extraordinary opportunity to witness the past not only through some fine essays but also through first class images. Even if they cannot replace travel, those who have the fortune of being able to visit the historic sites will discover that they also constitute a formidable guide for the visit of both museums and archaeological sites. In fact, some of them are presently sold in tourist offices and museums. They provide an historical understanding and perspective that cannot usually be achieved through the normal travel guides or even guided tours. If any Greek book is asked by mail it is convenient to specify the language in which the book is desired.

ART AND RELIGION IN THERA: RECONSTRUCTING A BRONZE AGE SOCIETY, by Nanno Marinatos (D&I. Mathioulakis, Andromedas 1, Athens 16231, Greece). Spyridon Marinatos, discoverer of Akrothiri, died as a result of an accident while excavating. His daughter, also an archaeologist, has dedicated this wonderful book to his memory. Its subject are the frescoes and objects found in the buildings and their religious and communal uses. She explores the symbolism of art and attempts to reconstruct the ceremonies. Even if the comments are rigorously written, following a thoroughly academical plan and style, both the grace and the passion of the author for the material turns it into a lively reading. Anyone interested in Minoan culture will find its many splendid figures, clear explanations and multiple insights fascinating. A must, independently of planning or not a visit to the island (it may be bought there).

MYCENAE-EPIDAURUS, by S.E. Jakovidis (Ekdotike Athenon S.A., 11 Omirou Street, Athens 106 72, Greece, 1978) A complete guide to the museums and archaeological sites of the Argolid. Jakovidis, a well known professor of archaeology, succeeds in bringing back the Mycenae of Agamemnon and Clytemnestra for us. Beautiful images and reconstructions of the city discovered by Schlieman, of its treasures, objects and frescoes. It also focus on Argos, Tyrins and Nauplion. It contains a large fold-out map of the region.

KNOSSOS-THE MINOAN CIVILIZATION. Text supervised by Sosso Logiadou-Platonos (D&I. Mathioulakis, Andromedas 1, Athens 16231, Greece). Beautiful photos of the palace of Minos. A wonderful pictorial survey of the Minoan civilization. Contains a brief history of Minoan civilization and of the excavations. It dwells on mythology, archaeology, museums and excavations. Visitors will discover that it also contains a proposed tour to Knossos.

DELPHI, by Basil Petrakos (Clio Editions, 20-22 Antiochias St., Athens 813, Greece). Having served as Ephor of Antiquities for Mytilene, Delphi, Patras, the National Museum and the Attica allows this archaeologist an exceptional vision of the ancient panhellenic sanctuary, from the time it was a small village in the hands of, in his own words, "the original owner of the place, goddess Earth", through the time Apollo pushed her over, to the last excavations. Wonderful pictures and reconstructions.

NATIONAL MUSEUM, ATHENS, by Semni Karouzou (Ekdotike Athenon S.A., 11 Omirou Street, Athens 106 72, Greece, 1977) An illustrated guide to the Museum by its former Honorary Ephor. Wonderful notes on the origin, history and meaning of the hundreds of objects and frescoes shown. A powerful pictorial history of Greece, from the time the Mother Goddess prevailed, passing through the arrival of the first male statuettes, relishing in frescoes and finds from the Minoan period, full with enrapturing photos of marvels from the classic era, ending with spectaculars works of the Byzantine Empire.

CELTIC MYSTERIES. THE ANCIENT RELIGION, by John Sharkey (Thames & Hudson, 30 Bloombury St., London WC1B 3QP, 1995) A delightful approach to the last tribal culture in Europe. It dwells on the traditions and lore of the ancient religion of nature with its symbols of death and rebirth. More than a hundred illustrations carries the reader to ancient Britain.

THE VIKINGS, by Howard La Fay (National Geographic Society, Washington, 1972) Well written, carries the reader to the world of the Norse gods. It brings compellingly to life heroic Viking leaders: Eric Bloodax, Leif the Lucky, Olaf the Stout, Harald Haardrada. Photos and illustrations are at the usual state-of-the-art National Geographic level.

MAGAZINES

For those readers interested in some particular point, readings from three magazines (*National Geographic, Scientific American* and *Archaeology*) are suggested. They have the virtue of carrying the reader straight to the point and usually providing some in-depth additional information. The articles are always splendidly written and the illustrations superb. The three can be found in public or educational libraries.

NATIONAL GEOGRAPHIC:

VIKINGS, H. La Fay, T. Spiegel, pages 492-542, V 137, 4, Apr 1970

THERA, S. Marinatos, O. Imboden, pages 702-726, V 141, 5, May 1972

APHRODISIAS, AWAKENED CITY OF ANCIENT ART, K.T. Erim, J. Blair, pages

766-792. V 141, 6, Jun 1972

HOMEWARD WITH ULYSSES TO THE IONIAN ISLES OF GREECE, M.B. Grosvenor, E.S. Grosvenor, pages 1-39, V 144, 1, Jul 1973

THE PHOENICIANS: SEA LORDS OF ANTIQUITY, S.W. Matthews, W. Parks, R.C. Magis, pages 149-189, V 146, 2, Aug 1974

LAST HARBOR FOR THE OLDEST GREEK SHIP, S.W. Katzev, M.L. Katzev, pages 618-625, V 146, 5, Nov 1974

THE RENAISSANCE LIVES IN TUSCANY, L. Marden, A. Moldway, pages 626-660, V 146, 5, Nov 1974

LIFE IN THE ENDURING PYRENEES, R. Laxalt, E.S. Grosvenor, pages 794-819, V146, 6, Dec. 1974.

EXPLORING THE MIND OF ICE-AGE MAN, A. Marshack, pages 62, V147, 1, Jan 1975

IN THE STEPS OF MOSES, H. Arden, N. Benn, pages 2-37, V 149, 1, Jan 1976

THE CELTS, EUROPE'S FOUNDERS, M. Severy, J.P. Blair, R.C. Magis, pages 582-634, V 151, 5, May 1977

ANCIENT EUROPE IS OLDER THAN WE THOUGHT, C. Renfrew, A. Woolfit, pages 615-623, V 152, 5, Nov 1977

GLASS TREASURE FROM THE EGEAN pages 768-793, V 153, 6, Jun 1978

MINOANS AND MYCENAEANS, J. Judge, G.W. Gahan, L.K. Townsend, pages 142-185, V 183, 2, Feb 1978

SEEKING THE TOMB OF PHILIP OF MACEDON, M. Andronicos, S. Tsavdaroglou, pages 55-77, V 154, 1, Jul 1978

BORDEAUX, FINE WINES AND FIERY GASCONS, W. Davenport, A. Woolfitt, pages 233-259, V 158, 2, Aug 1980

HUMAN SACRIFICE IN A MINOAN TEMPLE, Y. Sakellarakis, E. Sapouna-Sakellaraki, O. Imboden, S. Tsavdaroglou, pages 205-224, V 159, 2, Feb 1981

16TH-CENTURY BASQUE WHALING IN AMERICA, B. Curtsinger, R. Schlecht, J.A. Tuck, R. Grenier, R. Laxalt, pages 40-71, V 168, 1, Jul 1985

SAILING IN JASON'S WAKE, T. Severin, J. Egan, S. Mortimer, pages 406-421, V 168, 3, Sep 1985

THE ETERNAL ETRUSCANS, R. Gore, O.L. Mazzatenta, J.M. Gurney, pages 696-743, V 143, 6, Jun 1988

THE GOLDEN HOARD OF BACTRIA V.S. Sarianidi, L. Bogdanov, E. Terebenin, V 117, 3, March 1990

IRAQ: CRUCIBLE OF CIVILIZATION, M. Severy, pages 102-115, V 179, 5, May 1991

PASTURES OF HEAVEN, N. Polovsmak, C. O'Rear, pages 80-103, V 186, 4,

Oct 1994

WHEN ANCIENT GREEKS WENT WEST, R. Gore, S. Brimberg, pages 2-37, V 186, 5, Nov 1994

THE SILK'S ROAD LOST WORLD, T.B. Allen, Reza, pages 44-51, V 189, 3, 1996

SCIENTIFIC AMERICAN

MYCENAE, CITY OF AGAMEMNON, G.E. Mylonas, Dec 1954, pages 72-80

ETRUSCAN METALLURGY, A.N. Modona, Nov 1955, pages 90-100

THE INDO-EUROPEAN LANGUAGE, P. Thieme, Oct 1958, pages 63-79

THE EXCAVATION OF A DROWNED GREEK TEMPLE, M.H. Jameson, Oct 1974, pages 110-122

THE YEAR WITHOUT A SUMMER, H. Stommel, E. Stommel, Jun 1979, pages 134-143

A 16TH-CENTURY BASQUE WHALING STATION IN LABRADOR, J.A. Tuck, R. Grenier, Nov 1981, pages 180-196

GIANT VOLCANIC CALDERAS, P. Francis, June 1983, pages 60-69

THE SOCIAL ARCHAEOLOGY OF MEGALITHIC MONUMENTS, C. Renfrew, Nov 1983, pages 152-163

THE ERUPTION OF KRAKATAU, P. Francis, S. Self, Nov 1983, pages 172-181

A NEOLITHIC FORTRESS AND FUNERAL CENTER, R.J. Mercer, Mar 1985, pages 94-101

MINOAN PALACES, P.M. Warren, Jul 1985, pages 94-103

THE CONSTRUCTION PLANS FOR THE TEMPLE OF APOLLO AT DIDYMA, L. Haselberg, Dec 1985, pages 126-135

CROP STORAGE AT ASSIROS, G. Jones, K. Wardle, P. Halstead, D. Wardle, Mar 1986, pages 96-103

POSTGLACIAL FORAGING IN THE FORESTS OF EUROPE, M. Zvelebil, May 1986, pages 104-115

A ROMAN APARTMENT COMPLEX, D.J. Watts, C.M. Watts, Dec 1986, pages 132-141

A MESOLITHIC CAMP IN DENMARK, T.D. Price, E.B. Petersen, March 1987, pages 112-121

EARLY FARMING IN NORTHWESTERN EUROPE, J.M. Howell, Nov 1987, pages 118-127

THE ROMAN PORT OF COSA, A.M. McCann, Mar 1988. pages 102-114

THE TRIREME SAILS AGAIN, J.F. Coates, Apr 1989, pages 96-105

ORIGINS OF INDO-EUROPEAN LANGUAGES, C. Renfrew, Oct 1989, pages 106-117

THE WORLD'S OLDEST ROAD, J.M. Coles, Nov 1989, pages 100-107

THE MITHRAIC MYSTERIES, D. Ulansey, Dec 1989, pages 130-145

THE EARLY HISTORY INDO-EUROPEAN LANGUAGES, T.W. Gamkrelidze, V.V. Ivanov, March 1990, pages 110-116.

THE EMERGENCE OF MODERN HUMANS, C.B. Stringer, Dec 1990, pages 98-105

GENES, PEOPLES, LANGUAGES. L.L. Cavalli-Sforza, Nov 1991, pages 72-77.

THE RECENT AFRICAN GENESIS OF HUMANS, A.C. Wilson, R.L. Cann, Apr 1992, pages 68-75

THE MULTIREGIONAL EVOLUTION OF HUMANS, A.G. Thorne, M.H. Wolpoff, Apr 1992, pages 76-83

ORIGINS OF HUMANKIND: EAST SIDE STORY, Y. Coppens, May 1994, pages 62-71

WORLD LINGUISTIC DIVERSITY, C. Renfrew, Jan 1994, pages 104

LATE ICE-AGE HUNTING TECHNOLOGY, H. Knecht, Jul 1994, pages 66-75

ENVIRONMENTAL DEGRADATION IN ANCIENT GREECE, C.N. Runnels, Mar 1995, pages 72-83

THE TAPESTRY OF POWER IN A MESOPOTAMIAN CITY, E.C. Stone, P. Zimansky, Apr 1985

THE TREBUCHET, P.E. Chevedden, L. Eigenbrod, V. Foley, W. Soedel, Jul 1985

THE LOST TECHNOLOGY OF ANCIENT GREEK ROWING, J.R. Hale, May 1966, pages 66-71

ARCHAEOLOGY

BOYHOOD OF A GOD. (Cretan Zeus) H. Sackett, S. Mc Gillivay, Sep/Oct 1989, pages 26-31.

ANATOMY OF AN ERUPTION. (Thera) F.W. McCoy, G. Heiken, May/Jun, 1990, pages 42-49.

BREWING AN ANCIENT BEER, S.H. Katz, F. Maytag, Jul/Aug 1991, pages 24-33.

BODY IMAGERY OF THE ANCIENT EGEAN, L. Talalay, Ibid.

ART OF THE ETRUSCANS, L. Bonfante, A. Emiliozzi, Ibid.

WHO WERE THE ISRAELITES? N.A. Silberman, Mar/Apr 1992, pages 22-30

BIRTH CONTROL IN THE ANCIENT WORLD, J.M. Riddle, J. Worth Estes, J.C. Russell, Mar/Apr 1994, pages 29-35.

SECRET RITES OF LESBOS, H. Williams, Jul/Aug 1994, pages 35-40.

IMAGES OF THE ICE AGE, A. Marshack, Jul/Aug 1995, pages 28-39.

Mad Honey!, (hallucinogens) A. Mayor, Nov/Dec 1995, pages 32-40.
Winning at Olympia, D.G. Kyle, Jul/Aug, 1996, pages 26-37.
Warrior Women of the Eurasian Steppes, J. Davis-Kimball, Jan/Feb 1997, pages 45-51.

REFERENCES

Lettres, Madame de Sévigné (Garnier-Flammarion, Paris, 1976)

El hombre prehistórico en el Pais Vasco, M. de Barandiaran (Ekin, Buenos Aires, 1945)

Orígenes prearios del pueblo vasco, E. de Gandia (Ekin, Buenos Aires, 1943)

Los vascos, J.C. Baroja (Istmo, Madrid, 1974)

Breve historia de Euskadi, F. Letamendia Ortzi (Ibérica, Barcelona, 1980)

Vínculo de la lengua Vasca con las lenguas de todo el mundo, I. Aguirre (Ed. La gran enciclopedia Vasca, Bilbao, 1980)

Diccionario Vasco-Español, Español-Vasco, Hiztegula 2000 (Elkar, Donostia, 1994)

Aragón en el pasado, J.M. Lacarra (Espasa Calpe, Madrid, 1972)

Los Almogávares, J.M. Echevarria (Plaza y Janés, Barcelona, 1974)

Las sociedades secretas, S. Hutin (EUDEBA, Buenos Aires, 1961)

Los constructores de catedrales, J. Gimpel (Centro Editor de América Latina, Buenos Aires, 1971)

La herencia humana, J. Rostand (EUDEBA, Buenos Aires, 1960)

Tipos humanos, R. Firth (EUDEBA, Buenos Aires, 1971)

El pais de los Súmeros, H. Schmökel (EUDEBA, Buenos Aires, 1972)

El arte sumerio, A. Parrot (UNESCO - Hermes, 1969)

El totemismo, J.G. Frazer (Kier, Buenos Aires, 1946)

The Golden Bough, J.G. Frazer (Wordsworth, Hertfordshire, UK, 1996)

Gods, Graves and Scholars, C.W. Ceram (A. Knopf, New York, 1952)

Prehistoric Societies, G. Clark, S. Piggott (Penguin, London, 1970)

The Atlas of Early Man, J. Hawkes (St. Martin's, New York, 1976)

Tartessos, A. Schulten (Espasa-Calpe, Madrid, 1952)

Historia del pueblo etrusco, W. Keller (Omega, Barcelona, 1971)

Los etruscos, A. Hus (Fondo de Cultura Económica, México, 1975)

Dictionaire de la civilisation grecque, G.Rachet, M.F.Rachet

(Larousse, Paris, 1968)

GODS AND HEROES OF THE GREEKS, H.J. Rose (The World Publishing Co., New York, 1958)

THE GOD BENEATH THE SEA, L. Garfield, E. Blishen, (Corgi, London, 1977)

THE GODS OF THE GREEKS, C. Kerenyi (Grove Press, New York, 1960)

HISTORIA DE LOS GRIEGOS - HISTORIA DE ROMA, I. Montanelli (Plaza & Janés, 1973)

THE GREEK WAY, E. Hamilton (The New American Library, 1956)

THE WAR AT TROY, Quintus of Smyrna (Barnes and Noble, New York, 1996)

LA ILÍADA, LA ODISEA, Homero (Círculo del Libro, Caracas, 1972)

LOS NUEVE LIBROS DE LA HISTORIA, Herodoto (La Oveja Negra, Bogotá, 1983)

COMEDIAS, Aristófanes (Iberia, Barcelona, 1965)

DIÁLOGOS, Platón, (Porrúa, México, 1973)

SOCRATES, R.Silverberg (G.P.Putnam &Sons, N. York, 1965)

SÓCRATES, R. Mondolfo (EUDEBA, Buenos Aires, 1972)

RECUERDOS DE SÓCRATES, Jenofonte (UNAM, México, 1965)

HELÉNICAS, Jenofonte (Ed. Juventud, Barcelona, 1978)

LA EXPEDICIÓN DE LOS DIEZ MIL, Jenofonte (Espasa-Calpe, Madrid, 1976)

THE PELOPONNESIAN WAR, Thucydides (Penguin, London, 1965)

FRAGMENTOS, Leucipo - Demócrito (Aguilar, Buenos Aires, 1970)

HISTOIRE DE LA PHILOSOPHIE. LA PHILOSOPHIE GRECQUE. ENCYCLOPÉDIE DE LA PLÉIADE. Ed. B. Parain (Gallimard, Paris, 1969)

LES ORIGINES DE LA PENSÉE GRECQUE, J.P. Vernant (Presses Universitaires de France, 1962)

SEXUAL LIFE IN ANCIENT GREECE, H. Licht (Panther, London, 1962)

LA TRAGEDIA GRIEGA, A. Lesky (Labor, Barcelona, 1970)

TEATRO GRIEGO: ESQUILO, SÓFOCLES, EURÍPIDES, ARISTÓFANES, MENANDRO. OBRAS COMPLETAS (EDAF, Madrid, 1962)

GREEK TRAGEDY, H.D.F. Kitto. (Methuen & Co, London, 1971)

FORM AND MEANING IN DRAMA, H.D.F. Kitto. (Methuen & Co, London, 1971)

LA ESCULTURA EN LA ANTIGUA GRECIA, F. Chamoux (UNESCO - Hermes, 1968)

THE POCKET BOOK OF GREEK ART, T. Craven (Pocket Book, New York, 1950)

THE NATIONAL MUSEUM OF ARCHAEOLOGY, *Athens*, S. Meletzis & A. Papadakis (Schnell & Steiner, Munich, 1967)

THE PARTHENON, A HISTORY OF ANCIENT GREECE, P. Green (Newsweek, New York, 1978)

OLYMPIA, M. Andronicos (Ekdotike Athenon, Athens, 1976)

THE ANCIENT WORLD, T.R. Glover (Penguin, London, 1962)

ASPECTS OF ANTIQUITY, M.I. Finley (Penguin, London, 1975)

THE WORLD OF ODYSSEUS, M.I. Finley (Penguin, London, 1975)

THE ANCIENT GREEKS, M.I. Finley (Penguin, London, 1972)

HISTOIRE DU THÉÂTRE, V. Pandolfi (Marabout, Paris, 1964)

THE SACRED MUSHROOM AND THE CROSS, J.M. Allegro (Abacus, London, 1973)

TRANSFORMATIONS OF MYTH THOUGH TIME, J. Campbell (Harper & Row, New York, 1990)

A HISTORY OF GOD, K. Armstrong (Knopf, New York, 1993)

LOS ANALES, Tácito (Espasa-Calpe, Buenos Aires, 1952)

HISTORIAS - LA GERMANIA, Tácito (Aguilar, Madrid, 1961)

COMEDIAS, Plauto (Aguilar, Madrid, 1962)

LA ENEIDA, Virgilio (EDINAL, México, 1956)

LOS DOCE CÉSARES, Suetonio (Mediterráneo, Madrid, 1970)

THE GOLDEN ASS, Apuleius (Collier, New York, 1962)

LE SIÈCLE D'AUGUSTE, P. Grimal (Presses Universitaires de France, 1955)

THE COLOSSEUM, P. Quennell (Newsweek, New York, 1971)

DECLINE AND FALL OF THE ROMAN EMPIRE, E. Gibbons (Rand-McNally, New York, 1971)

JULIO CÉSAR, M. Grant (Bruguera, Barcelona, 1971)

THE ART AND LIFE OF POMPEII AND HERCULANEUM, M. Grant, (Newsweek, New York, 1979)

ROMAN SOCIETY FROM NERO TO MARCUS AURELIUS, S.Dill (Meridian Books, N.York, 1956)

VIDAS PARALELAS, Plutarco (EDAF, Madrid, 1972)

THE SATYRICON, Petronius (The New American Library, 1959)

LA GUERRE DES GAULES, César (Garnier - Flammarion, Paris, 1964)

CARTHAGE, M. Hours-Miedan (Presses Universitaires de France, 1959)

THE BYZANTINES, T. Caldecot Chubb (The World Publishing Co, Cleveland,

1959)

THE STORY OF ENGINEERING, J. Kip Finch (Doubleday, 1960)

WRITING, THE STORY OF ALPHABETS AND SCRIPTS, G. Jean (H.N. Abrams, New York, 1992)

THE SONG OF ROLAND, Anonimous (Penguin, London, 1971)

CANTAR DE GILGAMESH, Anónimo (Galerna, Buenos Aires, 1977)

THE FABRIC OF THE HEAVENS, S. Toulmin, J. Goodfield (Hutchinson & Co, London, 1961)

STAR NAMES: THEIR LORE AND MEANING, R. Hinckley Allen (Dover, New York, 1962)

QUAND DIEU ÉTAIT FEMME, M. Stone (Éditions l'Étincelle, Paris, 1978)

THE BARBARIAN WEST, 400-1100, J.M. Wallace-Hadrill (Hutchinson University Library, London 1952)

THE ANCIENT CELTS, B. Cunliffe (Oxford University Press, New York, 1997 QUAND DIEU ÉTAIT FEMME, M. Stone (Éditions l'Étincelle, Paris, 1978)

ESTUDIO DE LA HISTORIA *(Vol. I al XV)*, A. J. Toynbee (Emecé, Buenos Aires, 1968)

THE WORLD OF ANCIENT MAN, I.W. Cornwall (The New American Library, 1966)

A WORLD HISTORY OF ART, G. Pischel (Newsweek, New York, 1978)

EROS AND CIVILIZATION, H. Marcusse (Beacon Press, Boston, 1953)

MAN AND HIS SYMBOLS, C.G. Jung (Doubleday, New York, 1964)

MEMORIES, DREAMS, REFLECTIONS, C.G. Jung (Random House, London, 1963)

SIMBOLOGIA DEL ESPÍRITU, C.G. Jung (Fondo de Cultura Económica, México, 1981)

LA SIMBOLOGÍA, O. Beigbeder (Oikos-Tau, Barcelona, 1971)

NATURE AND HUMAN NATURE, A. Comfort (Penguin, London, 1966)

EL LENGUAJE OLVIDADO, E. Fromm (Hachette, Buenos Aires, 1972)

MYTHS, DREAMS, MYSTERIES, M. Eliade (Fontana, London, 1977)

THE MYTH OF THE ETERNAL RETURN OR COSMOS AND HISTORY, M. Eliade (Princeton, 1954)

EL ARTE PALEOLÍTICO, E. Ripoll (Grupo 16, Madrid, 1996)

MAINSPRINGS OF CIVILIZATION, E. Huntington (The New American Library, 1966)

LOS ORÍGENES DE LA CIVILIZACIÓN, V. Gordon Childe (Fondo de Cultura

Económica, México, 1954)

Sor Juana Inés de la Cruz o las trampas de la fé, O. Paz (Fondo de Cultura Económica, México, 1994)

The way of trascendence, A. Kee (Penguin, London, 1971)

The Medici, G.F. Young (The Modern Library, N. York, 1930)

Les intelectuels au Moyen Age, J. Le Goff (Éditions du Seuil, Paris, 1957)

The Renaissance, W. Pater (The New American Library, 1959)

Princes of the Renaissance, O. Prescott (Random House, New York, 1969)

Man and monkey, L. Williams (Panther, London, 1967)

Demonic males, R. Wrangham, D. Peterson (Houghton Mifflin Co, New York, 1996)

Los fundamentos de la evolución humana, W.E. Le Gros Clark (EUDEBA, Buenos Aires, 1961)

An essay on man, E. Cassirer (Doubleday, New York, 1956)

Orígenes de la familia moderna, J-L. Flandrin (Grijalbo, Barcelona, 1979)

Historia de Egipto, E. Drioton, J. Vandier Clark (EUDEBA, Buenos Aires, 1964)

The language instinct, S. Pinker (Penguin, London, 1994)

Dictionary of word origins, J.T. Shipley (Littlefield, Adams & Co., New Jersey, 1977)

Language, Ed. by R.C. Oldfield & J.C. Marshall (Penguin, London, 1968)

The mother tongue, B. Brysson (Morrow, New York, 1990)

Cows, pigs, wars and witches: The wars of culture, M. Harris (Random House, New York, 1974)

Index

Achean 72, 76, 78, 80, 107, 126, 130-136, 138-139, 141, 143-144, 147, 153-159, invasion 72, Achean kings 156, sacred kings, scheme of domination 158, takeover 134, trick 135, warriors 132, 139, 144, weapon (marriage) 131, success 132
Acheans 65-66, 72, 75-77, 80, 122, 124-125, 127, 129, 131-135, 138-139, 144.
Achilles 124, 139-140, 154, 237-238
Acropolis 65
actor 44, 58. See theater
Adam of Bremen 182
Adonis, Isis and 223
adornments 44
Adriatic 65
Aegean 66, 70, 72, 75, 80, civilization 66, Sea 99
Aegeus, King 135
Aegisthus 159
Aeneas 158
Aeneid 18, 158
Aeschylus 83, 110
Aetolian 126
Afghanistan 233
Africa 86, 98, 105, 107, 113, 116, 118, 122, 126, 196, 200-201, 210, 213, 218, 220, 223, languages 201
Agamemnon 74, 121, 124, 141, 144, 153-154, 156, 159-160, 175
Agni 142
agricultural tribes 209
agriculture 78, 101, 103-105, 115
Ahmad Ibn Fadlan 188, 189, 190
Ajax 140
Akkaddian 236
Alaska 62, 219
Álava 36
Alba Longa 50
Albacete 99
Alcmene 107
Alexander 79, 82
Alexandria, Library of 141

almogavars 29-30, 31
Alpin, Kenneth mac 44
Altamira 33
altars 68, 120, 132
Amazon 73, 131-134, 228, 235, 236-238, Hippolyte, the Queen of the 131, Hypsipyle 131, land 131, names 131, warrior women 131
America 16-17, 19, 34-35, 40, 48, 62, 89, 217-220, discovery by Columbus 19, North 19, 62, Solutrean discovery of 219-220, 222, Viking discovery of 182
American 19, 42, 47, 61-62, Revolution 229
Amerindian 42, 48
Amphictyon (father of Herakles) 91, 191
amphictyonic 90, 103, 120-121, 125-126, alliances 225, League 103, 121, 125-126, religious center 120
amphictyonies 126
Amyklae 151
Anahita, goddess 233
Anatolia 183
Anatolian 66
Anaxagoras 80
Anaximander 80
Anaximenes 80
ancient European names 204
Angel of Death 189
angels 59
Anglo-Saxon 37
Antenor 158
anti-European 86
antlers 98, 214
Apache 62
apes 201
aphrodisiac 192
Aphrodisias 73
Aphrodite 99, 102, 180, 233. See Venus
Apollo 126, 154, 184-186, 188, Lykaion 184, of the Wolves 184,

slained Pytho 188, below the temple of, 186, priestesses of 185,
Aquitaine 24, 26
Aquitanians 24
Arabia 241
Arabs 25-28, 30-31, 188-190, 218
Aragon 29, 31
Arana Goiri, Sabino de, 38-43, 46, 49, 60, 62, 65, 83, 90, 204, 206
Archelaus 80
architecture 20, 53, colonnades 121, pillars 121
architects, naval 81
Archon Basileus 108, 110
Arctic 219
Areopagus 108
Argival 72
Argonauts 107, 139, sons of the 139
Argos (city) 66, 73
Argos (ship) 107, sailors of the, 132-133, 140, 153
aristocracies
aristocracy, Athenian 78, male 91, male military 77
Aristophanes 83
Aristotle 79, 141, 184
Arkhanes 230
Armada Invencible 35
Armagnac 22
Arpeko Saindua (the saint woman of the cave) 180
art 17, 20, 27, 34, 57-59, 64, 71-72, 74, 102, 115, 137, 141, 231, 243, artists 99, 119, 141, 146, 150-152
Artemis 73. See , Diana, patroness of fishers and sailors
Arthur, King 103
Aryan 17, 63-66, 71, 74, 76-78, 80, 88-89, 209, 240-241, Europe 88, invasions 64, law 89, tradition 189, tribes 100
Aryans 33, 63, 68, 71, 93, 157, 211, 217, 222, crossbreeding 77, racial purity 78, four-chaste system 78,
pure 77
Asia 86, 196, 209, 213, 218-220, Minor 49, 66, 73, 75, 82, 223
Asian 107, American connection 219
Asiatic 33, 86
Assyria 233
Astarte, Phoenician. 183
Asterix 15-16, 25, 43, 48, 213, 218, 220
astronomer 104
astronomic 70, 104, 121, phenomenon 121, record 104
astronomical 103, 111, 126, 137, meaning 103
Athena 99-100, 105, 233, giant statue of 99
Athenaus 57
Athens 65-66, 68, 75, 78-79, 81-83, 91, 105, 108-110, 121, 125-126, 129, 135, 140, 141, 238, 243, father of 147, hegemony 126, throne 135, tribes 78, women 109
Atlantic 19, 34-35, 48, 62, 134, 220, 226, 229
Atlas 134
Aton-Rah 223
Atreus 121, 139, 141, House of 136, raise and splendor of the powerful house of 141
Attic dialect 75
Attica 82, four Ionian tribes of the 147
Augustus 158
Aurignacian 213-215, 222, culture 213
Australoid 42
Austria 207
Avignon 193
ax, double 68, 101, 237. See labrys, bipennis
ayatolahs' revolution 89
Ay-Mari 180
azkonas 29
Babylonia 127, 177
Balkans 216
Baltic 115

Index

Bandelt, Hans Jürgen 210
Baptistery 59
barbarians 59
Baroja, J. Caro 45
Basojaun, the Lord of the Woods 230
Basque 26, 31-38, 43-46, 60, 65-66, 68, 94-96, 98, 194, 196, 198, 204-209, 213, 216, 227, 230, family relationship 94, first-born inherited all 94, sisterhood 94, intellectuals 204, language 94, 162, 194, tongue 31, 36, 94, women 193, words 32, 46, 192, 194, 196
Basques 25-28, 31-43, 45, 47, 57, 62, 65-66, 68, 93-95, 106, 195, 212-215, 218, 225-227, 229-230, 246
Basse-Navarre 36
Batz, Bertrand de 22
Batz, Charles (d'Artagnan) 22-23
Baviera 208
Bede, Venerable 183
beer 104, ancient recipe 104, goddess Ninkasi 104
Berbers 26
Bergerac, Cyrano de 18, 23-24, 30, 62, 241
best of European cultures 243
Bidarray, stalagmite in 180
bipennis 52, 68. See labrys, double ax
Biscay 36
bishops 53, 150
Black Sea 140, 153
Black Virgins 225, and her Son 224
blade flint technology 213
Blanchard 104
blood–type groups 40, Rh 41-43
blue adornments and decorations 236
boats 189, small traditional open 219
Bohemian 198
Bolívar 38
Bologna 59
Bond, James 18, 44, 195
bone tools 213
bonnet 152

Bordeaux 34
Boyd, W.C. 42
Bradley, Bruce 219
Bran 107
Brantôme, abbé 242
breakwater 81
Britain 44, 57, 205, 207, 210, 212-213, 224
British 44, 67, 242, Isles 214
Briton 67
bronze 57, 66, 232
Bronze Age 122, 140
Buenos Aires 35
building 45, 54, 56, 67-68, magnificent 121, polychromatic 67
Bull 68, 70-71, bullfights 71, corridas de toros 71, leapers 71, toro de lidia 71, rectangular courts 121, highly domesticated breed 71, games 120-121, fighting 70-71
bull-leaping ceremony 121
burial 44, 232, 235-236, mounds 236, ships 231
businesses 88
Julius Caesar 16, 48, 229
Calabria 29-30
Caledonians 44
calendar 70, 106, lunar 104
Camito-Semitic 208
Canada 19, 62
Capitoline Hill 51
cardinals 150
Caria 73, 81
Carians 65, 73
Carnival 183
Carthage 54
Carthaginians 54
Cartier, Jean 19, 34
Cassandra 159-160
Castelmore 22-23
Castlerea 212
Catalonia 31
catastrophic episode 216
Catherine de Medici 242-243

Cato 54, 87
Caucasoid 42
Caucones 65
cauldron 118
cave dwellers 33, Ice-Age 119
cavern full of snakes and human skulls 189
Cecrops 91
celebrate 126
celebrations 88, 114, 137
celestial sphere 122
Celtic 43-44, 47--48, 71, 212, 216, 227
Celts 43-44, 46-48, 57, 65, 213, 228
Centaurs, Pelasgian horsemen 137, Cheiron 137, Nessus 137
ceramics 68, 88
cereals 104
ceremonial dresses 92
ceremonies 53, 68, 70, 82, 92, 105, 108, 111, 113, 115, 121, mimic 82
Cerne Abbas Giant 244-245
Cerveteri 58, 60
cetrum 52
Chalcas, the priest 175
Charlemagne 26-28, 30, 36, 229
Charles de Anjou 29
Charles the Lame 29-30
Charles VIII 24, 242
Charles IX 243
Charon 113
Chartres 224-225
chase 103, 105
Château wines 34
Cheiron (centaur) 137
Chemin of St. Jacques (Way of St. James) 225
Chimera 102, 129-130, 233, chimeric winged lions 235
chimpanzees 210
China 223, 233-235
Christian 37, 53, pilgrims 226, religious center 226, pre-Christian 37, 224-225
Christians 31, 158, Egyptian 183

Christmas 183
chromosomes 60
Chronicles of Fredegar 24
Church 224
Circe 243
citizens 16, 50, 53-54, 76, 78-79, 136-137
city 68-70, 72-73, 75, 77, 79, 81-83, 103-106, 109, 120-121, 125, 137, 140-141, 144, 149, 156-158, planning 20, 82, symbol 106, largest 67
civilization 53, 62-63, 66-68, 70-72, 74, 89, 95, 243, 245, affluent 70
civilized 68, 72, 80, 87
climate 70
Cloaca Maxima 51
Clóta, goddess, 224
Clovis point 219
Clytemnestra 159-160, 175
cognate 197-200
coition 102, public 189
colleges of priestesses 106, 130, 134
colony, placement of a 126
colors 68
coltell 29, 31
Columbus, Christopher 19, 35, 47, 201, 218
Combellack, Frederick 237
commerce 72, 74, 139, 243
commercial 17, 57, 70, 73, 78, 81, routes of the east 141
common ancestor 210
Communist Party 225
companions, king's 109
competitions, men's 120
composers 59
Compostela, Santiago de 225-226
confederacy 45, 51
Connery, Sean 44
consecration, horns of the 68
consort of Hera 107
constellation 100, 103
Constitution, Spanish 37
consuls 90, twin 90

Index

control of the eastern trade 140
copper 66
Copt 218
Cortes, Hernan 35
Cosa, Juan de la 35
couple 86, 88, European 88, love in the 88
court, central 70, 121
courtly love 241
courtship 240, 242
crafts 115
creation myths 102, 112
cremation habits 222
Cretan 67-70, 79, 99, 108, 118, 121, cities 121, goddess, 108, maritime empire 132, 153, thunder god, traditions 157
Cretans 65, 69, 157
Crete 66-68, 70-75, 82, 96, 99, 112, 116, 120, 130, 132, 135, 221-222, 230-231, 236, Achean invasion of 130
Mallia 121, central court of 121
Cromagnons 33, 199, 214-215, 222
Cronos 107
crowns, golden 152
cryptic language 142-143
cryptically 122
cult 53, 70, 83, 98, 100, 101-103, 105-108, 111-115, 119, 122, 129-131, 137-138, 223-225, 238, cult of the dead 53, 193, 199, two-season Goddess 137
cultural 17-20, 39, 43, 52, 63, 71, 85-86, development 82, disparity 81, exchange 83, habits 125, influence 80, shock 86, 136, 154
culture 17, 20, 34, 36-37, 44, 50, 54-55, 59, 63-64, 71, 73, 77, 81-83, 85, 86, 91-92, 155, European 85, Ionian 81
curiae 53
customary law 228
Cyclad islands 99

cycles 54, Earth-Venus 103, four-year 120, in nature 101, lunar and solar 126-127, nine years 121, menstrual 101, Metonic 134, moon 102, one-hundred-lunation 126, quadrennial Pythian Games 126, quadrennial religious festival 141, regal 120, 137, seven years 126, three phases 101, 103, three-season year 102, 130, 325-lunation 127, twenty years 134, two-season year 130, winter-solstice 184, nine men dying every nine years 182, summer solstice 183, yearly owl hunt 105
cyclic matrilineal systems 229
Cyclops 65
Czech 207, 222
Czechoslovakian 198
Dagda (Irish Herakles) 107
d'Artagnan 18, 23-24, 30, 45, 62, 185, 225
dance 36, 59, of the Goblet 36, wild 109
dancer 56, 58
Danish 195, 198
Danube 114
Daphne 186
Davis-Kimball, Jeannine 237
death and resurrection 231
death penalty 135
deflowering 131
deified 107, 116, 137, the only mortal 130
deity 106, 142
delirium 137
Delos 114, 175, League 126
Delphi 103, 186-187, 190, League of 126, sanctuary of 126, oracle
Demeter, the corn Goddess 102, 113, 120, 178, priestess of 120. See Persephone
democratic parties 79
Democritus 80
Dene-Caucasian 60, 62

Denmark 191
Diana 73, 99-100, 102, 105, priest of 105, temple at Nemi 105, temple at Ephesus 99
Diogenes 80
Dionysian festivities 83, Anthesteria 108-110, Chorus 185, Great Dionysia 83. See Hyeros Gamos, Sacred Marriage, Sacred Wedding
Dionysus 83, 108, 109, dethronement 184, married to 108, sanctuary 108, symbol of 186. See Dionysian festivities
Dionysus of Halikarnassos 50
discovery of America by Columbus 19, by Solutreans 219-220, 222, by the Vikings 182
dithyramb 109-110
divine child 102
divine couple, Dio and Dia 106, Sun and Moon 120, Tin and Tina 106
divinity 53, 102, 106
Djeus Pitar 123
DNA 33, 43, 210, 213, 216. See mitochondrial DNA, mtDNA
Dodona 73, 223
dolichocephalic 214
Dolní Vestonice 222
dolphins 68
Domboshawa 118
Dorian 73, 76, 78, 81, 91, 241
Dorians 47, 65-66, 72, 75-79, 81, 89, 124
Dorset 245
double ax 52
drainage 67
drugs, liposoluble 137. See hallucinogens
Druid 224
Dumas, Alexandre 18, 23
Dummuzi, Innanna and 223
Dutch 198
dwellers 105
dwelling 37

Early European 42
Earth Goddess 224
Easter 183,
Eastres (goddess) 183
Eastern Church 183
economic 141
economical 64
Egypt 66, 114-115, 218, 223
Egyptian 60, 183, 223, god Shu 107, mummy 60
Einsiedeln 225
Elcano, Juan Sebastián 35
Elche 99
Eleanor d'Aquitaine 241-242
emancipated slaves 229
Empedocles 80
engineering 55-56, marvel 82
engineers 67
England 35, 183, 190, 242
English 18, 61, 195, 197-198, 200, 227, 242
Eolian 47, 71, 76-77, 82-83, 123, 125-126
Eolians 65, 71, 77, 79-80, 106
Ephesus 73
epics 141
epidemics 192
Epiphany, feast of 184
equinoxes 108
ergot 190-192
ergotamine 190
erotic, couple 233, license 183
Eskimo 60, 219
Eteocretans 65
ethnias 76, 78-80, 82, 221, dethronement 126, groups 136
Etruria 50, 54
Etruscan 49-60, 62, 83, 88-91, 125, cities 125, League 51, 56
Etruscans 38, 49-57, 60, 65, 68-70, 81, 83, 88, 90-91, 106, 113, 189, 205, 208, 218, 228
Euripides 83, 109, 158
European, Community 246, mitochon-

drial gene pool 211, society 89, tribes 105, women 85-86, 88-89
Europeans, Mediterranean 85, modern 83, Old 86, Oldest 16, 18, 20-31, 33-34, 36, 38, 42, 44, 46, 48, 50, 52, 54, 56, 58, 60, 62
Euskaldunak 34
Euskalherria 34
Euskera 34, 45, 207
Euzkan 44, 47-48, 50, 52-53, 64, 68, 71, 74-75, 79-80, 82-83, 88, 91, 130-131, 134-136, 226, 228, 241-243, 245, burial traditions, cults 83, Goddess' cults 130, societies 79, system 135, tradition 189
Euzkos 34-35, 38-39, 42, 44-45, 49, 51-57, 59-67, 69-71, 73, 79, 82-84, 86, 88-89, 90-93, 95-96, 129, 187, 193, 195, 204, 206, 208, 218, 221, 227, 230, 240, 242, deepest and far-reaching legacy 89, from the sea 65-66, 69, matrilineal system, roots 90
Evans, Sir Arthur 67, 72, 91
Eve 210
ever-reigning queen 155
excavations 140
execution 137
fairytales, traditional, children's 93
Falerii 56
families 77, 79, 136, 236
family 20, 22, 37, 46-47, 52, 61-62, 87-88, 90, 93-96, 174, 183, 188, attachment 94, clans 96, family structure 79, family ties 94, Euzko 88
farmers 55, 209, 211-212
farming 56, techniques 209
fasci 51-52, 68
Fates, goddesses that controlled human life 102
Father God, 142
feast 109-110, 113, 183-185
feasts, Dionysian 108
female 209, 211, 214-216, 240, 242, 246, genitalia 214, influence 96,
female structured society 95
females 64, 87, 91
female-structured Paleolithic families 216
feminine 101, 104, movements 243
femininity 101
fertility 99, 101, 111, 114, 117, god 83,101, 114
fertility cult 185, 188, 245, celebration 185, 241
festivals 68, 81, 91, 137, 182-183, 243, annual spring 83, of Dionysus 183
festivities 104, 109, 115, 151, 183
Flamen Dialis 90
Flaminica 90
fleet 69
Fleming, Ian 18, 44-45
flights 185
flint off-cuts 219
Florence 57, 59, 243
Florentine 24
folklore 20, 184
foods 20, 56
fork 57
fortress 65, 68
Forum 51
founding fathers 123, 125-127, 238
Fra Angelico 59
France 15, 17, 22-27, 33, 36, 57, 104, 117, 183, 192-193, 205, 207, 214, 217, 219, 224-225, 241-242, 246
Franco 37
Franks 17, 26, 27-28, 241-242
Franklin, Benjamin 229
fraternities 109, 229, wolf 184
Frazer, Sir James 90, 105, The Golden Bough 90, 105, 110
freedom 228-229, personal 228
Freemasons 46, 229
French 16, 18, 20, 22, 24, 27, 32, 34, 47, 56-57, 155, 185, 192, 194-195, 197-198, 205, 218-219, 242-243,

Revolution 95, Revolutionaries 229
frescoes 58, 67-68, 70-71, 88, 91-92, 99, 100-101, 121, 150, 162, 230-231, Crete 99
funeral 53, 189, celebrations 137, traditions 222, of emperors 114
Furies, goddesses of vengeance 102
Gaelic 44, 195
Games, Olympic 114, 120, 238
Games, Pythian 104
Garay, Juan de 35
Gascoigne 24, 27
Gascons 24, 34, 242
Gauls 15-17, 43, 47, 56, 228. See Celts
gems, strings of 152
genes 89. See DNA, genetic
genetic 63, bottleneck 216, code 209, markers 43, 45, 212, 215. See DNA, genes
geneticists 196, 201
Genovese 35
German 66, 73, 198, 204-205
Germans 102, 110, 196
Germany 41, 57, 183, 192, 206-207, 210
Geronimo 62
Ghiberti 59
Gibraltar 26
girdle, maidens used a 131
glacial 44, Age 209, climate 213
Glaciation, Würm 213
goat 102, 109, skins 109
god 83, 99-101, 107-108, 111-112, 181-184, 186, thunder 142, to become a 137
goddess 99, 101-106, 108, 110-115, 117-122, 139, 142-143, 148-150, 152, 155, 159, 161-162, 222-224, 228-229, 233, 235, 237, 241, 246, and Her Son 223, consort 106, cult 106, 111, 129-130, 131, 137, Blue (or Black) 102, fertility 99, 150, married to the 106, naked 99, Red 102, richly dressed 99, symbol 129, 241 temples dedicated to the 114, triads of 101, Triple 101, 103, White 102. See Mother Goddess, Nymphs, Muses, Furies
godlike 114
gods 71, 100-101, 106-107, 112-114, 122, 126, 156-157
gold 69, brooch 152, crown of surprising portable design 233, jewelry 230, golden statuettes 233
Golden Girdle 131
goldsmiths 57
gorillas 210
Goscinny 15
Goths 17, 229, kings 241
government structure 125
Grabaulle Man 191
Graeci 65
grande cuisine 57
grapes, Bisturi 34
Graves, Robert 222, 239, The Greek Myths 222
Gravettian 222, culture 215
Greeks, educated 141, not-true 77, origin of the 123, pre-Greeks 77
Greenberg, Joseph 201, 202
Guadalete 26
Guernica 37
Guetaria 35
Guipúzcoa 36
Hades 139
Halikarnassos 66, 73, 81
Halloween 182
hallucinogenic brew 185, phenomena 186, power 185, substances 186, toxics 186, trips 190
hallucinogens 91, 104, 111, 116, 137, Amanita muscaria 186, bog mummies 191, bufotenines 186, collective hysteria 190, cobra snakes 186, ergotism 190, ethylene 186, frogs and toads 186, god of hallucinogenic trances 186, grayanotoxins 186, LSD 190, laurel, poisonous

Index

variety of 186, mescaline 186, Panaeolus papilionaceus 186, peasant madness 190, Pingri Village 186, priestesses holding snakes 187, Pythia fell into a hypnotic state 186, pythoness 187, 190, rye 104, rye bread 190, 192-193, snake-cult 186-188, toxic honeys 185, used in the Mysteries 191, voices and visions 186, wild sex in the open 191

Hamel, Elizabeth 204-207
Hannibal 54
harbor, Samos 81, planning 81
head of state 135
heavenly rearrangements 115
Hebrew 60
Hecate 102
Hekatontocheiroi—the one hundred hands 109
Helen 140-141, 144, 234, the most beautiful woman in Greece 140, Eleni, Orea 140, abduction of 141, Helesponto 162,
Hellanicus 237
Hellas 65, 162
Hellenes 65, 156
Hellenic 57, 64, 69, 78, 82
Hellenistic 73, 126
Helots 76, 78
henpecking order 92
Henry II 57, 242
Hephaestus (Vulcanus) 115
Hera 106, 131
Heraclitus 80
Heraeum—Hera's own zone 120
Heraia, girl's foot race 120
Herakles 106-107, 109-110, 112, 119, 121, 129-130, 132, 134, 137, 188, 235, 245, Deianeira 135-138, footrace winner 120, Golden Girdle 131, Hesperides' Garden 134, historic 107, horse and chariot races 121, Hydra of Lerna 188, instituted the Games 119, Megara 135, Ninth Labor 131, royal baby 188, only 137, shooting of the Stymphalian birds 130, Second Labor 130, 188, Sixth Labor 130, Sphinx's riddle 121, The Twelve Labors 109, 129, thousands of 107, two 107. See Hercules, Palemon.
Hercules 124, 129-131, 238. See Herakles, Palemon
Herminii 52
Hero 106-107, 111-112, 114, 118-122, 131-132, 135, 137, 139, 142, 147, 175, 188, 192, death 137, foot race 119, gain his kingship 119, honoring the sacrificed 114, Hero-King 131, only 137, royal titles of the 107, sacrificial death 132, to marry the 119,
Herodotus 49, 65-66, 69, 75, 77, 81, 83, 107, 111, 123-125, 129, 131-132, 138, 140-141, 222, 235-237, Father of History 132, Nine Books of History 123
Heroes 126-127, 129-131, 137, 148, 158, 238, bones 114, Bellerophon 129-130, 238, Iolcus, Peleus 131, Hercules, Theseus, Jason, Achilles, Agamemnon, Menelaus, Odysseus or Ulysses 124
heroic 59
Hesiod, 87
Hessen 206
hyeroglyphic 71
high priestess 159, 161
Hindu 78, 196
Hippo 80
Hippodamus 82
Hissarlik 67
histrio 58
homage 189
Homer 18, 66, 74-75, 77, 80, 139-140, 144, 221, 223, 225, 227, 229, 231, 233, 235, 237-239, Homeric 140

hominids 199
Homo sapiens sapiens 209, 213
hoplites 69
Horace 56
horsemen 31, 53
house 37-38, 52-53
human family tree 210
human sacrifice 91, 164, 185, all men yearly killed 130, 131 blood collected 116, bogs 192, ceremony 132, deifying 116, dressed with a skin goat 109, eucharistic meal 116, plunged into a sacred well 182, price of the full-grown cob 116, ritual murder 105, yearly in substitution of the king 93, 126-127, 182, 192, 223, woman 189, youths 116, 184, Zeus, sacrificed to 132
human-gene-markers 43
humans 210, 215
Humboldt, Wilhelm von 38
Hungary 57, 214
Huns 225
hunter-gatherers 209, 211, 216
hunters 201
husbands 86, 87-89, 95
Hydra of Lerna 130
Hyeros Gamos 100. See Sacred Wedding, Sacred Marriage
Hypolite 131
Hypsipyle 131
Iberian peninsula 25, 28, 46, 205, 207
Ice Age 32-33, 101, 106, 117, 216, iconography 228
iconography, Hercules 110
ideology 79
Iliad 18, 80, 121, 139-142, 144, 237, 239, copies of the 141
Ilion 140
impiety 134
Inchauspe 32
independence 68, 86
India 89, 223, 241
Indo-European 17, 19, 31, 38, 41, 46- 47, 49-50, 54, 60-61, 63-66, 68, 71-72, 74, 76-77, 83, 86, 89, 95, 100, 106, 109-110, 112-113, 119-122, 124, 155, 161, 195-199, 202, 212, 222, 224, 228, 231-232, 240-241, chieftains 122, invaders 124, 132, languages 195, myth 138, names 207, root 89, 195, 202, tribes 86, 142, 196,
Indo-Europeans 33, 43, 47, 64-65, 74, 77, 79, 82, 86, 89, 93, 95-96, 123, 125-126, 129, 137, 153, 205, 211-212, 217, 228, 232-233, 238, 243
Indra 142
Innanna and Dummuzi 223
intellectual, curiosity 81, influence 80
interbred society 71, interbreeding 83, intermarriage 122, intermarried 47, 49, 71, 77, intermarrying 79
interstadial 213, 215
Inuit 219-220
Iona, the sacred island 114
Ionia 79-80
Ionian 47, 71, 75-83, 88-89, 91, 123, 125-126, 147, 238, 243, cities 141
Ionians 65, 71, 75, 77, 79-82, 93, 106
Iphigeneia 175
Iran 89
Ireland 195, 212
Irish 43-44, 47, 106, 195, 227
iron 52, 57, 140
irrigation 20, 56
Ishtar 183, and Tanmuz 223
Isis, and Adonis 223, and her son Horus 223
Islands, Greek 183
Islands, Orkney 46
Italian 24, 49, 51, 53, 55, 57-59, 61, 63, 195, 198
Italians 88, 198
Italy 24, 49, 54, 56, 63, 75, 83, 105, 113, 134, 158, 205, 207, 242
ivory 98-99, 214, Ivory Period 214
Japanese 60

Index

Jasna Góra 225
Jason 124, 133-135, 139, 235
Jephte 174, 175
Jerusalem 183, 226
Jesus 183-184, official birth date of 184
jewelry 20, 68, 88, 230-231, 233, 238
Jonathan 174
Joseph 183
Jove 139, 142. See Jupiter, Djeus Pitar
Julius Caesar 16, 48, 158
Jupiter 90, 142, 223. See Jove, Djeus Pitar
Kamla Uppsala Kirka 182
Kharun (Etruscan Charon) 91, 113
king 90-93, 103, 106-111, 113-115, 118-122, 131, 134-135, 137, 140, 146-148, 154-156, 159, amphictyonic 90, could marry many queens 135, demotion of the sacrificial 229, extension of the life of the sacred 182, name of the 120, new 93, Norwegian 90, sacrifice 156, ritual killing of the sacred 120, sacrifice 156, Scandinavian 90, souls 114, unavoidable duty to kill the former 121,
kingdom 93, 134-135, 155, dead 113
Kings, Roman 90, Servius Tullius 90, Tarquin the Elder 90, Tatius 90
kingship 90-91, 107-108, 119, 121, 135, Etruscan 90, Roman 90
Knossos 67-70, 91-92, 100, 121, center of an amphictyonic league 121, central shrine at 152, Palace of 151
Kore and Persephone 102
Korynthos 66, 72
Kremlim 225
kurgan 235
laborers 55
Labourd 36
Labrador bay 34
labrys 52, 68, 101, 159, 237. See double ax, bipennis

labyrinth, Minotaur's 66, 135
Lacedemonia 69, 76, Queen of 140. See Laconia
Lacedemonian 132, 157
Laconia 69. See Lacedemonia
Lady and the Child 225
Laertes 140
Laima, the goddess of the woods 115
language 15, 17-18, 24, 31, 33-34, 36-37, 42, 44-50, 52, 59-62, 89, 92, 94, 96, 101, 106, 123, 125, 194-198, 201-202, 205, 209, 211, 213, 215, 217-219, cryptic 106, original language of the continent 204, specialists 195. See tongue
Languedoc 241
Laomedon 153
Lascaux 33
Last Glacial Maximum 216-217
Latin 17, 25, 31, 46, 63, 87, 95-96, 125, 174, 192, 194-195, 198, 202, 241, root 194
Latins 17, 49-50, 52, 54, 86, 88-89, 200
Latvians 183
Le Puy 225
leader, independence war 124
league 103, 120-121, 125-126, Delos 126
Leakeys 200
legends 20, 47, 71, 230
Legions, Roman 17, 20, 25, 51-52, 54, 228
Leleges 65, 73
Lemnians 83
Lemnos, sacred island of 73, 83, 131-133, women 132
Lerna 130-131, 188, traditions of the ancient, 130
Leucipus 80
levy 53
Liberté 229
Liberty Pole 229
Libya 222

Lille 23
Limoges 192
Lincoln, Abraham 124-125
Linear A 71
Linear B 71
linguistic 38, 60, 63, 204, 206-208, links to the stone, 221
linguists 31, 47, 61, 94-95, 195-196, 200, 205-208
lion 102, 110, skin 110, 245
literary 80, masterpieces 141
literature 27, 44, 59, 81, 87
Lithuania 207
Lithuanian 198
Lithuanians 183
Livy 53
locks 67, 70
London 212, 245
lore 63, 101, 105, 117
lotus eaters 170
Louis VII 241
Louis XIV 22
Loupiac—the city of the wolves 22, 185
love and hate prehistory 196
Love Revolution 242
Lucifer 58
Lulan beauty 234
lunations 214. See , cycles, moon
Lupercalia—the feast of the Wolves 185
Luperci 185
luxury 57, 91
lycanthropy 184
lyceum, 184
Lycurgus, the Spartan lawgiver 226
Lydians 49
Lysians 65
lyre 58
Maastricht 23
Macedonian 79
Macedonians 82
macho tradition 95
Maeatae 44

Maeonians 65
Magdalenian 222
Magellan, Ferdinand 35
Magi, three 184
magic 104
Magliano lead 60
malaria 56
male 64, 77-78, 86-88, 90-91, 94-95, 154, 156, 158, 160, aristocracy 126, -female relationship 86, 209, 240, genes 211, lover 241, power 87, male, from male to 215
Malnutrition 56
man 101, 106-107, 116-118, man, from man to 209
Mantova 59
manufacture 78
man-woman relationship 89
Mara, agricultural goddess 115
marble 99
Mari (city) 180-181
Mari (goddess) 180-181
Marie de Rabutin-Chantal, Madame de Sevigné 22
marriage 131-133, 136, approach 91, 131, counselor 136, to a princess 90, to the Goddess 223, marital differences 136, to the Queen 131
masterpieces 57
matria (instead of patria) 96
matriarchal influences 92, matriarchy 92, 95, matriarchy, hints of, 166
matrifocal 92, 96
matrilineal 90-94, 96, 126-127, 147, 154, 157, 159, 221, 223, 229, 231-232, 243, mark 93, royal houses 231, system 122, 135, 159, to patrilineal structures 221, tradition 154, matrilineality 189, 222
matrilocal 90, 96, 122, customs 122
matrimony 136
matriots 96
Mausolus 81, tomb 73
Medea 134-136

Index

Medici, Catherine de 57
medicine 137
megalithic 65
men 85-88, 94-96, 147, 149-151, 153, 162, 179, 181-182, 184, 187, 211-213, young 121
Menelaus 121, 124, 141, 146, 148, 153-157, 159-160
mercantile 72
merchants 70
metal 105, 194, 196, 199, artifacts 194
metallurgy 57
Mexico 35, 62, 219
Michelangelo 59, Pietá 59
Midas, King 73
Middle East 114, 211, 215
Miletus 82
Miltiades 83
Milton 37
mimically 109
Minoan 66-68, 72-73, 91-92, 230, 234, 243, civilization 66, 68, 234, nature religion 108, statuettes 187
Minoans 81
Minos, King 67, 69
Minotaur 129-130, 135
Minyans 132
misinformation 130, 137
mistletoe 184
mitochondrial DNA 210. See mtDNA
models of society 162
Modena 59
Monarchy 52
Mongoloid 42
Monroe, Marilyn 150
Montenegro 206
month, sidereal 103, synodic 103
moon 101-104, 119-120, 130, 148, 155-156, 241, 245, full 184, Goddess 101, Priestess 156
Moors 17, 45, 226, 229
moral writers 87
mortal 130, 132
Mother and Child 58

Mother Goddess 101, 105-106, 111, 117, 129, 222, cult 129, Gaia, the earth-Goddess 188, Goddess, 101-102, 106, 108, 111, 117, 121, Great Mother of all Gods 101, Lady 101, 110, Lady of the Lions 110, Mother of All Livings 101, Queen of the Fields 115, Queen of Heaven 101-102, Queen of the Woods 111, 115, Triple Goddess, 101
mothers 96
Mousterian 214
mtDNA 210-213, 215, 220. See mitochondrial DNA
multiplicity of powers 228
mummy 115, 191-192, 234
Munich (München) 208, 225
murals 114, 119
Muses, goddesses of the arts 102, 123, nine 102
music 57, 59, 81, ballet 243, drums 115, horns 114, 117, liticines and cornicines 114, musical instruments 199, Operas 141, singing, pipes 115, tubas 114, singing prostrated with their faces on the earth 189
musicians 59
Muslim 26-28, 85, 89
Mussolini 51
Mycenae 65-66, 68, 72, 74, 92, 99-102, 121, 140-141, 152, 156-157, 159-160, tomb at 152
Mysians 65
Mystery 59
myth 63, 66, 70-72, 83, 87, 94, 96, 101-102, 112, 117, 121, 126, 130-132, 134, 136-138, 153, 185, 188, 222
mythological beasts 129, being 102
Na-Dene 62
name 78, 80, 83, 87, 94, 96, 101, 106-109, 112, 114, 120, 123-125, ancient European, 204
Naples 29

Navarre 24, 31, 36
navies 51, 81
navigator 19, 34, 44, 47, 66, circle the globe 35
Nazi 17, 37, 229
Neandertals 199, 209, 213-214, 229-230
Near East 125
Negroid 42
Nemi, lake 105
Neolithic 46, 66, 99, 211-212, 218, Neolithic Europe 222
Nero 158
Nessus (centaur) 137
New Year 127. See Sacred Wedding
Nilo-Saharan 202
Nimrod, royal palace of 233
Ninkasi (goddess) 104
nobility 92, 95-96
nomadic high-tech 233
Non-Europeans 85-86
non-Indo-European 63, 65
Nordic 108, 111
Normandy 190
Norway 90, 207
Nuremberg, Gabriel Tetzel of 193
nymphs 104, 126, dryad 104, caryatid 104, hamadryads 104, helice 104, naiads 104, melia 104, oreads 104
Obedience to a strong central leader 228
Odin 223
Odysseus 124, 140-141, 144, 164-171, travels of 141
Odyssey 18, 141-142
Oedipus 121
Oenotria, 56
oil 70, containers 70, olive 56, whale 219
Ointments 137
oldest symbolic scripture 104
oligarchic minority 79
Olympias (Alexander's mother) 238
Olympic Games 114, 120, 238, original 119
Olympus, Mount 107, 115
Oñate, Juan de 35
One Hundred Years War 242
opulent 73, 79, 82, 140, cities 140
oracle 126, advice 159
oracular shrine 188
original language of the continent 204
Orkney Islands 46
orthognathism, 33
Oseberg ship 231
Oslo 231
Ottoman Empire 192
Ouranos 142
Out-of-Africa model 210
owl 105-106
Oxford 212
Padova 59
Paeonians 65
painters, cave 119
painting style 91
paintings 33, 53, 58, 141, 150, 238
palace 67-68, 70, 100, palaces 67-68, 72
Palaiokastrons 69
Palemon 130-139, 164-165, 170, 188, and his gang 131. See Herakles, Hercules
Paleolithic 19, 33, 36, 95, 101, 109, 211-212, 216, 218, 222, 227, DNA 227, man 101
Palestinian 66
Palio race 58
Pamplona 25, 68
Panathenea, central event in the 141
Panhellenic 120, ceremony 238
Pantheon 122
panties off 246
Paphos 238
Paris (city) 22, 57,
Paris, son of Priam 140
Parma 59
Parmenides 80
Parnassus, Mt. 126

Index

Parthenon 73, 99, 238
Patara 82
paternal authority 228
patria potestad, 87
patriarchal 89
patrilineal 126, 157, 159, 221-223, 232, patrilineal Indo-European 222, patrilineal societies 157
Pausanias, geographer and traveler 238
pearls 152
peasants 27, 30, 55
pecorino cheese 56
Pegasus 129-130
Pelasgian 65-66, 68, 71, 73-83, 123, 125, 149, 156-158, 224, life-style 80, power structure 91, rites 137, tongues 123, women 138, Pelasgian World 73-74
Pelasgians 38, 65-66, 71, 73-74, 76-80, 82-83, 102, 106, 112, 123, 125-126, 132, 138-139, 157-158, 218, 221, 228, Carians, Caucones, Eteo-Cretans, Leleges, Lysians, Maeonians, Mysians, Paeonians, Phrygians, Thessalians, Thracians 65, structures 125, and Etruscans 205
Pelasgic 66, 78
Peleus 139-140
Peloponnese 72-73
Peloponnesian War 79-80, 82
Penelope, 166, 168, 170-172
Penthesileia, the Amazon Queen 237
Pergamon 82
Perioeci 76, 78
Persephone (Demeter) 179
Persia 54, 73, 81-82, 89
Persians 81-82, 126, 196, 238
Perugia 59
Peter the Great 192
Phaistos 69, 121
Pharaoh 107, 115, 218
Phidias 99
Philippines 35

Phillip II 35
philogenetic tree 210
philosopher 80, philosophers 79-80
philosophical tradition 80
philosophy 17, 20, 23, 34, 79-80, Greek 79, school of 80
Phocis 126
Phoenician 106, traders 133
Phrygia 65, 108, 228-229
Phrygian cap 228-229
Piacenza 59
Picasso, Pablo 37
Picts 44-46, 236
pilgrimage 224-226
pious men 143
pipe lines 81, clay water-pipes, 67, pressure lines 82,
piper 57
pipes 57-58, 82, 115
pirates 69
Pisa 59
Pisistratus 83, 239
Pizarro 35
Plains, North American 71
planets. 103
Plataea 238
Plato 79, 87, Symposium 87
plays 20, 23
Pliny the Elder 54
Plutarch, 78, 121, 147-148
Pluto 113
poem 59, 81, 140-141, 154
poetical 74
poetry 228, 242, epic 140, Ionian 81
poets 34, 100, 110, 140-142, 143
poison 135, 137
Poland 207, 214, 225
Polish 195, 198, 225
political 17, 20, 27-28, 50, 55-56, 64, 76, 78-79, 81-82, 90-93, 131-132, 147, 149, 155-157, 159, 161, and religious status 131, dominance 139, guide 126, power 227, power among the Etruscans 90, rights 78,

political system 90
politics 74, 243
polychromatic buildings 67
Pontifex Maximus 158
Pope 150
population explosion 209
Populonia 57
Portuguese 194-196, 200, 217, 235
pottery 53, 57
power circle 122, game 136, structures 228, maritime 157, restriction of the king's 229
Pre-Columbian 35
pregnancy 102
pre-Greek 99
pre-Hellenic 108
prehistoric, Europe 221, murals 226
pre-Indo-European 54, 109-110
premarital 241
presidents 124
Priam 140, 157, 159
priest 78, 83, 90-91, 99, 105, 109-110, 147, 154, 156-157, 159, 161, 218, advice from the 159, Jupiter's 90, priestly king 106, 110, 113
priestess 92, 99, 104, 106, 111-113, 118-122, 129-130, 134, 148-149, 156-157, 159, 161, 231, 233, 238, of the tribe or clan 106, chief 156, chosen 120, election of both the Goddess' 120, old 118, post 135
priesthood 104
primitives 189
prince 90, competing 121
princess 90, 95
procession 52, 83, 105, 183
professions 115
prophecies 186
prophetess 159, at Delphi 187
prophetic trances 185
prosperity 108
prosperous 80
Proteus 134
public sacred coupling ceremony 216

Pyrenees 24, 27, 29-31, 33, 36, 44, 225, 246
Pyrgi 60
Pythagoras 81
Pythagoreans 103
Pythian Games 104, 126
Pytho, dethronement of 126, sacred serpent 187
pythonessess' oracular trances 188
queen 44, 90, 93, 131, 134-136, 138, 147-148, 151, 154-157, 159-161, 231, 233, 242, Apartments 151, daughter of the 93, ever reigning 155, King publicly copulating with the 217, of Lacedemonia 147, youngest nubile daughter of the 93
queendom 93
Quintus of Smyrna 237-238, War at Troy 237
race, men's foot 119, women's 120
racial theories 218
Ravenna 59
realm 93, 100, 108, 155-156
rebirth 75, 77, 79, 81, 83
red cap of liberty 229
reign 106-107, 115
Reilig Odhrain 114
relief 19, 59
religion 20, 34, 36, 51, 53, 55, 97, 99, 101, 103, 105-109, 111, 113, 115, 117, 119, 121, 125, 218, 224, 226
religiosity 37, 53, 226
religious beliefs 98, books 238, combat between genders 239, religious hierarchies 64, influence 222, 224, relationship 125, structures 136, symbol 187, ties 125, traditions 134, war 143
religiousness 68
Remus 185
Renaissance 58-59, 75, 94, 242
Republic 52
Republican 90
resurrection 184

Index

Rhine Valley 192
Riff Valley 201
rights 76, 78. See women's rights
ritual 53, 60, 68, 70-71, 77-78, 83, 92-93, 104, 109, 113-115, 120, 137, 231, 240, 246, games 236, mating 192, mimic 83, Pelasgian 78, role 92
rituals 53, 71, 77-78, 83, 104, 109, 113-115, 120, 231, mimic 83, Pelasgian 78
river names 47, 207
Roderick, King, 25-26
Roland, Song of (Chanson de Roland) 18, 27-28, twelve peers 28
Roman 15-17, 20, 24-26, 30, 34, 44, 46-47, 50-58, 67, 73, 82-83, 87-88, 90, 102, 106, 113, 115, customs 90, legions 17, 20, 25, 52, 54, 82
Romans 15-17, 20, 24-26, 31, 39, 43-44, 47, 49-51, 53-54, 56, 59, 65, 81, 87-88, 90-91, 106, 114, 141-142, 185, 205, 228
Rome 25, 49-52, 54, 56-57, 59, 73, 82, 87, 90, 158, 223, 226, 229, founders of 185
Romulus 52, 185
Roncesvalles 25, 27-28
roots 194
Rostand, Edmond 23
royal 23, 25, 44, 52, 147, 155-156, 159, blood 159, hair with lapiz lazuli 236, houses 96, 155, rights 134, sons 93, status 106, women 233
ruling class 132
Rumanian 194, 198
Russia 189, 207, 235-236
Russian 195, 198, peasants 192
Russians 196
rye, contaminated 190
Sabines 49, 52, 54, 63
Sabrina 224
sacred 60, 102-104, 106-111, 113-118, 120-122, bands of fifty or a hundred members 109, boats 115, books 141, coupling 111, grove 182, name 162, places 190, sex rituals 191, royal couple of the league 121, war 157, writings 122,
Sacred island 83, 114, 126, 131, Leuce 114, Lemnos, Delos, Pharos, Samothrace 114
sacred king 90, 106-107, 111, 113, 115, 118, 120, 134, 158, 223, 245-246, had extended his survival period 134, of Rome 90, longer period for the 126, pastoral 108, sacrifice of 113, sacrifice of substitute 126-127, 192, 223
Sacred Marriage 128, 130, 132, 134, Paleolithic 217. See Hyeros Gamos, Sacred Marriage
sacred number 103-104, Eight 103-104, 107, five 103, four-year 104, King Arthur and his twelve knights 103, nights between the first crescent and the full moon 103, nine 103, number of the celestial bodies 103, seventy-two-day 103, The judge and the twelve jurors 103, thirteen months 103, three 99, 101-103, 113, 115, 119, triad 102, triple triad 104, twelve of a kind plus a different one 103, 189, 237, week of seven days 103
sacred queen 131, 134-135
Sacred Son 223-224
sacred trees 104, ash 104, oak 104, 110, 113, 117, nut 104, willow 104
Sacred Wedding, 108, 110, Paleolithic 217. See Hyeros Gamos, Sacred Marriage
sacrifice 83, 105, 110, 113-117, deifying 116, goat 109, ritually killed 90, 130, 132, substitute victims 93, 126-127, 182, 192, 223, victims 53, 135, 190, yearly 127
sacrilege 134-135

sadistic times 190
Sagas of the Norwegian kings 90, Heimskringla 90, Ynglingar family 90
Sailors 17, 19, 34-35, 54, 132, 134
Salamis 54
Samos 81
San Fermin 68
sanctity 106, 110
sanctuary 126, 223
sanitation 67
Sanskrit 195, 198
Santorini 92, 157. See Thera
Saragossa 27
sarcophagus 52, 58, 60
Sardinians 215
Sarich, Vincent 210
Saudi Arabia 212
Saule, Ligo festival of 183
Saxons 197
Scamander 157
Scandinavia 43, 70, 90, 188-189, 223, 231-232, caverns 190, countries 205, village 189
Scandinavians 38, 40, 43, 65, 90-91, 103
scepter 90, Roman 90
Schliemann, Heinrich 66, 67, 74, 140
science 20, 34, 104
Scotia 47, 70
Scotland 41, 43-44, 46, 114, 195
Scots 38-40, 43-44, 47, 65, 90-91, 195, 227
Scott, Walter 44
scroll 60
sculptors,
sculpture 59, and paintings of goddesses 187, realistic 99, best sculptors 99-100
Scythians 235
sea people 54
seasonal 103, changes 214
seasons 101-103, 111, 118, three 101-102

seat, stone 120
secrecy 45
secret 18, 44-46, 149, 161, ceremony 108, a most valuable 133
seer 79
Seine 224, 232
Selene 102
Senate 50, senators 50, 52
Seneca 53
sepulchre of two ladies 231
Sequanna 224
Servia 206
Servocroatian 198
Seti I 245
Seven Sages of Greece 175
Seven Wonders of the World 73, 81, 99
Sevigné, Madame de 23, Marquise de 22
sex 241
sexual 98, 111, power 111
sexy Minoan statuettes 188
Shah 89
sheep 34, 44, 46, 56, 195
shepherds 19, 34, 39
ships 35, 48, 54, 114, 133, 140, 144, 162, miniature 114, sink their 133
shoes 57
shrine 126, 224-225
Shu, Egyptian god 107
Siberia 98, 220, 223, 234-235
Sicily 29
Siena 58-59
silver 69
singers 27, 59
Sino-Caucasian 60, 62
Sinope 238
sk 38, 49
Skara Brae 46
skin suits 219
skulls 33, 44, 66, 114, 189-190, 214, narrow 66
slaves 55, 57
Slavs 183
smith 115

Index

Smyrna 73, 237-238, Izmir 73
snakes 99, 105, 152, 186, Cocullo 105, Angitia 105, Ankisia 105, San Domenico of Foligno 105, supernatural 188
social 37, 50, 52, 54-56, 78-79, social psychic instability 136, structure 78, 125, upheaval 129, economical, religious and political turnover 126
Socrates 79
solstice, rebirth of the sacrificed Sun God, the 183, summer 68, winter 108, 110
Solutreans 219-220, 222
son of a god and a mortal 184
song 18, 28, 36, 80, 109, 140, 234, 238
Sophocles 83, 110
sorcery 192
sorgin (Basque witch) 191
Soule 36
South and Central America 217
South Pacific Islands 220
Southern Rhodesia 118
Space Age 246
Spain 24-28, 33, 36-37, 45, 99, 117, 183, 192, 205, 207, 216-217, 225-226, 230
Spaniard 95, 198
Spanish 18, 35, 37, 60, 71, 116, 194-195, 198, 200, 217, 226, 235
Sparta 75-76, 78, 81, 161, 243
Spartacus 55, 228-229
Spartan 69, 72, 78, 226
Spartans 69, 76-79, 82, 226
Sphinx 121
spirits 104
spiritual 71
spouses 87
spring 108
St. John's Eve 183
stadium 120
Stanford, Dennis 219
state procession 150
statues 88, 99-100, 230, 238

statuette 71, 98-100, 102, 121, 150, 152, 222, 233, Faience 152, male 100
steatopygy 98-99, 222
stone 17, 31-33, 35-39, 45-46, 48, 51, 65-67, 69, 94, 98, 105, 111, 120, 194-196, 198-202, roots 94, stone-cutters 45-46, stone-cutters and Freemasons 46, precious 69, workers 219
Stone Age 17, 31-32, 36, 38, 105, 194, 199, Man 196
stories, prehistoric 93
Strabo 76, 95, 237
Stymphaly 130
Styx, river 113
subuli 57
Sulla 55
Sumer 223
Sumerian 236
sun 103, 111, 119-120
supernatural 109, 114, 116, benefits 135, locus 188
Swedish 18, 195-196, 198
Switzerland 57, 207, 225
Sykes, Bryan 210
symbol 37, 52, 103, 105-106, 110, 117, 129, 137, 151, 155, 187, 228-229, 233, multicolored 151
symbolic moles 151
symphony 58
Syria 222
tablets 60
taboos 90, 105, 113, 155
Tagliata Etrusca 56
Tammuz, Ishtar and 223
Tantalus 175
Tarchinians 51
Tarik 26
Tartessos 165
technology 34, 66
Telamon 140
temple 46, 48, 51, 53, 73, 114, 116-117, 180, 182-183, 186

tenants 55
terracotta 102
Teutonic 38
thalassa 66, thalassocracy 54, 69
Thales 80, 82
theater 82, actor (formerly the king) 83, 110, bacchantes or maenads 109, chorus 109-110, chorus from 50 to 12, 110, chorus up to 15 110, dramatic festival 110, tragedies 136, fifty members of the Chorus 109, lecherous satyrs 109, modern 110, playwright 110, second actor 110, song and dance 109, tragedy 109, Thespis 110, hallucinogenic trance 109
Thebes 245
theologians 184
theological 115, 151
Theopompus 87
Thera 68, 92, 99, 101, 236. See Santorini
Theseus 72, 78, 124, 129-131, 135, 235, 238, Minotaur 129
Thessaly 65, 66
thinkers 80
Thrace 73, 108
Thracians 65, 228-229
throne 135-136, 147-148, 155, 158-159, candidates to ascend the 136
Thucydides 77, 80, 82, The Peloponnesian War 82
Thyestes 121
tiara 152
Tiber River 158
Tillya Tepe 233
Tiryns 65, 68
toga, palmata 52, Etruscan royal 90
tomb 51-53, 58-59, 114-115, 230, 233-234
tongue 17, 26, 31, 36-37, 41, 44-46, 83. See language
toponyms 37
torture 133

totem 105, 109, 112, 184, fraternities 109
towns 140
trade 78, 80, 82, routes 133, 139-140, 153, 156, 164, trademarks, registered 70
traditional tribes 93
traditions 19-20, 35, 41, 47, 51, 63, 73, 77, 79-80, 99, 111-112, 114, 117, 120, 122, Pelasgian 77, 79
trees 104, 106
trial madness 192
trinal 102
trinity 103
Trois Frères 117
Trojan 72, 75, 80, 228-229, seer 159, War 72, 80, 229
troubadours 242
Troy 51, 66, 75, 80, 140-141, 143-144, 146, 150, 153-155, 157-159, 161-162, founder of 153, windy 154
Tulius Hostilius 50
Turk 225
Turkey 73, 75, 77, 79
Tuscan 59, 242
Tuscany 49, 52, 57-59, 75, 242-243
Tutankhamen 233
Tyrins 72, 92
U.S.A. 62, 124, 197, citizens 124, South-West 62
Uderzo 15
Ukraine 214, 205, 236
Ulysses 124
Unamuno, Miguel de 38
unify 135
Uppsala, gold-gleaming temple of 182
Urals, western side of the 89
urn 59, 231
Uttar-Pradesh 186
Vandals 17, 26, 229
Varuna 142
Vascones 24-26, 31, feroces 69
vase 59, 228, 238, of Vix 232
veneration 103, 114

Index

Vennemann, Theo 204-208
Venus (goddess) 215. See Aphrodite
Venus figurines 98-99, 215, 222, Cycladic 99, African origin 98
Venus of Willendorf 97
Venus, Planet 103, 183
victim, "of every living thing that is male" 182. See human sacrifice, sacrifice
Viking 44, 188-189, 214-215, 218, blood 214, ship 231
villages 105, 120, 140
vine 70, 83
Virgil 158
Virgin Mary 58, 180, 224-225, and the Child 58, of Czestochowa 225
Viscayan 33, 36
Visigothic 25-26, 30
Visigoths 17, 25-26
Volumnii 52
Vosgos Mountains 204
Vulcanus (Hephaestus) 115
vulva 222
Wales 41, 47, 212
Wallace, Douglas 220
walls 65, 68-69
war, civil 125, Carlist 37, Medic 81, Persian 123, war-prone 72
Wascones 24
Washington, George 124, 225, 229
water, running 67
Way of St. James 22, 225-226. See Chemin de St. Jacques
weather 101
weights and measures 70
Welsh 43-44, 47, 227
werewolf, loup-garou 185, fraternities 184
whales 34
wife 87
William of Malmesbury 246
William the Conqueror 190, 197
Wilson, Allan 210
wine 20, 22, 34, 36, 56-57, 70, 83, 232, bread and 179, 191, Cabernet Sauvignon 34, Chateau 34, Consule Planco 56, Falernian 56, Latour 34, Mouton-Rothschild 34, Haut-Brion 34, Margaux 34, oinos 70, transformation of water into 184, and ecstasy 108
wisdom 189, test 121
wise woman 189
witches 39, 174, 182, 186, 191-192, in Portugal 186, sorginguaiza (witch's scissors) 36-37, trials 185, witch-hunts 190,
wolf, city of the wolves 22, female 185, man-eating 185, fraternities 184, werewolf 185
woman 64, 68, 70, 85-96, 98-99, 101, 109, 113, 118-121, 131-132, 138, 146-150, 154-155, 158, 161-162, 174-175, 180, 186-187, 189, 222, 230-241, 243, 245-246, army 238, artists 119, court 230, European 85, from woman to 209, high status of 232, independent, self-assertive 85, in office 231, kin 96, nubile 152, pre-nubile, nubile and post-nubile stages in 102, rider 235, youngest nubile 93, warlike 235, woman-centered society 95
women's rights, 20, 87, 89, 96, age 89, best rights 89, choose their future partners 240, disposing of women 154, divorce at will and then retain property 231, dowry 95-96, education 87, father's authority 86, high status 231, gradual decrease in women's rights 212, high status of their women 90, 222, if not married 89, independent existence 89, inexistent by themselves 89, inherited kingdoms 90, inheritance 94-96, higher education than men 232, legitimate children 87, marriage of the brothers 95, maternal, paternal

names 96, millennial rights 138, property 87-88, 95-96, right to live 89, Roll of Benasque 95, Scandinavian 231, status 86, 94, social rights 86, 125, social scale 86, widows still burn themselves
words 194-203
workshops 59
World War II 17, 37, 86, 218
worship 114, 120
wrestling match 119
writer, moral 87

Xinjiang Uygur Autonomous Region 234
Y chromosome 210-211, 213, 215
yearly, amphictyonic king, chosen 90
youngest royal daughter 147, 159
Zagreb 60
Zakros 69
zatricchion (Minoan chess) 70
Zeno 80
Zeus 142, 223-224, Olympian 120, sanctuary devoted to 223
Zurbarán 45